S0-BYU-611

PRAISE FOR
KNOCK-OUT NETWORKING!

"*Knock-Out Networking!* is an absolute must read. If you're looking to grow your business or land a new job, Michael Goldberg's pragmatic approach to networking will serve as an invaluable resource in accomplishing those goals. Many of the philosophies discussed in this book are embraced in BNI chapters worldwide for good reason—they work! If you're anxious to learn strategies you can put into action today for immediate results, look no further."

—*Ivan Misner,*
Founder of BNI and Referral Institute

"If networking is part of your success plan, *Knock-Out Networking!* is not an option, it's a must buy, must read, must implement book before you attend your next meeting."

—*Jeffrey Gitomer*
Author of *Little Red Book of Selling*

"This book shows how you can accomplish just about anything through networking. Goldberg shares a "what works and what doesn't" approach to implementing successful networking techniques. It is a must read for anyone looking for more business."

—*Maribeth Kuzmeski*
President of Red Zone Marketing, Inc

"I always thought I was a good networker but I found so many important ideas in Michael's book that I had to rethink all the events I've been to and how I handled them. Michael is a funny, engaging teacher and writes as if he's speaking to you in person. His knowledge is obvious, and his style of sharing the information makes this book so easy to read. Knock-Out Networking! is a MUST for all salespeople!"

—Gail B. Goodman
President, ConsulTel, Inc.

"I have known Michael Goldberg for many years and I know very few people that have a better grasp of what networking is and how it can impact not only ones career but their entire life. Michael truly is a networking master and everyone that has spent time with Michael and learning from him has been benefited. Michael has not only assisted me but also many advisors at my firm as well as within our industry. The lessons in this book if applied will be a difference maker in someone's life."

—Edward G. Deutschlander
CLU, CLF, Co-President, COO, North Star Resource Group

"Michael Goldberg has created the quintessential field guide for effective networking and prospecting. His field-tested strategies will help any sales professional, regardless of their career stage, to take their game to the next level!"

—Joey Davenport
Principal & Chief Development Officer, Hoopis Performance Network

"Many people take networking for granted. They don't realize what a valuable tool it can be. Michael Goldberg's book *Knock-Out Networking!* identifies the easy ways to implement networking into your everyday business practices. By following his Rules of Networking, your business will grow substantially. Mine did!"

—Christopher Galati
Senior Account Executive, Cortel Business Solutions, Inc.

"Michael's book offers a common sense, tactical approach to networking which is relevant to all. The techniques and tools provided in the book are instantly applicable and have helped many of our top sales people take their game to the next level. It's a Knock-Out!"

—*Tye M. Elliott*
Vice President, North Territory Director, Aflac

"*Knock-Out Networking!* is an exciting introduction to the world of networking. Michael takes a complicated concept like networking and makes it simple and easy to understand. A must read for all financial services representatives"

—*William Shea*
Agency Training Director, Barnum Financial Group, Top MetLife Agency

"*Knock-out Networking!* is a necessity for anyone trying to make a good impression. Michael's networking techniques are the best tools for drawing people toward you and closing the deal, whether it's selling a product or selling yourself."

—*Laurel Pickering*
MPH, Executive Director, Northeast Business Group on Health

"The recession has caused the longest term unemployment in 70 years. Finding the right job is not done the way it used to be. Recognizing this, Michael has redefined networking. His program retrofits and adapts the art of networking to the myriad of challenges facing folks struggling to re-career. *Knock-Out Networking!* is both informative and empowering for America's job seekers."

—*Joseph M. Carbone*
President & CEO, The Workplace, Inc.

"Michael not only defines the true meaning of 'Power Networking', but also teaches how to do it do it right and to be an effective networker. Michael's Pool Rules strips the fear and unknown of networking and provides a clear understanding of the do's and don'ts…"

—*Kisha Pugh*
Field Marketing Consultant, MetLife

"*Knock-Out Networking!* is the perfect blend of practical ideas, interesting stories, and call to action. Goldberg gives you the best roadmap I've seen to creating sales success through networking. You won't be disappointed."

—*Bill Cates*
President of Referral Coach International

"Michael's refreshing perspective on networking is an instructive work that identifies practical ways to succeed where so many others have failed. At our organization, his work has been instrumental in more than doubling our bottom line since our sales team focused on his tips and tactics. *Knock-Out Networking!* is the perfect bridge between Michael's energetic and enlightening presentations and his down to earth reality about networking."

—*Vincent Ashton*
Executive Director, HealthPass

"*Knock-Out Networking!* provides the clearest, most concise information on networking I have ever heard. Michael provides the reader with an action plan and ways to achieve true goals. Wish I read this book 20 years ago!"

—*Lee B. Salz*
Sales Management Strategist

"Michael's book *Knock-Out Networking!* is a must read for anyone who believes networking is an integral part of their business plan. His #1 rule that networking is a proactive approach to meeting people and helping them is the most important and overlooked rule of networking. Applying this principal alone has helped me grow my business immensely."

—*Michael Sullivan*
Vice President, Parker, Remsen & Sullivan Insurance

"If you want a step by step guidebook to mastering business development through networking, then *Knock-Out Networking!* is a MUST read. Michael not only knows the subject matter, it is his approach to building his own business."

—*Jeff Golan*
Regional Managing Director, The Principal Financial Group

"Networking is a major ingredient in growing a successful business, this book has done a great job identifying key rules and activities to assist. Whether you are new in your business or a 20 year veteran, there are some excellent principles in this book which can help enhance the growth of your business. "

—*Michael S. Chille*
Vice President - Northeast, Aflac

"With nearly a decade of experience in this highly competitive business, I can genuinely say that no one knows networking quite like Michael Goldberg. With an uncanny knack for transforming the "work" in networking into actionable, successful and enjoyable strategies, Michael can turn almost anyone into a networking natural. For professionals seeking to grow their business and see more clients, this page-turner and delightful must-read, *Knock-Out Networking!* offers uniquely insightful tips and strategies to turn almost any situation into a successful networking opportunity!"

—*Amy M. Guettler*
Editor, ProducerseSource.com

"The concepts Michael teaches in *Knock-Out Networking!* are brilliant. Any advisor or manager looking to grow their business through networking needs to master them."

—*Paul Blanco*
Managing Director, Barnum Financial Group, Top MetLife Agency

"I don't know anyone who has a more firm grasp of networking for business than Michael Goldberg. He is both a student and teacher of the art (yes, networking is an art!) and has a true gift for communicating his keen insights and real world applications culled from years of battle-tested experience. Michael's value proposition to those wishing to learn relationship building is immense. *Knockout Networking!* delivers! It is a rally cry for those who believe that success in business is determined by our ability to form and leverage professional relationships. This is a guy who steps out, pulls no punches (pun intended!) and gets your business adrenaline surging!"

—*J.D. Gershbein*
CEO, Owlish Communications

KNOCK-OUT NETWORKING!

More**Prospects** | More**Referrals** | More**Business**

Michael Goldberg

Printed in the United States of America

This book is available at special quantity discounts to use a premiums and sales promotions, or for use in corporate training programs. For more information, please write to the Director of Marketing and Business Development, Building Blocks Consulting, PO Box 606, Jackson, NJ 08527.

Published by:
Prime Concepts Group Publishing
7570 W. 21st Street N., Suite 1038A
Wichita, KS 67205 USA

Library of Congress Cataloging-in-Publication Data

    Goldberg, Michael, 1966-
      Knock-out networking! : more prospects, more
    referrals, more business / Michael Goldberg.
      p. cm.
      Includes index.
      LCCN 2010943513
      ISBN-13: 978-193690104-3
      ISBN-10: 1-936901-04-8

      1. Success in business. 2. Social networks.
    3. Business networks. I. Title.

    HF5386.G65 2011   650.1
                 QBI11-600028

DEDICATION

To Frank Goodman, Dorothy Goodman, Ralph Winter, and Vince Ashton for helping me get it right.

To Paul Blanco, Ed Deutschlander, Tom Delaney, Don Brown, Tye Elliott, Mike Chille, Laurel Pickering, Elizabeth McDaid, Alan Knepper, Bruce Liebowitz, Mike Shipley, and Willow Shire for helping me get it started — way before I knew what "it" was.

To Jimmy Walsh for helping me to fear nothing and go after everything both in and out of the ring. Elbows in — you win!

To mom, dad, and my brother Glenn, my absolute best friend and the funniest person I know.

To my girls Julia, Jessica, and my wife and business partner (or is it business partner and wife?) Lainie, thank you for putting up with my schedule and putting up with me. I never said it would be easy! Progress continues…

PREFACE

"Networking is an essential part of building wealth."
—Armstrong Williams, Political Commentator

I've always been infatuated with the jump rope. Well, not the rope itself. But with people who can jump rope and look pretty cool doing it. Like boxers. One day, I approached a guy in my gym off in a corner, in front of a mirror, jumping rope. And man, did he look cool! He was in his own world listening to an iPod while doing his thing. What impressed me most was how easy he made it look.

I approached him and after introducing myself, asked if he could show me how to jump rope. He looked at me baffled and said that I already knew how to do it. "Not like you!" I said, and he laughed. He said, "Yes, this took some time." He told me to jump rope once just to see what I had. Once I did (reluctantly), he said, "Not bad. My name is Dan. Come back to me once you can jump rope at least 20 times in a row." I appreciated the dare and promised I would. And I did.

It took a couple of weeks but I did get up to almost 100 jumps in a row. As it turned out, Dan had been a boxer and still had nifty footwork. He and I became good friends and I gained a great workout partner out of the deal. Also, as a result of my training with Dan, he improved my footwork and started teaching the rudiments of boxing and I was hooked!

I then decided that if I was going to box and be able to become proficient, it was necessary for me to hire a boxing trainer who would also be able to improve my jump roping. By coincidence, my obsession with boxing actually led me into a conversation with a woman I met at a bus stop (of all places), while commuting into New York City from New Jersey. The woman I was speaking with was someone that I had met in the gym where I met Dan. She suggested that I speak with her trainer Jimmy, who as it turned out, was someone that I already knew.

Jimmy was in the business of selling commuter bus tickets and over the years, I had purchased tickets from him. I never suspected nor would have guessed that he was a former professional boxer and a hell of a trainer. That commute to the city changed my life and Jimmy changed the way I view almost everything. That was over 4 years ago. The rest as they say…well, you know the rest.

You're probably saying to yourself, "Nice story, but what does any of this have to do with networking?"

There are several perspectives here so bear with me. In a matter of speaking, networking gave me my "jump start" into boxing. Hey, if it wasn't for the "guts" it may have taken to approach Dan in the first place, I never would have had the opportunity to pursue my goals in the ring. I'm guessing most people don't approach complete strangers in the gym to ask for pointers about jumping rope. (I'm funny like that). Also, all the connections I have made in the most unlikely of places, is in itself a networking story. We all have stories like that.

Of course, boxing, like networking, is a contact sport. The more and better *contacts* you make while boxing or networking, the more successful you're going to be!

It does take a high level of conditioning and training to fair well in both a boxing ring and at a networking event.

With boxers it is obvious but with networking not nearly so clear. But we'll get to that. And that's probably where the comparison between boxing and networking ends.

Although boxing lends itself to a couple of warriors battling it out for the win and maybe the knockout, networking shouldn't be a battle at all. It should be a win-win. You help me and I help you!

That's actually what networking is but most people don't understand that, at least not at first. But we all started out barely being able to get over that jump rope or unable to muster up enough confidence to introduce ourselves to strangers at a networking event. Some of you are still there. No worries, that's why you're reading this book!

My hope is *Knock-Out Networking!* will give you the one-two punch needed to get you to go to the right places, say the right thing and meet the right people.

Networking is the single best way to meet people, build relationships, grow your client base through referrals, land the job of your dreams, and meet the love of your life. I know this because, over the past 10 years, I have built and grown my own successful consulting and speaking business exclusively through networking.

The reasons for you to strive to excel at networking are compelling—*The Wall Street Journal* has stated that 90 percent of all new business comes through networking—and the international outplacement firm Lee Hecht Harrison reports that 76 percent of those who find employment do so through networking.

Networking is simply a proactive approach to meeting people with a view towards learning something and potentially helping others. The process involves face-to-face interaction! Being active on social-media sites can facilitate networking, but there is so much more to it than that.

Few people engage in networking, and even fewer are good at it. Why do people avoid this low-cost proven means of making exponential gains in their personal and professional lives? Funny you ask! It's mainly because of fear! Some people shy away from networking because they think it involves selling or politicking, but those activities run contrary to the positive relationship-building aspect of networking. Others simply don't know what to do and are intimidated by meeting people in person. The myriad fears associated with networking can be defused simply by knowing the "rules to networking" or, what I refer to in Chapter 2, as "The Pool Rules of Networking."

Some people take networking for granted—they don't realize how powerful a business tool it can be, when done correctly. It's not about asking for business or pitching your wares to others but rather, it's about building and maintaining positive relationships.

Others recognize the intrinsic value of networking but aren't sure how to execute it. I have written this book for the people in both of those camps.

I understand that networking can seem daunting, even overwhelming, to the novice. I was there once—the lone soul hovering near the coffee station at a networking function, terrified of talking to strangers. (Remember, mom told us not to talk to strangers!). By working at it and practicing basic networking strategies, I have become a professional speaker on the subject. I'm hired to present all of the material in this book in workshops and I give hundreds of speeches all over the country each year, to large, well-known organizations and companies. Also, as an adjunct instructor at Rutgers University, I impart to my undergraduate students the information and ways to help them acquire the ability to network and other "secrets of the trade", to hopefully gain internship opportunities and to land employment. And, in my consulting practice, I have helped thousands of sales professionals move beyond mediocrity to excellence by following my guidelines for networking.

Anyone who is willing to make a concerted effort to devote the time and has the perseverance and patience to practice the art of networking will have the ability, over a sustained period of time, to master the skill and will become much more successful and confident as a result.

Every tip, recommendation and story in this book is based on my personal experience with networking. There are no theories here—only proven approaches and programs that have worked for me. And if they worked for me, they can work for anyone!

This book will teach you all the networking strategies you need to know, such as how to deal with sticky situations, develop a target market, perfect your "elevator pitch" and generate referrals to build your book of business. You will learn where to go and what to say to whom. You will learn how to land your dream job through networking, start your own networking group and develop your own detailed networking plan. You will learn how to greet people effectively, exchange business cards, end conversations tactfully, follow up, create an ongoing strategy and most importantly—create key relationships.

By purchasing and reading this book, you have taken a major step forward in your quest to take your business (and in many cases your life), to the next level. I am honored to accompany you on your journey to networking success. If I can offer further guidance, please feel free to visit www.BuildingBlocksConsulting.com for more information.

Happy networking! And keep the left up!

Michael Goldberg
Jackson, New Jersey

FOREWORD

I had the pleasure of meeting Michael over 10 years ago at (what else but) a networking event. A mutual colleague had been trying to connect us, and despite several exchanged emails and phone calls, neither Michael nor I could find a time that worked for us. We were both very busy, but that was a good thing.

One evening at a networking event I noticed a really good looking guy (he'll love me for saying that) standing and schmoozing with a few people. I looked at his name badge and it said "Michael Goldberg." Could this be THE Michael Goldberg I wondered? I meandered over and hovered nearby. Michael glanced at me and said, "Sheryl Lindsell-Roberts, I can't believe we're finally meeting each other." (There aren't too many people with a name like mine, so he had no doubts.) Since that serendipitous meeting, Michael and I have become close colleagues and good friends. We've presented together and collaborated on several projects. I've developed the utmost admiration for Michael—both professionally and personally.

Michael is the quintessential networker. I thought I was a savvy networker until I met him. I had been living in the community where we met for nearly ten years and knew lots of people. Michael was living there for a short while and knew more people than I did. I knew he was someone I could learn from. So I became his Kung Fu "Little Grasshopper."

I strongly encouraged Michael to write this book because his wisdom and know-how need to be shared. For those of you who are fortunate enough to have heard Michael speak, this will be a constant reminder of all the valuable strategies and tactics you learned. For those of you who haven't heard him up close and personal, you'll find great wisdom within these covers. After reading this book, I guarantee (there's no money back, by the way) that you'll close more business, land more job interviews, get more information, solve more problems, meet more friends, and maybe, just maybe, meet the love of your life.

If you're standing at a bookstore reading this, close the book right now and take out your credit card. By the way, don't lend this book to anyone. You'll never get it back.

Sheryl Lindsell-Roberts
Author of 23 books

TABLE OF CONTENTS

CHAPTER 1:

Why Don't More People Network?

*"The greatest mistake you can make in life is to
continually be afraid you will make one."*
—Elbert Hubbard

It is my belief that, other than possibly curing a disease,
you can accomplish almost anything through networking.
If you know with whom you need to speak, where you need
to go and what you need to say, you can make tremendous
progress. Networking is a gateway to solving problems and
meeting the people you need to meet, with everything you
do, in every aspect of life.

My definition of networking is **a proactive approach to
meeting people so that you can learn something and
potentially help them.**

That's it! Networking is simply about learning and helping.
Not you—them. Let me repeat, not you—them. If you do a
great job at learning about the business people you are with
and helping them, they will help you right back. That's what
networking is all about! It's a collaborative effort toward
helping one another achieve a goal, whether it's selling a
product or service, landing a job, solving a problem, learning a thing or two about something or meeting the love of
your life.

By the way, these are the five primary reasons why people network — to grow a business (promote products and services, recruit, fundraise), to land a job (internships or other career opportunities), to solve a problem (find a realtor or a good painter), to brainstorm or learn something (learn about the real estate market), or to meet friends (a workout partner or your dreamboat).

Networking can happen serendipitously (you meet someone at the airport whom you just happen to connect with) or strategically (at a networking event). Either way, the same definition applies.

Despite all the important reasons why more people should network, there are even more reasons why people don't (or won't). What gets in your way?

Fear of Failure

What's the worst thing that can happen when you meet new people? Maybe you will say something you shouldn't say. Maybe you'll do something you shouldn't do. Maybe things won't work out the way you planned. Maybe you will make some other mistake that compromises protocol, etiquette or whatever. So what? We all make those blunders from time to time. The key is in recognizing your mistakes (not getting discouraged by them) and doing better the next time. Simple? Now repeat!

You have to get out there and try it (like with anything!). So if you know why you're at any event, know how to introduce yourself and ask some questions of people, that's at the very least a good start. Don't you think? Then, as you do this, you'll notice things, like "I should have spoken to this person longer" or "I should have asked more questions" or "I should have followed up on that" or "I should have had more business cards." There are a lot of shoulda, woulda couldas.

It's the same thing with public speaking. I speak between 10 and 15 times a month, yet I'm always thinking about what I could have done better (and there's plenty!). You have to start somewhere. As Nike says just get out there and do it.

One very effective way to take the fear out of networking is to picture the worst thing that can happen, and then plan to recover with poise if such an incident happens. (Of course, an even more effective way to eliminate the fear is to picture what the best thing is that can happen.)

What's the worst thing that ever happened to me while networking? Well, there's plenty. Where do I start?

I remember having to travel and co-present with a woman named Jackie. She is older than me, very cerebral, with a much different speaking style than mine. While I consider myself kind of off the cuff and dynamic, she is very structured and even. We were supposed to travel from the East Coast to the West Coast and co-facilitate a full-day seminar. If our presentation went well, we would ultimately work on other projects together. If the presentation didn't go well, maybe not so much.

So we ended up flying together, which was awkward. We struggled to make conversation. And for me to struggle to make conversation with somebody is saying something. But we made small talk—"How's this whole thing going to go?"—and got through it.

The next morning, we both spoke and did our thing with our audience. From my standpoint, we were OK—not great, but

OK. It just didn't feel that our chemistry was very good. I felt that what we had to say was all right, but that it could have been better. So lunch came, and of course food always adds yet another dynamic to networking. It was a buffet-style lunch, with limited space. Most seats were taken, so we had to stand up.

So I found myself two inches away from Jackie. Here we are face to face, nose to nose, belly to belly. And we're each balancing a Styrofoam plate, a plastic fork and knife and a beverage—somehow, somewhere. I remember on my plate there being grilled chicken, steamed string beans and something that I recall as being orange.

Jackie is about my height and has really large glasses, which make her eyes look even bigger. So I am speaking with her, and I bite down on this steamed string bean, and what do you think happens? You guessed it. Piping hot water shoots out of that string bean at def con nine, probably about 80 miles an hour, knot seven, and it takes this downward trajectory rather suddenly, at about a 30-degree tailwind and glazes her glasses, leaving a line of steaming hot water as it—get this—flies into her soda! So now the large, magnified eyes of Jackie that were once looking at me are now cross-eyed, fixated on the line of steaming hot water on her glasses. An awkward moment, yes?

So I do what any self-respecting person probably would have done in that situation—I pretend that it didn't happen. No, really. Now you have this awkward lull. You know someone has to say something, and obviously she notices it now. Finally, she kind of smirks. And for the first time since I have known her, she actually smiles. I have a horrible poker face, so I know that I'm just holding it in. Finally, I say, "You saw that, huh?"

"Yeah."

"OK. Now what?"

That was my brilliance as a professional communicator: "Now what?"

She takes her glasses off and actually chuckles, saying, "Awkward, huh? Tell you what. Let me clean my glasses. You get me another soda, and we'll call it even."

I answer, "Fair enough."

Suddenly, we both seemed to morph into different people because we were laughing over this. All of a sudden, it was like we had a great connection. Lunch from that point on was awesome. Our afternoon of speaking together was even more awesome and our event was a complete success! And we ended up doing additional work together.

What's the worst possible thing that could happen to you in a networking situation? It doesn't really get much worse than spitting food in somebody's face. I might not have had string beans since that incident, which has become known as The String-Bean Incident, however, the point is that it can never get any worse, really. Everything can be repaired with an apology, or "I didn't know," or whatever it is. Then you move on. And an incident like this can actually break the ice and make the situation better in the end.

Fear of Public Speaking

For many people, the simple act of talking in front of others paralyzes them with fear, and they avoid networking because of it. In fact, public speaking is the No. 1 fear of

Americans—death is No. 7! As comedian Jerry Seinfeld says, "At a funeral, you'd rather be lying in the casket than delivering the eulogy."

A lot of people have fears and challenges with networking for the same exact reason that people have fears and challenges with public speaking: they're afraid they're going to look stupid. They're afraid they're not going to know what to say. They're afraid they're not going to know how to handle the questions. They're not confident. They don't feel good about themselves. "The spotlight is on me. What if I screw up?"

So what does this have to do with networking? Networking is a form of public speaking. (I'll discuss public speaking more in-depth in another chapter.)

For more than six years, I have taught a public-speaking class at Rutgers University. One of my former students, Nicole, almost withdrew from my course because she was so terrified of getting up to speak in front of the class. (Students can simply withdraw from the class. Sales producers end up failing as sales producers. Job searchers don't work and therefore can't pay the rent.)

Nicole was really quiet and sat in the back of the room. In my first class, I have the students get up and speak about themselves. (It is a public speaking class you know.)

At the end of the first class, Nicole came up to me after everyone else left and said, "I have to apologize. I just have to let you know—I don't want to waste your time. I can't take this class." I asked her, "Why? Did I mess up already?"

She chuckled and answered, "No, no. It's just that I'm absolutely terrified."

I said, "Yeah, but you did so well. And you need this class to graduate."

"Yeah, I do. I'm going to have to figure something out."

"No, I can't allow you to do that," I said.

Right then, her mother called on her cell phone, and as Nicole spoke with her, she was almost in tears. She didn't know what to do. It was a little awkward. Her mom was trying to convince her to stick it out. Then I said, "Nicole, do me a favor, hand me the phone."

I said, "Hello, Mrs. Nicole's Mom. This is Michael Goldberg, the instructor. Listen, your daughter is beside herself. I want to make a promise. I want you to help me keep her in this class, and I promise that she will overcome this fear, and she will be one of the best in the class. I will work with her—I will do whatever needs to happen, otherwise this is going to haunt her forever. And I can't allow that. So if you can work with me on keeping her in this class, I will do the best that I can, and I will even put in extra time with her."

Nicole got back on the phone with her mom, and it became an emotional moment (or a Kodak moment): "OK, I'll do it."

So throughout the entire semester, the class knew that she was struggling and had confidence issues—although they didn't know about that conversation we had the first night of class. The one dynamic I really try to create in the classroom is that the speaking is not a competition—we're pulling for each other, rooting for each other. Despite this, it was evident that she was struggling.

That particular semester, we were videotaping students as they gave speeches and we would often start the class by critiquing a taped presentation from the previous week. Sometimes we would critique a newscaster or even a celebrity. So I popped in a DVD and we watched Conan O'Brien deliver his monologue. And suddenly there's Nicole — right there on Late Night with Conan O'Brien! (This is before he took over and ultimately got booted from The Tonight Show.)

At the end of the clip, Nicole stands up in class and gives a presentation about how she has overcome her fear, what happened, what was going through her mind and how appreciative she was of the class.

By overcoming her fear, Nicole had an incredible experience that she will never forget. And she will have many more. She will meet people she would otherwise never meet and have experiences that she would be too fearful to have otherwise.

Other than national television appearances on a talk show, what are the Top 10 (David Letterman reference) opportunities you're missing out on?

Fear of the Unknown

For some people, not knowing what will happen is the fear that keeps them from networking. (It's the fear that keeps on giving.)

However, the more skilled you become with the science of networking (and at speaking with people), the less likely you will be confronted with surprises. If you learn as much as possible about the clients you wish to work with most, you will get to know about the culture of a given industry, profession or market segment. What great information to effectively build your expertise, your skill and your book of business!

Fear of Being Too "Salesy"

I hear about this fear a lot from financial advisors (a marketplace I do a ton of work with).

Sales and networking are two different monsters. Sales (or selling) is about assessing needs, qualifying, overcoming objections and making the big close. Networking is different. Aside from selling yourself (which we do every time we get dressed in the morning and show up somewhere to do something or talk to people), networking is about meeting new people, learning about them, offering to help them and developing strong relationships over time. If you're good (and a bit lucky), sales and other opportunities will just happen.

Lack of Confidence

Fear can cause a lack of confidence, too, and that is a huge networking deterrent (among other things).

Typically in a networking environment, I find a lack of confidence among not just newer and younger financial advisors and sales reps, but also the more seasoned ones. They are not confident in what they are doing, what they're supposed to be saying, what they're not supposed to be saying, how to deal with awkward situations and how to navigate a conversation in a networking manner, rather than trying to pitch their wares, sell their product or just talk about the weather.

And the biggest reason that people lack confidence in networking? It's because they don't have a strategy. They don't have a mission. They don't have a goal.

Another reason for a lack of confidence is inexperience—looking young or being young. One financial advisor said to me recently, "I don't even have any facial hair!"

So people who are new at networking often ask, "How am I supposed to navigate my way and have businesslike conversations with confidence and conviction at a chamber event, conference, convention or association meeting, with people who may be a lot more seasoned, a lot more knowledgeable and experienced, hence a lot more confident, than me?

You gain confidence developing a strategy (even if you end up adjusting your strategy later—go in with something) and with practice. Focus on doing one or two things well—deliver your elevator pitch (discussed later), ask a few questions. If you have a specific purpose, then you're more likely to have confidence.

Having a measurable strategy—such as asking three questions to three new people (again, discussed later) whom you haven't met yet—helps defuse fear, and that is why it helps you become more confident.

Not Understanding the Goal

Many people don't know what they're looking for, and that is another huge networking deterrent.

At just about any cocktail party or chamber event, you can always find at least one person who is standing by the coffee station or somewhere else speaking with nobody. They have put themselves in a corner, and they are terrified. They are there because they told someone they would go or because, at some level, they realize that they should be there. But they don't want to be there. Or completely understand why they are there. They know they want more business but what does that mean? What kind of business? Helping with what?

And how do you answer all those darn questions people ask about you, your business and how you add value?

If you don't have the answers to these questions and have a specific goal set for yourself about what you need to accomplish, it's no wonder you won't network. (Or why your networking is not-working.)

It's Too Time-Consuming

Just the other day, I was at a firm working with a sales producer. He had been reluctant to network because he thought it took too long to produce results. He said, "I would network but I don't want to wait 30 months to generate new business." I said, "If it really takes you 30 months to generate business through networking than you really do need my help." Yes, networking can be time-consuming (not 30 months). But if done properly, it's well worth the time. The idea is to strike a balance between your networking time and the time spent operating the other aspects of your business.

If you're a new sales producer—you're probably in a situation where you have way more time than market (actual business). If you're a more seasoned producer, then you may not have as much time to devote to business development and networking. Then again, if you're well networked, it won't take as much time.

A lot of producers tell me, "I need to focus on product knowledge," and I tell them, "Yeah, you do. But now you have all the time in the world to get good at networking because you're going to level off otherwise. So get good now while you have the time to practice."

Yes, it takes time. But I believe that the return you get from networking is directly proportionate to how skilled you become at it, the places you go and the people with whom you speak.

People who say it's too time-consuming may not be as skilled at saying the right things, going to the right places, speaking to the right people or following up in the right way. (Right makes might.)

You're Too Busy

Just about everyone is way too busy. When will that ever change? And are you "good" busy (writing a lot of business or studying a lot of information) or "bad" busy (keeping yourself occupied or doing busy work)? If you're waiting for the time when you're not too busy, good luck! Truly busy people (the "good" kind) always make the time to get the right things done.

Lucille Ball said, "If you want something done, ask a busy person to do it."

Are you too busy because you're doing all the business you want, with the clients you want, with the margin you want, on the terms you want? Or are you too busy because you're busy trying to become busy? There are two types of busy— there is activity busy and there is the kind of busy where you're getting paid for what you do. Which do you prefer? If the latter is the case, networking is absolutely the best way to meet the right people, ask the right questions and ultimately work (as in get paid) with the right customers.

People who are new at what they do or struggling in their area of business very often kid themselves into thinking they're too busy, or they do things for the sole purpose of being busy.

So my question is always, "If you have more business than you can handle, then maybe networking is not for you." That always gets a laugh. Are you in that situation?

You Think You Can't

Many times, people think they can't network. They say to me, "OK, speaker boy, we know you can get up there and put a word or two together. We know you can do all of these different things. But you know what? I'm more of an introvert, kind of shy, a little introspective. I'm more on the analytical side of things. So this isn't for me."

I get what they're saying. It might come across better from someone who's a bit more outgoing, but many of the people I know who are brilliant networkers are also analytical, introspective and introverted. You don't need to be the life of the party (I'm certainly not) to be a good networker. You just need to know what to say, with whom to say it and where to go.

Being introverted or analytical should be an incentive rather than an excuse. I actually consider myself an introvert and if I can network than anyone can do it. (Look at me I'm networking!) I'm not saying networking is easy. Yes, starting conversations with complete strangers may be easier for someone who's outgoing. But it doesn't make them a good networker per se. It actually could lend itself to them being a bad networker. Heck, outgoing people can chit-chat, have a good time and socialize. But are they paying attention to the strategic aspect of what networking is? Are they trying to help people? That's an important distinction. I find that analytical people are better at taking an initial conversation and parlaying it into an ongoing process — following up, staying in touch and ultimately generating business, a job or whatever.

I spoke at a CPA event recently. I talked about how a lot of people think they can't network. I wanted to address this because I knew that it was on many of their minds—many CPAs are introverted and analytical, left- vs. right-brained. I knew if I didn't speak about that right up front, that is what they would be wondering. And they might be discounting what I was saying because they couldn't get past that—"We know you can do this, but it's not for me—I'm a debit and credit guy."

If this is your belief, you're right!

Not Sure Where to Go

On the one hand, anywhere that people hang out is a good place to go. On the other hand, it pays to be particular about where you go to meet the right people. The question then becomes, "Who are the right people?" Let's just say you decide that as an insurance agent or financial planner, it's a good idea to meet accountants. That makes sense because accountants tend to work with people looking for financial advice. So, what next? For starters, ask friends and those close to you if they use an accountant and if so, could they provide you with an introduction? Other places to meet accountants may include state accounting societies, chambers of commerce, accounting association meetings, community groups and networking organizations. You may want to start by asking your own accountant!

There are tons of networking organizations, business groups and association meetings for accountants and pretty much any profession you can name. Just visit Google, press the buttons and go.

Not Sure What to Say

The best thing you can do when you meet new people is to ask them questions about them. A new concept, I know! People love to talk about themselves. When you are networking, you should be in the business of learning about people. The more genuine interest you show in others, the more they may show genuine interest in you! Interesting, huh? What's the best way to learn about other people? Ask questions about their work, play, goals, accomplishments, interests, associations and skills.

In the upcoming chapters, I'll give you battle tested strategies that will help you overcome any fears or obstacles you may have around networking. My goal in writing this book is for you to demystify your fears so you can have networking success! I will address the strategies necessary to engage in an effective networking campaign to help you grow your business, land that job, solve all of life's problems (well almost), learn a thing or two, or make a few friends. The emphasis will mostly be on the growing your business part but feel free to tailor the approaches to meet your objectives. Happy networking!

Takeaways

- *Networking* is a proactive approach to meeting people so that you can learn something and potentially help them.

- One way to disarm fear is to imagine the worst thing that can happen to you while networking and then accept that fate, imagine how you might recover gracefully and vow to move on.

- Another way to disarm the fear is to just try it once—you have to start somewhere. As long as you know why you're there, know how to introduce yourself and have a list of questions to ask of people, you are ready to begin networking.

- There are five primary reasons why people network: To get more business, to land a job, to solve a problem, to get ideas or learn something and to make social connections.

YOUR "CALL TO ACTION" PLAN

Why Don't More People Network?

1. What prevents you from networking more? Check all the deterrents that apply to you personally.

- ❑ Fear of failure
- ❑ Fear of public speaking
- ❑ Fear of the unknown
- ❑ Fear of being too "salesy"
- ❑ Too time-consuming
- ❑ Too busy
- ❑ You think you can't
- ❑ Not sure where to go
- ❑ Not sure what to say
- ❑ Not sure how to ask for business
- ❑ Too busy
- ❑ Not sure how to follow up
- ❑ Not sure how to start a conversation with a stranger

2. What specific steps can you take to address and eliminate these networking fears and other deterrents?

_____

_____

_____

_____

3. Which of the following are reasons that you would like to begin networking? Check all that apply.

❏ To get more business
❏ To land a job
❏ To solve a problem (What is the problem?)
❏ To get ideas or learn something (About what?)
❏ To make social connections

4. What is a measurable strategy that you can use as a guideline at your next networking event? _____

_____

_____

Another way to disarm the fear is to just try it once—you have to start somewhere. As long as you know why you're there, know how to introduce yourself and have a list of questions to ask of people, you are ready to begin networking.

There are five primary reasons why people network: To get more business, to land a job, to solve a problem, to get ideas or learn something and to make social connections.

Your Turn

The first step in networking is just getting out there and doing it—unless you are finding it difficult to do so. If that is the case, your first step is to identify what fear or other deterrent is keeping you from becoming a networker.

The following checklist can help you get started with your own networking plan.

CHAPTER 2:
The Pool Rules of Networking™

"The first rule is not to lose. The second rule is not to forget the first rule."
—Warren Buffet

I have always been intrigued by the concept of rules. There are those who follow the rules and those who break them. Rules of the road, rules of engagement, a rule of thumb, slide rule, rule of inference, hard and fast rules. You rule!

Rules separate right from wrong in all aspects of politics, health, business, ethics, economics, law, mathematics, driving, sports, medicine—even sports medicine! There are even rules for how we use rules. And we all know that rules are meant to be broken.

Remember the movie *Fight Club*? Fans of *Fight Club* remember some of the brutal fight scenes, as well as some of the classic one-liners. What fans (and even non-fans) of the movie seem to remember most is the name of the Brad Pitt character (Tyler Durden) and the *Rules of Fight Club*. The first two rules seem to be the most memorable. Here's a refresher.

1st RULE: *You do not talk about FIGHT CLUB.*

2nd RULE: *You DO NOT talk about FIGHT CLUB.*

3rd RULE: *If someone says "stop" or goes limp, taps out, the fight is over.*

4th RULE: *Only two guys to a fight.*

5th RULE: *One fight at a time.*

6th RULE: *No shirts, no shoes.*

7th RULE: *Fights will go on as long as they have to.*

8th RULE: *If this is your first night at FIGHT CLUB, you HAVE to fight.*

I was thinking of Tyler Durden and *Fight Club* one day when reading the Pool Rules and Regulations at a public swimming pool. It seems that all public pools have the same rules—no running, no jumping, no splashing, no food or beverages, no diving in the shallow end, no swimming, no fun—you know the routine. And there's always a rule saying that horseplay isn't allowed. I don't even know what horse-play is—but whatever it is, you can't do it. The rules are in accordance with the Department of State Division of Code Enforcement and Administration, so they have to exist, for both safety and liability reasons.

Often, when entering the public pool area, you have to show a picture ID, have your bags checked (no food or alcohol), sign an agreement stating that you understand the rules and regulations, get dusted for prints—the usual. It's like being at the airport. And you can have comfort in knowing that the rules are strictly enforced by the lifeguard on duty.

What does any of this have to do with networking?

Wouldn't it be great if everyone splashing around you at a networking event knew what they should and shouldn't be doing? If registration at a business event were treated the same way as entering the pool area, more of us would know the rules of the game upon entering.

Better yet, imagine if everyone who attended association events, networking groups, chamber mixers, conferences, conventions, trade shows, holiday parties, client-recognition events and cocktail parties had to read, understand and sign off on The Pool Rules of Networking™.

We'd do a ton more business and be much better networkers overall. In fact, more of you would just jump right in the deep end! Without knowing "the rules," it's no wonder so many sales reps, business owners and job searchers are fearful and uncomfortable when it comes to wading into even the shallow end of the cocktail party or other event.

Here are The Pool Rules of Networking™ to help you navigate the waters at future events. But before we dive in (pun intended), it's important to keep a few things in mind.

For starters, The Pool Rules of Networking™ are in no particular order, but some set the tone for others or overlap. Also, some of the rules may allow more flexibility than others, depending on the type of event you attend or a specific circumstance that you experience. I'll cover this in later chapters. Like the rules at the swimming pool, some of The Pool Rules of Networking™ may seem like common sense or even silly, while others are more involved and logical. Yet others may stop you right in your swim trunks—a revelation of sorts!

Remember from Chapter 1, we discussed the five reasons why anyone would ever network: to do business, to land a job, to solve a problem, to learn something or brainstorm and to make social connections. The Pool Rules of Networking™ apply to all five of them.

We WILL talk about networking.

1. No Selling—Ever!

Most people can't define networking. Can you? Well, it's not your fault because it is not clearly defined (or even mentioned) in most college textbooks. Do you remember covering it in your marketing class? MBA program? How about in law school? You would think networking would be a rite of passage of sorts in college, given how important it is to business and to a job search. But it's not. In the public-speaking class that I teach at Rutgers University, I have been incorporating networking strategies as part of my curriculum. The information is a revelation to most of the students, most of whom are majoring in business communication—an irony in itself. At the end of the semester, students get to share anonymous feedback about the class, and my networking segment receives the most honorable mentions. It's no wonder why students have such a difficult time making important business connections early on—no one teaches them how!

Many recent college grads and others end up in sales positions. But even most sales reps haven't a clue when it comes to networking and effectively building relationships. Sales reps are typically taught sales skills to push products and services, but most fail because they aren't taught the right way to make connections or to establish and maintain great relationships through networking.

Networking <u>Is Not</u> the Same as Selling

As we stated in Chapter 1, networking is **a proactive approach to meeting people so that you can learn and potentially help them (as in the other person)**—not to sell your product or service.

Years ago, a friend of mine invited me to a trade show. He insisted that there was great networking to be had. The trade show was in a huge convention center, and much to my surprise, my friend was there to greet me at the door. Without giving me time to get acclimated, he shuffled me through several exhibits and across an aisle or two, insisting that he introduce me to someone. Of course, I was interested and excited. As we made our way, we finally found our destination as my friend introduced me to a guy named Dave. As Dave and I shook hands, I realized my friend who had just introduced us disappeared. So it was just Dave and me—face to face, nose to nose, belly to belly.

Anybody ever do that to you? Just leave you standing there with someone you don't know, for reasons unknown? I'm not the shyest guy in the world, so I was more than fine. I was just curious about why we were introduced in the first place.

I realized that, when Dave shook my hand, he slipped me a business card at the same time (the kiss of death by the way). I looked at Dave and he asked, "Do you own a home?"

I said, "Yes I do."

He said, "Great! What's your mortgage rate?"

I couldn't help myself. I said, "Interesting question, Dave, but I have a question for you. How much money did you make last year?" I could see that he was confused. I said, "Level with me, Dave. We're becoming fast friends here. What type of scratch did you pull down last year?" Dave just stared at me. I said, "Let me be fairly clear. I'm here to network, not to be sold products and services — or to refinance my house. I'll let you go. There may be others you should be speaking with, and I don't want to take up more of your time. Good luck today and I look forward to crossing paths."

I have bumped into Dave on several other occasions at trade shows and other networking events over the years, and he won't even talk to me. Not a word!

So was Dave networking or selling? Nobody likes to be sold, and certainly not at a networking event. I try to keep things simple. At networking events, you network. At sales meetings (sales appointments, job interviews), you sell. Easy, right? Well, to many sales reps, it's not. It's hard to snap yourself out of the mindset of selling, but to be more effective at building relationships, you must.

Think about how you might feel at one of those time-share meetings in Mexico. Have you ever attended meetings like that? Usually, you'll be bribed with a free massage, boat tour or some other incentive. But the sales reps there are relentless and trained to be that way. It's uncomfortable to be the target of such sales tactics. You don't want to be the one to do this to someone else, either. In some cases, you might get the sale, but you'll have a tough time getting referrals, renewals and a good reputation.

The only thing you should be selling at a networking event is your interest in and willingness to help others, your likeability, your smarts and your competence. If you do that, you'll sell plenty!

2. Everyone Is *Not* a Prospect

If everyone is a prospect (like they may teach you in sales training), then you have to sell them something. Again, as sales expert Jeffrey Gitomer says, "People don't like to be sold, but they love to buy!" Do you see the difference? People want to make (or feel like they made) their own decisions. So you can't assume that everyone is a prospect.

A *prospect* is someone who knows you or knows of you, has an interest in your product or service and is open to making a purchase today or in the future. That's it!

So contacts you meet at a networking event are not prospects. Family members and friends are not prospects. Leads on lists that you purchase are not prospects. People you make cold calls to are not prospects. And certainly businesses in the Yellow Pages are not prospects. So what's my point?

Networking is one of the best ways to find prospects (as you meet people who present themselves as such), or you could be referred to prospects—that neighbor who's looking for life insurance, that woman in the grocery store who's looking for a wedding planner or that guy at the gym who needs a mortgage (incidentally, I would never refer him to Dave).

3. It Is Never About You

As we discussed in Rule No. 1, networking is a proactive approach to meeting people so that you can learn something and potentially help them. It is always about meeting people, making a great impression and helping them. And it is always about somebody else. The questions that you ask and the comments that you make all have to be focused on them—what they do and potentially how you can help them.

It is never, ever about you unless somebody makes it about you.

So if I'm speaking to someone at a networking event, and I'm asking all kinds of questions—"How long have you been in business?" "What brings you here?" "What is it that you're looking for?" and that person says, "You're so kind. I appreciate your interest, but enough about me. What about you?" I will say, "Funny you should ask" and tell them a little about myself. I answer their questions; I don't want to come across like I'm being guarded, and I do want engagement. But I always keep them top of mind and will steer the conversation back to them when I can.

So I never get into a conversation about myself unless someone asks me to.

4. Decide on a Target Market

My definition of a *target market* is whom you serve best and therefore wish to serve most.

It's important to have a target market because it makes it much easier to become an expert at helping *someone at something.* That way, at a networking event if you are asked, "What brings you here?" you can be very specific and say something like, "I'm here to potentially meet or be connected to managing partners, managing directors, branch managers and general agents in the insurance industry because those are my best clients." (Hey, at least that's what I would say.)

Often, I would even mention the specific name of a company or firm.

When you are specific about your market like that, it creates what a friend of mine refers to as *marketing gravity*—a situation in which someone is being drawn to you. (Marketing gravity is an interesting concept, isn't it? Think about what you would need to do to create such a gravitational pull.)

Having a target market helps present more opportunities because you're pinpointing the type of business that you like. Someone might say, "You know, it's funny—my brother works for that firm." If I had never brought up my target market, and specifically the actual name of a firm, the opportunity may never come up.

For more details on creating a target market, see Chapter 4. There, we will look at how to go about developing a target market, how to know which market is right for you, what happens if you find that it's not right for you and how to create marketing gravity and a good reputation within that market.

5. Create (and Use!) Your Elevator Pitch

You need to have something brilliant to say when somebody is interested and kind enough to say, "Enough about me. What about you?" You need to come up with something that's great and takes only 20 to 30 seconds to rattle off. The elevator pitch should not come across as a script or sound like it's been rehearsed a billion times. I teach it as a script so that people will practice it until it comes naturally to them. But once you get it, it becomes a mindset. And second nature.

In Chapter 5 there are more details about developing your elevator pitch, including a model that I created to help you accomplish that task.

6. Be Positive, Professional and Respectful—Always

Not everybody will follow this rule. Sometimes we run into people who aren't positive, professional and respectful. But it doesn't mean that you shouldn't be. So always be very positive. Say something like, "Oh, what a great business you're in. It sounds like you are doing well. Things are going well for me, too."

When networking, a conversation should never be about complaint or venting. The absolute last thing you want to do is vent about your problems, how slow business might be, how frustrating your job search is, or how bad the economy and housing market is. (Is that really what you want to be discussing?)

Again, your goal is to create marketing gravity. But if you indulge in negativity, what will happen is that positive people will not gravitate toward you; negative ones will. So stay positive! Then, you will either attract people who want or need to hear your message or those who do not want to hear it because they want to be in their negative place, and they will go away. In both cases, it's good. You want to be able to speak with other positive, like-minded people. Nothing good can be accomplished by spending time with negative people that always seem to be down on their luck.

The typical networking event is a business event, even though there is a social flair, so you want to conduct yourself as a business person. Who knows—you might end up face to face, nose to nose and belly to belly with your next client, or somebody who knows you and can refer you to your next client. (That is, if you play your cards right.)

Of course, you always want to be respectful to people because it's the right thing to do. Also, you don't ever want to end up in an embarrassing situation where you're disrespecting someone, something or a company and you're speaking to somebody who has a connection there. (I have some experience with this.) The world is a very small place so be nice and mind your manners.

7. Look the Part

Dress appropriately for the standards of the event and the market that you are either part of or are looking to serve. For example, if I'm going to an event, and my niche market is police and fire departments (which it was once upon a time), I don't think that they would think too kindly of me if I showed up at the small town fire station in a suit. It just wouldn't fit, so I might want to dress more business-casual instead (at least that was the case in the small New England towns where the fire and police departments that I worked with were located).

Know your audience, know what the dress code for the event is and then perhaps kick it up a notch or half a notch as appropriate. (Although networking shouldn't involve "selling", your appearance is the fastest way you "sell" yourself at an event or meeting.)

8. Know About Contacts, Leads and Referrals

First of all, know what the terms mean. A lot of people use them interchangeably, but they mean different things.

A *contact* is simply a person with whom you have very little, if any, connection. "I got a guy who's got a guy who's got a gal who's got a dog who's got a guy." Someone might say to you, "I know of somebody you should talk to. I used to work with him when I worked at Staples. He probably doesn't remember who I am. Here's his name. I don't even know if he's still there. But see if you can track him down." That's a contact.

A *lead* is a name you acquire through someone you know. I might say to you, "You should talk to my friend Hal. He's a really good guy. And I know he has been thinking about hiring someone who specializes in your area of expertise. Just give him a call and use my name." That's a lead.

A *referral* is a contact you make when someone else introduces you to a person. You might say to me, "Michael, can I ask you a favor? Would you mind putting a call in to Hal to see if he would be interested in speaking with me about helping him?" And then I would contact Hal and come back to you and say, "Yes, Hal is expecting your call." That's a referral.

Ironically, networking (like boxing) is a contact sport. And like boxing you can't be good at it without making contacts—or at least making contact. It's also very important to play the game of referrals. I give referrals, and I expect them in return. But you have to educate people because most people don't know the difference between contacts, leads and referrals, and you can't assume that they do. So you have to consider that when you speak to people and get to the point when you can make a request of them. (I'll get into this in more detail in Chapter 5.)

9. Know Your Chickens and Eggs

"Eggs"—golden eggs—are your prospects. They are the people who hire you to do your job.

"Chickens"—golden geese—are referral sources. They are people who fish (Fish? Chickens?) in the same pond as you. They are looking to meet the same people you are, but for different reasons. They are not competition; they are collaborative partners. They are constantly coming in contact with the golden eggs. For example, a "chicken" for a financial advisor would be a CPA—an excellent and constant source of referrals.

A person could be both an egg and a chicken—that person might play a dual role. He might hire you while being involved in the same target market that you are involved in and, therefore, in a great position to refer more business to you.

10. Eat and Drink Strategically

There are a few ways you could interpret this. It could be that you don't kick back too many dirty martinis—and I have stories of people who did and shouldn't have and said all kinds of things that they shouldn't have—bad. Drinking, bad.

But a larger part of it is that a lot of people get lost or caught up with the food and the drink, and it ends up taking them out of the networking game, or it becomes an obstacle. So how do I balance the Styrofoam plate, plastic fork, beverage and napkin, and at the same time go out there and present myself, give a business card, shake a hand, kiss a baby and all of that? It can definitely seem awkward — especially if you're nervous to begin with.

So "eat and drink strategically" means to consider that and then determine your strategy. For example, I like to get to networking events a bit early if I can. That way, I can eat and have one or two beverages—usually non-alcoholic—and now I'm free to move about the cabin (so to speak). Now I can really focus on the "work" aspect of "network."

Other people I know will wait until the end of a networking event to eat. Or they will be very good about incorporating when and how to eat with whomever they might be with. Or their strategy might be to stay near the bar or near the buffet table because people have to go there eventually. And maybe that's not a bad strategy.

So be strategic about it. Don't let the food and drink distract you from networking.

Now, some people may think, who cares? Everyone's got to eat, so why make such a big deal out of it? It's because most people, I find (as we learned in Chapter 1) are a bit nervous. Some find networking a daunting experience, and they don't want to be there in the first place. But maybe a boss told them that they need to be there, or they know in their heart of hearts that they should be there, and the awkwardness of the food and drink situation becomes yet another thing that prevents them from getting out there, meeting people and saying what they need to say. The last thing that we want is something that seems so commonplace, like eating and drinking, to become a big networking deterrent.

11. Have Your Tools of the Trade

When you are networking, you have to have your networking tool kit with you. I know that when I meet people for the first time at a cocktail party, networking event or wherever it might be, I expect people to be prepared—to have tangible, physical things with them that would make them networkers. That sounds basic, but you'd be surprised how unprepared many people are.

Tangible Tools

First of all, you need a couple of pens—throw-away pens. Why throw-away pens? Because if someone walks away with one of them, who cares?

Also, you must have business cards with you at all times — especially at business events and functions. Business cards are your true "calling card" as a networker and as a business person. And if you're a student or job searcher — you're not off the hook! There are many online printing resources that you can have a business card made with simply your name, contact information, and profession (or major if you're a student about to graduate).

I threw my brother his bachelor party many years back. It turned into 10 guys going to Vegas from Thursday to Sunday. My brother returned the favor a year later; he threw my bachelor party in New Orleans—same idea, different group of guys, Thursday through Sunday. I'm just saying.

Anyway, here we are at the Hard Rock Café Hotel, a gorgeous day outside, and now it's Friday morning. A friend of mine named Steve, who is a financial planner, is out in the swimming pool, and we see that he's talking to somebody. We all look over to see who he is talking to and it looks like he is engaged in a business conversation. We're thinking, "He doesn't know anybody here, but there he is. OK, go Steve!" After a couple of minutes, Steve reaches into the pocket of his swim trunks and pulls out a plastic bag, which contains business cards, and hands a business card to the person he is talking to.

Steve was just starting his business at that time. Today he runs a thriving practice and has people working with him. That day at the pool, he ended up closing a very large group client because of that transaction. He was told later that what sold them, other than him being a good guy who seemed to know what he was talking about, was, "Anybody who was that prepared to talk business, hence presenting a business card at a bachelor party in a swimming pool, is the person I want managing my portfolio."

So business cards breed business—regardless of where you may be. It doesn't hurt to keep them with you at all times. I keep them in all of my briefcases, my car and my wallet. I even keep them in my softball bag and gym bag.

Also, add index cards to your tool kit. Keep a stack of index cards with you so you can take notes on them. You may not remember everything that happens at the event and everyone you meet. But if you promise somebody that you're going to do something as a follow up, you want to be able to jot that down. It also makes a good impression on the person you're speaking with because you are writing down what you're saying you're going to do. The task is now noteworthy, and, therefore, it's going to get done.

Be careful about technology—a Blackberry, Treo, iPhone or whatever you're using. Don't get caught putting more focus on your PDA—emailing, texting, Tweeting—than on speaking with the person who is right in front of you. That's just disrespectful. You can use your device as a resource. If you need information right then and there, that's fine, but don't use it as yet another networking deterrent. It's also just rude to be more preoccupied with your technology than you are with someone that's standing in front of you live and in person.

One thing that happens in my own networking as I'm speaking with people is that I might forget to turn my cell phone off, or to at least put it on silent mode, so it will ring. I will say, "Excuse me for one second. Let me just see who this is, and I'll shut it down. If it's my wife, I might have to take it." That usually gets a chuckle. So now I look at the cell phone to see who is calling. Unless it is my wife, I'll put it on "ignore," shut it down and say, "I'm so sorry about that." People are very nice. They'll say, "No, go ahead and take it" because we've been conditioned like this now. And I'll say, "No, no, that's quite all right. I do appreciate that. But I have only one conversation at a time."

What ends up happening is that now they're flattered. They realize that the conversation that I'm having with them is numero uno. It's the most important thing going on right now! And invariably, without me having to say that they should—they will shut their phone down, too. So now you have mutual respect for one another's time and attention.

It is also wise to have a name tag with you. Sometimes at events they're given to you. Keep one with you, just in case you're not given one because that puts people at ease, having your name right in front of them. And put the name tag on your right side so that when you shake someone's hand, it presents the name tag at eye shot.

Intangible Tools

Business cards, pens, index cards, breath mints, PDA's, name tags, your favorite hat, yada yada — those are the tangible tools of the trade.

There are also intangible tools—the primary one is to know why you're there. You have to have a goal, and it can't be just that you're "looking to do more business."

Remember the five reasons why people network, from Chapter 1? To get more business, to land a job, to solve a problem, to get information or learn something, and to make social connections. Know what your goal is, and again, know who your target market is.

Another intangible tool is having an array of questions to ask people. Or, as Pool Rule No. 13, "Have Good Questions to Ask," suggests, you can have a list of questions with you at an event, which would make it a tangible tool and perhaps easier to use.

12. Initiate Conversations by Introducing Yourself

When I meet somebody for the very first time, I'll say, "Very nice to meet you. So what type of work do you do?" That seems obvious, but I get a lot of a-ha's from my clients about that. People will say, "You go right into that?" Absolutely. If it's a business event, no doubt. If you think that's too direct, then maybe start off with something like, "Very nice to meet you. So do you know anybody here, and if so, what is your connection to being here?" Or something like that. And then you can move into, "So, tell me, what type of work do you do? Who do you work for? Do you like what you do?"

By the way (I'm tempted to write BTW), research has found that 66% of people who are lucky enough to be working right now do not like what they do. And I find that the lion's share of them happen to be attorneys. Many attorneys seem to hate what they do. I often will ask, "Do you like what you do?" And if somebody replies, "I love what I do," I'll say, "That's really good to hear because I love what I do, too. Great." And then I'll ask, "What is it about the work you do that you love?" People love talking about that. And I love hearing it. Of course, if they don't love (or even like) what they do, you might be in a position to help them. (If not, consult an attorney.)

13. Have Good Questions to Ask

The best way to start a conversation, carry a conversation and learn from a conversation is to ask questions. Lots of them! You don't want to come across like you're conducting an interview, but you do want to appear interested. Hopefully you are.

But what should you ask? Will you come across as nosy? Pushy? Or just naturally curious? If you are naturally *interested*, you will become naturally *interesting*. And those you meet will become interested about you, too. (Interesting, huh?)

It makes a lot of sense to be prepared with a list of questions you plan on asking others as you meet them and network. You can even have them written out on an index card until you get the hang of it.

Asking questions is the best way to start a conversation; to learn something; to maintain a conversation; and to stay focused, collaborative and comfortable. You don't want to talk about the weather or have to make small talk. You want to have a very specific reason why you are talking to people and have a road map to follow.

I will often start out by saying, "It's very nice to meet you. What type of work do you do?" and "Do you like what you do?" If they like what they do, I'm thrilled, and I'll say, "Well, that's really great to hear because I love what I do. Tell me what it is about your work that you love." Now, if they say, "I'm really having a tough time right now—you know, the economy" or "I don't like what I do"—I will say, "I'm so sorry to hear that. What is it about your work that you would change if you could so that you would like it?"

That's important for two reasons. First, you're making it OK for them to say they're not enjoying what they do, and you're allowing them to reflect on what would make it better. Second, it's a recruiting opportunity — especially if you're a sales manager or someone looking to grow a team. You can say, "You know, after I learn a little bit more about you, perhaps I might be able to avail you of a career opportunity."

Recruiting is not my purpose for asking the question, "Do you enjoy what you do?" but it is an outcome.

Other questions I may ask are, "How did you learn about this event? Are you a first-timer like me, or have you been here before?" Now, if they're a first-timer like me, I'll say, "Oh, that's great. Good. Sigh of relief. How did you find out about the event?" So now I'm learning about other events that perhaps I should go to, or maybe I'll learn about an upcoming conference or another person I should know—it's all about learning—which is the definition of networking!

If they have been there before, I'll say, "That's great. What keeps you coming back?" They may reply, "Oh, I'm a board member," or "I've been a member a long time," or "I do a lot of business here." Now I know that somebody here probably knows more people than me, especially if I am, in fact, a first-timer.

Another question I love to ask is, "If I were going to meet a perfect prospect for you, how would I know?" People love that question (or at least I do). This question brings the discussion to their target market, and now I'm really drilling down and asking questions that people don't often ask.

Another question I would ask is, "What do you do for fun when you're not at networking events or cocktail parties, and when you're not working or focused on your business?" I can talk about my little girls and Disney princesses all day, or I'll talk about my dogs, about sports, or about boxing. You need to try to have fun at business meetings and networking events. (Even if you have to fake it at first.) As The Joker said in The Dark Knight, "Why so serious?" (Pool Rule No. 21 — Have Fun!)

Even if you don't talk a lot about business but are having a great conversation, and you hit it off, I know you could get into a business discussion—if not now, then at some point later. I might say, "Look, I've taken up a lot of your time. Are you OK if we continue talking? I know we've been talking about Disney princesses. I could talk about this all day, but do you want to do the business-card exchange, and then circle back? I'd also like to hear more about your business, and perhaps there might be a way that I can help you." Of course that conversation is going to take place because I've already hit it off (despite the Disney princesses).

Then, if I really like the person, I'll say, "You sound like you're really good at what you do. You sound like you're really into it. I would love to be a resource for you. Tell me how I can help you." I don't ask everyone that—one-third of the time I will like someone enough to ask that question, but two-thirds of the time I won't. (I don't like everyone I meet. Do you?)

Other questions I will ask are "How long have you been in the business?" "What brings you to this event?" "Who do you know here, and what is your connection to them?" "What is your goal in attending this event?"

Tailor the questions to what you think is most appropriate and how they might fit you. Notice that all of these questions are completely about them. They're not about me or you.

Here is a recap of the questions I typically use when I'm at a networking event, cocktail party, mixer, conference or golf outing, as appropriate.

- *So what do you do?*
- *Who do you work for?*
- *How long have you been at it?*
- *Do you like what you do? Why?*
- *Anything about your work you don't like?*
- *How do you market your business?*
- *What brings you to this event? Have you been here before?*
- *What are you looking to accomplish here?*

- *Who would you love to meet? Why?*
- *How do you help your clients (or customers)?*
- *What do you do for fun (other than working or networking)?*
- *How can I help you? (If I happen to like them.)*

14. Have a Goal and a Plan

My goal is typically to meet two or three *quality* people. Two or three — that's it! Not 10 or 20. I'm not looking to "work the room". If you meet more than two or three, great! But your targets should be low — two or three *quality* connections (with the emphasis on *quality*) is fine. Why put so much pressure on yourself? Think of how daunting it is to show up at an event and look at an entire room of strangers that you think you have to meet. Just look to meet two or three quality people (at a quality price — kidding). If you're on a roll, look to meet more. (Feel better?)

So, what is a quality person anyway? To me, a quality person is somebody I like, somebody I can help (best if we can help one another), somebody that's smart, and often enough — somebody I have something in common with. Remember, think *quality*, not quantity. What good is there in meeting a lot of people if they are not of quality (my interpretation anyway)? And *quality* people tend to hang out with more *quality* people. I'm just saying.

> **Tip:** Be very choosy about the networking events you visit and where you ultimately become active. *Quality* events tend to attract quality people.

15. Listen More, Talk Less

Very often, I am accused of being an over the top, outgoing, gregarious person who's bouncing off the walls. But really, that's not who I am. I'm more on the reserved side — sometimes even introverted. When I'm at a networking event or cocktail party, I am not "working the room". That's not me. It's also not networking (learning about and helping people).

Let me be clear — I'm not shy, but when I'm speaking to people, I'm asking great open-ended questions, and I shut up and listen. If I don't shut up and listen, I'm doing all the talking. (Do you know anyone like that? If not, maybe it's you!) If I'm doing all the talking, it makes it very difficult to learn about and help others.

I am often described as an exceptional listener, easy to talk to (at least in business circles). The reason for that is that I don't do a lot of talking, other than asking clarifying questions or just weighing in, conveying a similar experience. But I really try to make most of the conversation about them. I find that, whereas most people do 70 percent of the talking and 30 percent of the listening, I flip it around. I try to do 30 percent of the talking, if I can, and 70 percent of the listening. How can I figure out how to help someone and have a valuable business conversation if I'm not listening the way I should be?

16. Keep Your Eyes Focused on Your Conversation

There is an episode of "Will and Grace" in which Jack and Karen—two of the most obnoxious people ever—are at a cocktail party, socializing with some folks. Their pinkies are up in the air, they've got cocktails and are eating *hors d'oeuvres*, and they see new people come into the room. They look at the people they're speaking with and say, "Gotta go. Better people!"

You don't want to "better people" anybody. If you're speaking with somebody, make sure that you maintain eye contact as appropriate. You don't want to look for somebody "better to speak with" because the people you are speaking with will find it rude and disrespectful. However, if there's somebody in the background that you happen to have had eye contact with or that you need to speak with, just address that.

Say something like, "Bob, can I excuse myself for one second? I just need to say hello to that person. I haven't seen him in a long time. There's a question I need to ask him, and I'll circle right back." And that would be perfectly OK. Or you could wave at the other person and say, "Hey, Ed, how are you doing? I'll catch up with you in a second." Then say to the person you're talking with, "I'm sorry about that, Bob." And now you can bring the conversation right back to where you left off. But you don't want to be scanning the room. (Scanning the room for "better people" — rude.)

17. Introduce Others with Passion

Be passionate about introducing people to one another. Have you ever introduced two people to one another and they ended up dating? Or married? Don't you love telling the story of how you connected the two? Well, it's almost the same thing in business.

It's a cool thing to be able to give somebody else's elevator pitch to a prospective client. So I might introduce Hal to

Bob by saying, "Hal is a CPA. He is a great friend of mine. And Bob is a financial planner, and I think it's ideal for the two of you to speak with one another. I see a lot of potential value here because you serve the same markets and tend to work with the same kind of businesses." Make it evident as to why you're introducing them.

At a networking event, I can introduce two people once I have gotten to know a little about both of them and have learned what they do. I would mention to both of them why I think it's a good idea for the two of them to meet, why it's a good connection.

18. Implement a Time Limit

At a networking event, I try not to speak to any one person longer than six to eight minutes—without ever looking at my watch. That's just rude. So it's not like I'm always in a rush to go some place else; I just don't want someone to feel obligated to stay in a conversation with me if there is no good reason to do so. (This often happens because neither party knows how to tactfully break away or end the conversation.)

As I've mentioned, I box as a hobby (yes, boxing gloves, a ring, someone hitting me!), so my life has actually become a series of three-minute rounds. I try not to talk to any one person for longer than two rounds (as in three minute boxing rounds — ding ding). That's just a guideline, though, and there are a couple of exceptions. If it makes sense to continue a conversation, certainly I'll do it. If it doesn't make sense, I won't.

I will speak with someone for six to eight minutes if we have a good connection. I won't speak to *everybody* for that length of time. If it's not a great connection, I will speak to them for only a minute or two, and then I will excuse myself respectfully and professionally. I don't want to monopolize the other person's time if there is no need.

If I'm having a grand old time speaking with someone, after a couple of "rounds" have gone by, I might say, "I'm having a really great time speaking with you, but I don't want to hold you up if there are other people you want to speak with. Are you OK continuing to keep me company here? Or we could continue our conversation elsewhere—we could do the whole business card thing. It's up to you. I just don't want to hold you up." And that person will be flattered and feel good that I'm giving them that option. They might say, "No, I'm really into our conversation, but I really appreciate you asking."

If I do need to move on, I will say, "There are a couple of people I need to catch up with, but I would love to do the business card thing and continue our conversation soon. It sounds like there's a lot for us to talk about."

> **Important note:** Always be honest! Only say there are others you need to meet if in fact there are. Offer to continue the conversation at another time only if you seriously plan to. You don't want to blow someone off. I'll discuss this more in-depth in the next Pool Rule and in the next chapter.

Listen to your gut. If you feel a great connection there, the conversation is easy (and fun!) and there is a lot to talk about, they probably feel that, too. But if you feel there is not a good connection, they probably feel the same way. A mirror image of sorts.

19. Terminate Conversations Politely

Do you connect with everybody you meet? Of course not! I have determined that one-third of the time, we do; two-thirds of the time, we typically don't.

You know how it is when you go to a wedding, and you are coupled out with somebody? You're at one of these round tables, and you're there with three or four other couples. Nobody knows one another. If you hit it off, it's great. It's just a night out. You're eating and drinking; life is good. When you don't hit it off—which is two-thirds of the time— does anybody ever come back to the table? No! You're off talking to people you know, dancing, doing your own thing.

But at a networking event, you can't disappear like that—not really. So two-thirds of the time, you probably will not get to the six-, seven- or eight-minute point (your proverbial time limit). If you are speaking with someone you don't feel a good connection with, your conversation might last just a couple of minutes, then you will probably want to terminate the conversation—like I did with Dave (the mortgage guy), from the trade show.

I would say to Dave, "You know, frankly I'm not looking to refinance my house right now. That's not my purpose for being here. So let me let you go. There are probably other people you want to speak with. I don't want to get in the way of that and waste your time. It has been great meeting you. Good luck today and I'll see you again soon." And you're out of there — no muss, no fuss, professional, respectful.

If I do not have a good vibe, if I feel that someone is trying to sell me something, or if I just don't like them, I will end the conversation pretty quickly — always in a professional and respectful manner.

20. Follow Up

You have to go into a networking event knowing and thinking that there will be a follow-up component. You are not going to write business at the event or close a sale, probably. Doors are opening (opportunities presenting themselves that is), so now you have to figure out how you are going to keep them open by following up.

Your intention at a networking event has to be to follow up (this is actually an intangible tool of the trade). You can't rely on somebody else to do so. So if you and I are speaking to one another somewhere, and we're approaching our six to eight minute time limit, if and when we exchange business cards, I'll say, "It has been great chatting with you. I look forward to following up with you over the next couple of days to see if we can explore how we might be able to help one another." After that, I'm going to take the initiative to follow up.

> **Important note:** When people tell you, "Oh, I'll be back in touch," they never will. Unless you happen to be a prospect for them! Otherwise the promise to follow up becomes a blow off or an exit strategy rather than a way of continuing the networking process.

Following up also means following through on your promises and commitments. If you tell someone you will get that article or information to them, do it—and get it done within the next 24 hours. I get a lot of questions from people, even seasoned networkers, about following up. So we will go into follow-up more in-depth in another chapter.

21. Have Fun!

OK, back to the having fun thing. This may be the most important rule. If you are not having fun at networking, there's something wrong. Not with you necessarily but there has to be some element of fun in your networking approach otherwise you won't do it. Network that is. And you'll never get better at it. I'm not saying networking is for everybody, but once you find your style, approach, market, process — it should at least become more fun over time.

The Pool Rules of Networking™

1. No Selling—Ever!
2. Everyone Is Not a Prospect
3. It Is Never About You
4. Decide on a Target Market
5. Create (and Use!) Your Elevator Pitch
6. Be Positive, Professional, Respectful—Always
7. Look the Part
8. Know About Contacts, Leads and Referrals
9. Know Your Chickens and Eggs
10. Eat and Drink Strategically
11. Have Your Tools of the Trade
12. Initiate Conversations by Introducing Yourself
13. Have Good Questions to Ask
14. Have a Goal and a Plan
15. Listen More, Talk Less
16. Keep Your Eyes Focused on Your Conversation
17. Introduce Others with Passion
18. Implement a Time Limit
19. Terminate Conversations Politely
20. Follow Up!
21. Have Fun!

We cannot be held responsible for accidents or injuries. Thank you for your cooperation.

If networking is painful and grueling for you, the people you meet will see that a mile away. If you look like you're toughing it out or you don't want to be there, no one will want to talk with you, help you, refer you and certainly not work with you. I certainly wouldn't.

I know the word "work" is in "network," but in my mind, if you're doing it the right way, it should be fun—or become fun, over time with practice.

None of The Pool Rules™ mean anything unless you dive right in. It's important to at least get your feet wet. These rules (and other concepts we discuss) may not be second nature at first, but as you become more skilled, more confident, and more focused, you will get better and enjoy it more.

People who behave in the ways I have described tend to be extraordinary networkers and really good with people. And I also find that they tend to be pretty successful at what they do.

Takeaways

- *Networking* is a proactive approach to meeting people so that you can learn something and potentially help them.

- Your *target market* is whom you serve best and therefore wish to serve most.

- Always try to create *marketing gravity*—that situation in which someone is being drawn to you.

- A *contact* is simply a name of a person with whom you have very little, if any, connection. A lead is a name you acquire through someone you know. A *referral* is a person to whom someone else introduces you.

- In a networking conversation, ask a lot of questions related to your target market. Questions help you enter conversations gracefully and also will result in valuable information that moves you closer to your set goal.

- Talk only 30 percent of the time; listen 70 percent of the time.

- Always be professional and respectful, even when terminating a conversation or relationship.

Your Turn

Ideas are useless without action. The Pool Rules of Networking™ are meant to give you a pragmatic approach—specific steps—toward networking that you can implement right away. As with any skill, you won't notice a difference until you get out there and do it.

The following "call to action" plan will help you get started.

YOUR "CALL TO ACTION" PLAN

The Pool Rules of Networking™

1. What group or industry would you like to reach out to by networking (i.e., who is your target market)? _____

2. Name a networking event that you could attend in the near future to reach this group or industry. _____

3. What specific goal(s) would you like to accomplish by attending the event? _____

4. Who are some specific referral sources, prospects, clients (remember chickens and eggs) you should contact?

5. How do you plan to follow up with the people you meet at the event? _____

6. How can you help people you meet at an event—prospects, clients, referral sources—and how can they help you?

CHAPTER 3:

How to Deal with Sticky Situations

"The rate at which a person can mature is directly proportional to the embarrassment he can tolerate."

—Douglas Engelbart, American Inventor

When you are in a networking environment—or at any event or party where others are mingling around—sticky situations can arise. People are keenly aware of that, and a lot of the fear that surrounds networking, which we discussed earlier, is tied up in not knowing what to do if something unfortunate happens.

If you can overcome such situations, networking will be less intimidating, and you will do more of it, which will increase your chances of meeting people who can further your career and your cause. In this chapter, I'll discuss the questions I get most often about networking and how to handle what can be difficult situations if you don't have a lot of experience with them.

Don't feel like you're the only one who is concerned about doing something stupid. Recently, I was consulting a group of managers and agents who work for a highly sophisticated company. These are very seasoned professionals, some of whom are quite successful, yet they had myriad questions about how to introduce themselves, how to excuse themselves if they didn't want to continue a conversation and what they should do if they forget someone's name. So even the most sophisticated, extroverted and intelligent professionals who are masters at problem solving have questions about these issues.

How Do I Introduce Myself?

It is handy to know this—not just in a business setting, but also in a social setting, such as at a holiday party. Even though it sounds basic, a lot of people have a hard time walking up to a total stranger and introducing themselves. Again, I think it's mom's fault because she told us not to talk to strangers.

First and foremost, I need to discuss the handshake — the mutually acceptable way to greet someone in this country in both business and social settings.

I know learning how to shake somebody's hand sounds very basic but you would be surprised how many times I am asked about how to do it. (By very smart and successful people mind you.)

When approaching someone, use common sense as it applies to their physical size and strength, as well as yours. Remember, you don't want to hurt someone. (Keep in mind that there may be times that you encounter someone with an injury or disability.)

I invented The Scale of Fate (I had some time on my hands — literally.) The Scale of Fate dictates that from a scale of 1 to 10, 1 is the weakest handshake possible (the dead-fish) and 10 is ripping someone's arm out if it's socket (Haiko — a Dutch term). Somewhere around 7 to 8 on the scale is acceptable for firmness (as in a firm handshake) in both business and social situations — for men and women in this country.

Women seem to know the concept of the handshake better than men. It's probably because women tend to be better networkers than men. I've been at many a cocktail party or networking event where an assertive business woman walks up to a business man and introduces herself — offering her hand.

The man always seems to hesitate (probably not so much if another man would approach him and introduce himself). He hesitates as if taken by surprise. Reluctantly, he'll follow her lead (or so he thinks) and offer a dead-fish type of handshake (1 on the scale if you're following along at home) and she crushes him with an 8 or 9. Again, women seem to know the concept of The Scale of Fate better than men.

By the way, I call this rating system The Scale of Fate because often enough the handshake sets the tone for the conversation and ultimately for the relationship. (This is outside an injury or disability.)

No one likes the dead-fish handshake. It's kind of creepy. But you also don't want to kill somebody with the G.I. Joe/ Kung Fu grip — or a Haiko grip.

What is Haiko? I worked with a guy at a Wall Street firm many years ago named (you guessed it) Haiko. He was huge — 6'8" and very Dutch. He wouldn't just shake your hand hard—he would jerk your whole arm. One day, he did that to somebody and actually dislocated the guy's shoulder. The guy had to be rushed to the hospital. No, Haiko, no! Dead fish—bad. Haiko—worse.

Again, on a scale of 1 to 10:

1   =   the Dead Fish
7-8 =   Where the firmness of your handshake should be
           (at least in the U.S.)
10   =   No Haiko, no!

After your greeting and handshake, you can then proceed to ask the questions that we covered in Chapter 2.

Here's how you introduce yourself. Basically, you walk up to someone that you think wants to be greeted. If they're not speaking to somebody, say, "Good morning. My name is…," and have a smiling, engaging demeanor. Give them a 7-to-8 handshake and say, "It's very nice to meet you." Then continue with an engaging question or comment. If they're speaking to someone already, say, "I'm sorry to interrupt," then proceed with your greeting and name. I know this sounds very basic but if you're an introvert (and many extroverts struggle with this) or don't get out much; the mere thought of introducing yourself to a stranger at an event may seem daunting. As you can see there's nothing to it!

Even if you're at a social event, you can still talk about business—and sometimes you can even do business.

(It's not the actual act of introducing yourself that's difficult. I think most adults with a sound mind can do that. It's what happens after the introduction that seems daunting. OK, now what? That's where the questions we discussed earlier come in.)

This past year, I moved into a new home. I live on a large cul-de-sac. There are about 40 houses in this loop. One of my neighbors invited my wife and me and our other neighbors to a holiday party at his house. We showed up and knew a few people as acquaintances but certainly didn't know everybody there.

You know how you first get to a party and it's kind of lame? People just aren't quite in the spirit yet. It's just gearing up, and there is a sense of awkwardness. It was like that when we walked into No. 30 (as in house number 30). I shook hands with some folks and greeted the person who lives there. He was stocking ice in coolers. I told him, "I appreciate the invite. You remember me, No. 19, right?" I asked him if there was anything I could do, and he said it would be great if I would help him with the ice so that he could be free to meet and greet people. (Talk about your ice breaker!) After I finished with that, my wife looked at me and said, "Not the liveliest of parties." She knew I was thinking the same thing. She elbowed me in the ribs and said, "Do something!" (I get that a lot.)

So I walked back up to the host and said, "Anything else you need me to do?"

He replied, "No, I really appreciate it."

Then I began asking him questions: "So tell me, when you're not delegating ice duties to complete strangers, what kind of work do you do?"

He told me that he was an IT professional, and he asked me what I did. I said, "I *are* a professional speaker." He laughed, and I told him a little about what I did and threw a crafty elevator pitch at him.

He said, "You know who you need to speak with?"

"No, who?"

"You need to speak with No. 14. He heads up compliance at a major insurance company." He introduced me and my wife to the residents of No. 14, and everyone started talking about their work. All of a sudden, the mood at the party escalated, and people started having fun. One person was a finance guy; one was a doctor, etc. It turned into a great party where we got to know everybody very quickly and had plenty to talk about, and people started talking about business, including me. It ended up becoming a great situation, and my wife gave me an "Attaboy!" wink, which is always a good thing.

I asked the same questions I would ask at a networking event: "Do you like what you do?" "Where do you work?" "Who else do you know here?" I tweaked the questions a little bit, since this was a party and not a business event, but you still have to have great questions to ask people. And most often, even in a social situation, the conversation will gravitate toward work because people are comfortable with it, and typically they like to talk about what they do. We also spoke about kids, schools, soccer leagues, what was going on in town and those types of things. But talking about work literally broke the ice (and kept the ice chest full).

I used to say that you can do great networking everywhere that there's people, other than funerals. But now I've reneged on that because networking happens at funerals, too—funeral-goers just shouldn't be your target market (depending on your line of work of course).

I've even asked my softball team these questions. I've played in the same league for six years already. I know what everybody does for a living, and they all know what I do. They're all businesspeople. But one of the reasons people know about one another, really, is because I ask them the first couple of weeks, "What does everybody do when we're not playing softball badly?" I helped somebody on the team land a job, and some people have done business there. Asking those questions brought what we do to a different level of consciousness.

Remember, it's always about them. It should never be about you until they make it about you.

How Do I Start a Meaningful Conversation?

To have a meaningful conversation, you must ask meaningful questions. If your questions are about the weather and other topics that aren't significant, your conversation will not be meaningful—unless we're about to have a big storm.

Even if you don't feel like you're in an environment that is a true networking environment—like a holiday party—it's still an opportunity to consider the five reasons people network: to get more business, to land a job, to solve a problem, to get ideas or learn something, or to make social connections.

The extent to which your conversation is meaningful is directly proportional to the quality of questions that you ask. That's always what it comes down to.

One great way to start a conversation is to mention something that is on your mind that is relevant no matter who you're with or where you are.

A few years ago, I was at a cocktail party with small business people in Philadelphia. It was right when the new Rocky movie was coming out. I'm not only a boxer but a real Rocky Balboa fan.

Since 1983, when *Rocky III* came out, there has been a lot of hubbub about the Rocky statue. In *Rocky III*, there is a scene in which a bronze statue of Rocky stands at the top of the 72 steps of the Philadelphia Museum of Art—the steps that Rocky runs up in all the movies. Well, in real life (I love that phrase), the statue remained at the top of the steps for a while. It created a lot of controversy at the time (and probably still does) because the art museum did not consider the statue art, even though it's a beautiful 800-pound structure. They considered it "commercial" and didn't want it to be on the top of the steps because they felt that it detracted from the art and culture of the rest of the museum. So it kept going back and forth, from the art museum to the Spectrum (now the Wachovia Center), which was a sports arena in Philly where Rocky had some of his fights in the movie.

When Rocky Balboa came out in theaters in 2006, they were showing all the different Rockies on the side of the art museum, almost like an in-your-face type thing, and Sylvester Stallone was there. He was meeting people, and it was a big deal. The statue ended up back at the art museum, and it's there today. But instead of being at the top of the steps, the compromise is that it's now at the bottom of the steps. You have to look for it to find it. But where the statue used to be, there are two footprints of the sneakers that "Rocky" wore in the movie (remember those high top Keds?).

There was a lot of hype in town with the movie coming out and the buzz of film crews visiting many of the Philadelphia landmarks. Since I was in city during the day working with a client, was in the thick of Rocky-land, and knew a little about boxing myself, I was sure I would have plenty to talk about.

As I went to meet people and introduce myself, I would ask about the statue: "Good evening. My name is Michael

Goldberg. Very nice to meet you! OK, I've got a very important question for you. Where the heck is the Rocky Balboa statue?" That was my lead-in. It was relevant and in the moment, and I was genuinely interested in it. I knew it would be a fun conversation. And I knew that before I left the city, I was going to touch the Rocky statue.

That opened up unbelievable conversations because not only were people saying, "That's a good question" or "Let me tell you about it," they would call other people over and say, "Hey, Barry, come over here!"

So not only did I become involved in conversations with all of the people there—about 25 of them—I was working the room. Bartenders got involved, and the manager of the place joined in the fun. The cocktail party ended up being a blast, and that conversation changed the tone of the whole event.

That night, I ended up becoming friends with people I'm still friends with now—I didn't do business, but I made some great connections. And I was escorted to the Rocky statue. We all went in convoy, and people took pictures of me. It was a great night—all because I asked a question about something that was relevant to the moment — and to me.

I covered the other questions, too. We got into business discussions; that's why we were there, but the Rocky questions made it easy. The conversations flowed and it helped make everybody more comfortable. And I got to touch the Rocky statue!

Remember the last Pool Rule?

How Do I Introduce Others in a Conversation Without Being Rude?

This question comes up often, too. If I'm speaking to somebody and someone else enters the conversation, rarely does it happen that they introduce me. Either the person I'm talking to forgot my name (as opposed to their own name), they forgot the new person's name or they just don't know what to do next. In some cases, people just get caught up in the new conversation and fail to introduce the new person to the person they were already talking to—they're kind of being rude but probably don't mean to be.

What you do in this situation is use one another's name. And if you don't remember their names, just ask. Say, "I'm sorry— your name? OK, Barry. Barry, this is Rudy. I have known Rudy since way back when we worked together. I think it would be good for you guys to talk because…" and tell them the ways you think they would be able to help one another.

You can load it up that way. Or you could just give a quick synopsis of how you know one another, and maybe some of the details will come out during the introduction—"Oh, you work for that company, too?"—and all of a sudden, they have something to talk about. So you're making the conversation easy for them.

My purpose is to be a good host, at least for that conversation. People know that I'm a networking guy, so I want that to come across. But more importantly, I want them to feel comfortable in the moment. And if I can avail them of an opportunity to make a great business connection, of course that's a great thing, too.

In Chapter 5, you'll learn about the elevator pitch. If I know someone well enough, or if I have learned enough from the conversation already, I will deliver each of their elevator pitches *for them* and explain why I think it makes sense for them to continue a dialogue.

How Do I Introduce Others and Walk Away?

If you do a good job of adding value to two people by introducing them to one another, then you may feel that their new conversation is more important than the conversation you might have with each one of them. If that happens, then you can let them go. Just say, "It sounds like you have a lot to talk about. I don't want to get in the way. Let me circle back with both of you later. If I can help out in any way, certainly track me down, but good luck and I'll speak with you later. Have fun." So now I'm out, and I've made it evident that it's value added time for them. It's not like I'm blowing them off. I'm letting them do what they need to do, but I make a promise to circle back. Sometimes people struggle with excusing themselves like this because they think they're being rude by leaving. This is not the case because the conversation is more of a benefit to them, not to you.

But again, going back to The Pool Rules of Networking™, it's not about us, it's about them. You will probably find that people will appreciate the kindness that you extend by introducing them to other people. They will probably thank you for helping them make that connection. You've made them feel comfortable. People in these settings want something to do. They often don't know how to load it up themselves, so if you can do it for them, everybody wins.

I especially love helping job searchers connect with others. They tend to be reluctant to begin with because they may not know how to network and they're frustrated about being job searchers. If I can ever help someone in job search I'm always happy to. But for those networking to land a job, it's the same deal. I'm going to introduce them to one another and brainstorm with them about how they might help one another. Then I'll walk away and say, "I'll circle back if there's something you need, but I think you have a lot to talk about."

What Should I Do if I Forget Someone's Name?

The obvious response is, don't forget their name! Try mnemonic devices to remember names—simply associate their names with someone or something you know. When someone introduces themselves to me, I will repeat the name and even spell it or have *them* spell it. Now I own it (the name is committed to memory for at least the short term). In some cases, if it's a common name like Bob or Bill, I'll ask that person for a business card right then so that I have a visual to reinforce the name. I will also associate that person with a friend or someone else I know who has the same name. So if I meet someone named Ted, I'll associate him, in my mind, with the guy named Ted who does my printing. That makes me less likely to forget his name.

I do forget people's names, though. People always introduce themselves to me after a presentation because I'm the speaker, and sometimes I can't remember all of them. But forgetting someone's name is not the end of the world.

If someone is offended because you forgot their name, let them get over themselves. It has happened to everybody. I will say, "I'm sorry, when you get to be my age, you forget things. Your name again?" I always take the shot. And if they're older than me, it always gets a laugh. It's disarming, they give me their name and that's it. If I can make fun of myself in the process, so be it.

I do ongoing work for a St. Louis based financial services firm. Given the frequency of my visits over the course of a year, I've gotten to know the firm quite well. I know most of the advisors by name. Many of the advisors come over and shake my hand when I arrive at the firm (thankfully no Haiko grips). One advisor in particular will come over to me and re-introduce himself — both first and last name. Every time! "Hello Michael Goldberg, Bill Smirnoff here." He knows who I am, and I know who he is but he still offers the friendly reminder. It's nice of him because he knows that I come into contact with a lot of people, and he figures he's just one advisor, so how could I remember him?

I started busting his chops about it. This last time, I said, "Bill Smirnoff, I know who you are. How come every month you introduce yourself to me?"

He said, "I do that, don't I? I do that with everyone. I don't know if it's a good habit or a bad habit."

I told him, "I think it's a *great* habit, but just not with me because I know who the heck you are." He has great social grace because he is very personable. He just made the assumption that people don't remember names. He wanted to be proactive and keep it from being awkward. So kudos to Bill Smirnoff! I'll still bust his chops — but I'll never forget him. Or his name.

If you are at an event and you don't remember someone's name, be proactive. Simply ask them their name again.

Or tell them your name, and they will probably tell you theirs. Just assume they don't remember you, either. "I know we met the last time. I'm Michael Goldberg…." They will chime in with their name, and now you're on equal ground.

The bottom line is the fear of forgetting names shouldn't be a networking deterrent. People are bad with names because they're nervous, have other things going on and meet a lot of people. As long as you're up-front with it and you take it on the chin yourself, you're good. If you try to dodge the issue— you wait for them to introduce themselves to somebody else or hope that you catch their name at some point—it just makes you that much more nervous. And if they call you on it, then you will come across as lacking confidence.

I sat next to a gentleman on a plane recently who looked like a gang member—a very "street" looking 26-year-old with dreadlocks. Somehow we hit it off. As we were talking, I learned that his name was Tremont—I asked him to spell it, and he did. I also mnemonically associated his name with a street in Boston because I don't know a person named Tremont, and that's how I remembered it. We spoke quite a bit during the flight. Every so often after I said something, he would remind me of his name. He told me he had never been to New York or New Jersey, so as we were leaving the plane and heading for the baggage claim, I directed him. As he left, he shook my hand and re-introduced himself yet again, even though he was leaving. (Maybe Tremont was afraid of forgetting his own name.)

So I think the best way to not forget somebody's name is to be proactive about trying to remember it. And if you do forget their name, just ask them for it again. That is, if you remember!

How Do I Ask Someone for a Business Card?

Really, this is a problem? OK, here we go: "Do you have a business card?" That's it! That's how you do it. OK, somebody role-play with me here. "Do you have a business card?"

The reason some people have a hard time asking for a business card is they're afraid they're going to come across as salesy. One sided. Self centered. You know the deal.

Very often, the best way to have somebody take your business card is for you to ask them for theirs. Often, if it's someone I want to continue the conversation with later, I will say, "Perhaps we should exchange cards." I make it a "we" thing instead of a "me" thing. And, because it's about them and not me (a Pool Rule), I typically do not give out a business card unless someone asks me for one. Hey, if they wanted my card they would ask!

Ask for a business card only if there is a good reason for it; don't ask for one just as a reflex. My reason for asking for a business card might be that I want to remember their name. Or maybe it's because they seem like a good person, and I am interested in learning a little bit more about what they do. These are the early stages of a business (and maybe personal) relationship.

It is very important not to feel obligated to ask for a card. There should always be a reason. And you don't want to run into someone like me who will qualify you. If you ask me for a card, I will be flattered, but I will say, "Absolutely, I have a card, and I appreciate your asking. Tell me what it is that you have in mind." I want to know why you're asking for my card. I want to know if maybe you are just asking because you think you should. I bring it to a level of consciousness.

You might say, "Well, a friend of mine hires speakers," or "I want to be able to follow up with you because I think we might have a discussion about…." It qualifies the interaction and puts any kind of follow up into perspective.

If someone asks for your business card, I think it's polite to return the favor and ask for theirs. But it depends on a number of factors. If I'm in a networking situation, and we're on even ground—we're both at the same event and don't know each other—in the spirit of being polite, I would probably ask for one in return, especially if there's a good reason why they're asking for mine.

If someone just wants to add me to their database, to me that's not a good reason to ask for my business card. In that situation, I wouldn't ask for their card. In fact, I may even say, "I appreciate that, but there's really no need to put me in your database." Or I might ask him to tell me a little more about the database and what he does with it. Maybe he plans to subscribe me to his blog. If it's something I'm interested in, then of course it's a different story. But if it is not something I am interested in, I will say so politely, and then bow out of the situation.

But if they're saying they can connect me with someone and we can help one another, I will ask for their card. Or, if it's just that they're pleasant, I might ask for their card just to be polite, only because we're on even footing. I don't want to make anybody feel uncomfortable. It's a bit subjective but I always want to clearly define why I'm giving or taking a business card.

However, if you are not on equal footing as the other person (you're the speaker at the event) and they ask you for your business card, you don't have to ask for theirs in return. I don't think it's rude in that situation.

Be careful! You also don't want to take someone's card and give them false hope. Some people think that if you ask for their card, it's for a compelling reason, and something is in it for them.

It seems like business-card exchanges should be simple and cordial, but you can see how they can get a little dicey. If acquiring business cards can perpetuate staying in touch with people or help you build a relationship, that's good. If it's just so somebody can put you in a database and try to sell you stuff that you don't want or need, or they're just collecting your card because they don't know what else to say or do, that's bad.

One last thought about your business cards: Make sure they are of high quality. It may not be as important for job searchers as it is for other networkers, but business cards do make an impression.

I was at an event recently in Chicago, and there was another speaker who took the stage after me. He handed me a business card, and it was horrible—it was flimsy and had perforated, jagged edges. On the back, it said "Fuji Color Professional." Maybe I am just a networking snob but what kind of image does that present? What kind of image do you want to present?

How Do I Take Notes on Someone's Business Card?

When I exchange business cards with someone, I will look at the card, read it, take a mental snapshot of what I need to remember and try to think if there's something I need to ask. As I'm doing that, I'm exchanging information with the other person. As we end the conversation, I'll say, "I will get that article to you." Or "I will absolutely connect you with this person." Or "I'll absolutely get back in touch with you so that we can continue our conversation about…."

And then I will ask, "Would you object to my writing a note or two on the back of your business card?" I always ask that because once, I was speaking to a Japanese business professional. I had his beautiful business card in my hand the whole time, with a tree insignia on it, and it was made of a really nice, heavy stock. But I didn't compliment it. I didn't hold it the right way. And then I scribbled on the back of the card. The man was horrified. Maybe he shouldn't have been horrified because we weren't at a Japanese business event. Then again, maybe I should have known better. It's a cultural thing. I saw the expression on his face, and I said, "I'm doing something wrong, aren't I? I apologize if I am offending you. Please educate me."

He apologized and said, "You wouldn't know." And then he explained that in Japanese business culture, a business card is a matter of status. You should compliment the color, the graphics, and the heavy card stock. The entire time you're speaking with that person, you should frame the card in your hand because it keeps that person in the moment—and you never write on the back of it. That is a sign of disrespect. It's like you are defacing his personal image. I told him,

"I appreciate knowing that. I will never again write on somebody's business card — at least without asking."

So now I *always* ask those I meet (Japanese or not) through networking if it's alright to write on the back of their card, and they are flattered that I have asked. Now I have gone above and beyond. They're thinking, what's the big deal, but at the same time, they're thinking it is kind and courteous of me to ask. Also, they're flattered by the fact that what we've just discussed is noteworthy enough for me to want to write it down.

And then what I find is that people will say the same thing to me as I'm writing something down on the back of their card—"I guess you wouldn't mind if I wrote something on the back of yours?" So now I've raised the consciousness about the issue, as well as the quality of our discussion, just by doing that.

Writing notes on business cards also serves as a filtering process. I will return from a business trip or a meeting with a stack of business cards, and they will all have notes on the back of them. The others (no notes) get discarded. Why? Because there is nothing "noteworthy" to discuss. Those notes constitute the follow-up I will do with people after an event. (Of course it will get done! I've written it down.)

Some of the notes I might write down on a card will be a characteristic about that person—I might write that the person is attractive and wearing a navy suit with an orange tie. Or I'll mention that they are a sports fan and like a particular team. I'll jot down anything that sticks out in my mind at the moment so that I can remember them.

When I follow up, I do so with a hand-written card. I want to make mention of some of the details I have written on the back of the card.

I met a woman at an event recently named Evelyn, but our running joke is that she's "Orange Jacket" because when we met, she was wearing a bright orange jacket that really stood out. The way we ended our conversation was that, when she saw me writing on the back of her card—and gave me her permission, of course—she said, "If you don't remember anything else, just remember that I'm the very pretty lady in the orange jacket."

So I chuckled and said, "Yes you are." So now our email correspondence relates to the orange jacket, and of course I mentioned it in my follow-up note. That sets me up to remember who she is (and for her to remember me). It also sets me up with a running joke, the next time I see her, "Where is your orange jacket? You're not prepared." We'll have a chuckle, and then we'll be off to a cool conversation.

It's important to have fun with this even if it's a bit goofy. I don't take this stuff all that seriously. I'm really light with it. But from a business standpoint, I also want to be on my game.

How Do I Know When to End a Conversation?

This goes back to Pool Rule No. 19, "Terminate Conversations Politely." Obviously, there are exceptions, but for the most part, when the conversation is going well, use a six- to eight-minute guideline for speaking to someone.

But if somebody is trying to pitch you or sell you and you don't want to be talking to them or you just don't get a good vibe, you don't have to wait six to eight minutes to try to end the conversation. After a minute or two, you can politely end the conversation and excuse yourself. "Well, it was very nice meeting you. Good luck at the event today. If I can be of help in any way, just let me know. Have fun!"

How Do I Excuse Myself Politely Without Offending?

Be direct. Just chime in and say, for example, "Dave, I have to be honest with you. I'm really not in the market to refinance my house right now. That's not why I came to this event. I came here to network. Let me let you go. There are probably other people you want to speak with, and the last thing I want to do is get in the way of what you've got to do here." Then I offer my 7-to-8 handshake and say, "Good luck today. I look forward to crossing paths again."

Or if it's somebody who's nice, but they're just not the one you need to speak with—maybe it's the Mary Kay lady who is speaking to you, and you just don't see a business connection there—I will say something like, "I don't want to take up your time. I know where you're coming from. My wife used to sell Mary Kay products. But let me see if maybe we can connect you with somebody who might be a better fit and you can dialogue about something that might make more sense business-wise." Even though you're ending the conversation, you are offering an introduction to try to connect her with someone it makes sense for her to speak with.

The level of directness that you should use to end a conversation should be in direct proportion to the level of rudeness with which someone approaches you. If somebody is pushy with me, and it's very blatant—almost to the point where I

feel that I'm at one of those time-share pitches in Mexico—
that's when I'm pretty direct, too. I will say, "Look, I have to
be honest with you. That's not why I came here, and the last
thing I really want to have happen to me is to be sold to. But
I don't want to take up your time. Let me let you go. Good
luck with your business. I look forward to crossing paths."

Most people are very nice but just don't know how to network
so I don't take it personally or too seriously. (But I do get
plenty of stories to share with audiences and plenty of blog
material.) The reality is most people simply don't know The
Pool Rules™. I get that. I'm usually pretty gentle with it, but
I'm direct to the point where I want to let them know where
I'm at and let them know where they might want to be.

If it's someone I just don't like, I'll say, "Look, Sparky, I
understand what you're saying. But I have to be honest with
you. I'm not really sure that I am the one to help you. I don't
really want to take up any more of your time. There are a
lot of other people here, and I want to allow you to be able
to speak to some other folks. There are some other people
I need to get with as well. Good luck today. It was great
meeting you, and I look forward to seeing you again."

Also, you don't want to introduce somebody you don't like
to another person (as funny as it might be). That person may
not like Sparky either and might resent you for having introduced them to each other. You always want to look good
and make a great impression. In fact, one of the comments
that I get when I refer people, which is very flattering, is
"You always refer me such great people." That's what I
want to be known for. That's what good networkers want to
be known for. If you hobknob with great people, hopefully
you're a great person yourself, and that's the impression
(and personal brand) that you want to create.

But I find that people who are kind of shady, people I don't trust, people I know a lot of other people are wary of, tend to flock together.

Naturally, I also trust the opinions of people I really respect. If they say, "You want to watch out for Dave. I know some folks have had bad experiences with him. I hate to say that, but it's true," then I'm going to be a bit cautious with Dave.

Important note:

Frankie Dunn (Clint Eastwood) may have said it best when he says to Maggie Fitzgerald (Hillary Swank) in the boxing movie *Million Dollar Baby,* "Protect yourself at all times." This is another example of how boxing and networking are alike. At networking related events (as opposed to in the ring) I'm always looking to have fun, make a good connection or two and help people. But just know that everybody is not like that. People do have their own agendas. I hate to say it but not everybody is honest or very nice. There are people who have fallen on hard times (or have always been on hard times) and desperate to make a sale. Heck, some people are just out to take advantage of others and to say all the things those people need to hear. Networking is a great thing (done correctly it may be just about the best thing). Networking can be a good time and can help a lot of people make a few bucks, land a job, and make a friend. I have done all of the above through networking. But there are some people out there that are more than happy just to take your money or pull a fast one. So *protect yourself at all times* and keep the left up (as we say in the ring).

Sometimes you need to end a conversation for the simple reason that you need to use the restroom. That can be awkward for some people (believe it or not). But it's less so if you'll just be direct with people. I will say, "Can I excuse

myself for one second? I need to go powder my nose." I get
the chuckle, and they get it, and if it's a good conversation,
I'll ask if I can circle back.

Now, you don't want to use that as a shtick (just to terminate a conversation) if, in fact, you don't need to go to the
restroom. If you're just using that as an excuse to end the
conversation, that person will either circle back with you
later, or they might follow you into the bathroom. Or they'll
be on to you! End your conversations as honestly and
tactfully as possible (short of telling someone you don't like
them). If it is, in fact, a bathroom break that you need, then
that has to be true. If you need to grab something to eat or
drink, then you have to be up front about that, too.

Or maybe you see someone you need to talk to. Again,
you can be direct about it and say, "You know, I just saw
somebody who just arrived that I absolutely need to reconnect
with. Would you mind if we continued our conversation in
a little bit? I don't want to be rude, but I don't want to miss
him." And that's OK.

Just make sure that you are polite and respectful.

I screwed this up a few years ago. I left a conversation a little
more abruptly than I should have and had to do damage control.

I was at an upscale cocktail party at a big hotel in Newark, New
Jersey, with a group of meeting planners. I knew a handful of
people there. I was hobnobbing and doing my thing. I was
introduced to someone named Joe who is a consultant but
does something different than me. As I was talking to him,
I saw in the distance this woman named Laura whom I had
worked with in Boston five years earlier. I had not seen her
since then. We had a great working relationship back in the

day. It was a shock to see her there, especially since we were in New Jersey, not Boston, so I sort of blew Joe off. I don't think I was terribly rude—I said, "May I just excuse myself for one second?" And I ventured over, and it was hugs and kisses as Laura and I reconnected and caught up.

About 15 minutes later, I realized that I had sort of left Joe hanging. I felt really badly because I talk about how rude it is to do this, and now I've done it. I looked for Joe but couldn't find him. I didn't even have his card. I tracked down the person who had introduced me to him in the first place. I told her, "Jo Ann, I have to apologize. You introduced me to Joe, who was so nice, and I was rude to him." She assured me that I probably wasn't rude at all, and she gave me his contact information.

I called him that night, from my cell phone on the way home, knowing I'd get his office number. I said, "Hey, Joe, it's Michael Goldberg. You may not remember me. Jo Ann introduced us. I was the guy who was completely rude to you when we were speaking. I caught up with this woman named Laura whom I had not seen in years, and my excitement overcame me. I might have been rude to you in the process, and if that was the case, I am so sorry. I got your information from Jo Ann, so I'm hoping we can reconnect on the phone and continue our conversation." And I left my contact information.

The next morning, Joe called me. He said, "I am really flattered that you thought you were rude and thought enough to contact me. It never entered my mind. I just thought it was really cool how you reconnected with someone you hadn't seen in so many years." I am still in touch with Joe now.

Hey, circumstances like this could happen to anybody. And I think you can fix anything you might do that is rude or inappropriate, nine times out of 10, with an apology.

Important note:

When *won't* an apology fix the problem? An apology probably won't work if you do something unethical, that lacks integrity, or if you speak badly about someone or something. Of course, personal insults rank right up there. Keep in mind that all of these instances are intentional — not an accident. Remember, it's a small world.

Now think about this: Have you ever been at a networking event or cocktail party, and you are speaking to someone but don't want to be? The person corners you and drones on and on and on, and you can't get away? If that has never happened to you, it's you! (I'm just saying.)

What Should I Do if I've Done Something Embarrassing or Stupid?

This is coming from somebody who does a lot of stupid things. Remember the story from Chapter 1, about how I spit food (hot water from a string bean) in Jackie's face? My first piece of advice is, just try not to do anything stupid!

The chances of you doing something stupid or embarrassing are greatly diminished if you are armed with good questions, speaking to somebody with high integrity, genuinely looking to help them, and look at the conversation as being added value and fun.

Again, if you do happen to do make an honest mistake, a genuine apology should take care of it.

Sometimes people appear stupid or foolish because they come across in a way that they don't realize. For example, I've seen people exaggerate or talk about how much money they have or how successful they are. It's not enjoyable speaking to someone who is full of themselves, who divulge information they shouldn't have, who say something that's inappropriate in mixed company, who know it all, who offer unsolicited advice, or who give bad advice. (Can you think of people that do some of these things on a regular basis?) Saying something negative or something that makes somebody else feel uncomfortable or compromised is also a bad thing.

Stay positive. You don't have to lie and speak well of somebody if you don't feel that way, but just refrain from speaking badly of them.

Important note:
The exception is when your honest opinion prevents someone from getting hurt or ripped off. This is especially true when someone asks you for your advice.

(Should I re-finance my house through Dave?)

What If We Just Don't Click?

Remember, in Chapter 2, I said that two-thirds of the time, people just don't click with one another? If you don't click, don't feel that you have to force it. If you feel that there is not a good vibe, the other person probably feels the same thing.

If I'm going through my questions, and the other person doesn't take to me or doesn't want to be bothered, and I think it is not a good use of our time, I will bow out of the conversation. I will say, "Look, Larry, it has been great learning a little about your business. Good luck today. If there's something I can do, certainly call on me. I'm meeting people for the first time here, but I'd be happy to help you any way I can." I will give him my 7-to-8 handshake and say, "It's great to meet you. I look forward to seeing you again."

Initially, be *interested* in everybody (*interested* equals *interesting*). And if they are just not interesting or they're not interested in where to go next (there's no love connection) end the conversation politely and respectfully. Then position yourself as a resource—"If there's anything I can do for you and you want to call on me, please do. Good luck today and I hope to see you again."

I hate to say it but you won't connect with everybody. That's just the way it is.

If your intentions are good and you follow some of these guidelines, the percentages may be in your favor — at least a third of the time!

Takeaways

- Even the most seasoned, successful people need networking charm school.

- The extent to which your conversation is meaningful is directly proportional to the quality of questions that you ask.

- It is important to know how to introduce yourself so that you can engage in conversations easily at both business-related and social functions.

- People often don't know how to meet new people, so if you can introduce them to one another, everybody wins.

- Use pneumonic devices to try to remember people's names—associate a person's name with something or someone you know. If you forget someone's name, be up-front about it and ask for it again. Don't try to dodge the situation.

- Very often, the best way to get somebody to ask for your business card is to ask for theirs.

- Ask for a business card only if there is a good reason for it; don't ask for one just as a reflex or just to see how many you can collect, and don't feel obligated to ask for one. Also, don't feel obligated to give someone your business card just because they ask for it. It is OK to ask their reason for requesting it.

- Take a page from the Japanese book of business etiquette and ask permission before you write on someone's business card.

- If you're enjoying speaking with someone, continue the conversation for six to eight minutes (but don't look at your watch—just estimate the time you've spent talking to them). If you are not enjoying the conversation, politely excuse yourself after one or two minutes.

- The level of directness that you should use to end a conversation is in direct proportion to the level of rudeness with which someone approaches you.

- If you do something embarrassing or stupid, apologize. If you've done something blatantly unethical or something that lacks integrity, an apology probably won't help.

- If you feel that you don't click with someone, they probably feel the same way. Don't feel that you have to force the conversation. Just excuse yourself politely and find someone else to speak with.

Your Turn

The dynamics of human relationships can be complicated. Conversations and interactions may not always run smoothly. Instead of letting that deter you, think of worst possible scenarios, and plan how you would handle them.

YOUR "CALL TO ACTION" PLAN

How to Deal with Sticky Situations

1. What are some sticky situations you've encountered at business or social events? How did you handle them?

2. How well did you handle those situations?

3. Now that you have read this material, how would you handle such situations differently?

4. What do you think is the worst thing that could happen at a networking or social event?

5. If something like that were to happen, what is the best way for you to handle it?

CHAPTER 4:

Developing a Target Market

"The richest people in the world look for and build networks; everyone else looks for work."

—Robert Kiyosaki, Entrepreneur and Author

If everyone is your target market, then no one is your target market.

Remember the definition of a target market, from Chapter 2? Your target market is *whom you serve best and, therefore, wish to serve most.*

It is absolutely critical to have a target market, especially if you are just starting your practice or business, or if you're looking to take your business to the next level. I don't think having a target (or niche) market is the only way to grow your business or to take it to the next level, but I do think it's one of the easiest and most effective ways.

If you walk over to someone at a networking event and after chatting with them a while you say, "Help me get more clients," they will wonder, "What type of clients?" You have to be very specific about what type of clients, what type of job, what type of company, and what type of information. And having a target market helps you to be much clearer about what you are looking to accomplish.

How I Discovered My Target Market

My favorite groups to work with are composed of people in the insurance and financial services industry. Financial advisors have a dynamic that's similar to mine—high-energy, sales-oriented, smart (not that I'm all that smart), and open to learning new ways to grow their business. (Of course, these dynamics exists in many industries.)

But I didn't discover that the financial services industry was my target market until a few years ago. I had what you might call a false start with an entirely different target market.

When I started my own business many years ago, I knew of the concept of target marketing (niching). I knew that, from a conversational standpoint, it was important to have something to aim at, something specific to say. I knew that the more specific I could be — the more others could help me connect with and help the right prospects (and yes, there is such a thing as wrong prospects).

I thought an obvious target market for me was police and fire departments, for a number of reasons. My dad is a retired New York City police officer, a 20-year veteran of the police force who worked in some tough neighborhoods and therefore was pretty tough himself.

Given the environment I grew up in, I knew I would be very comfortable being in front of tough groups. Police officers and firefighters are tough because they have to be to do their jobs—there's no question about it. I knew I would have credibility because of my dad and my upbringing, but also because I can be a tough, direct presenter without getting rattled. I thought it made perfect sense for police and fire departments to be my target market.

Also, one of my best friends is a fire chief. When he was promoted into that position, he was the youngest person to ever become a fire chief in Massachusetts. He made it very easy for me to have that target market because of all of the attention and respect he had earned with his promotion. He quickly put me in touch with other fire and police departments, and one would refer me to the other.

What really cemented it for me is that he helped me get an opportunity to be the keynote speaker before the Massachusetts Police Chiefs Association. I was in front of every single police chief in the state, giving a presentation on sexual-harassment prevention, one of my target areas at the time.

A lot of those police chiefs hired me to do leadership and communication training and consulting in sexual-harassment prevention. It turned out to be a huge gig for me. That's the beauty of having a target market. You know where to go, what to say and to whom. You become more referable, and you become an expert in an area. It got to the point where police departments were saying to other departments, "You're insane if you don't bring this guy in. Look what he's doing for us," or "He works with cops and firefighters. He gets us." Again, that's the beauty of having a target market.

It also enables you to better spend your marketing time—how to direct your Revenue-Producing Activities, or RPAs. Your RPAs are much more effective if you know what your target market is. It tells you what events you need to go to; what you need to say, read, learn, write, join, subscribe to; and whom you need to meet to create more marketing gravity.

After a while, I found working with police officers and firefighters to be very difficult. Even though I had established a good reputation with my target market and was doing a lot of business, I was getting burned out. I was even beginning to dislike the nature of my work with these groups. I was just taking on the work for the sake of taking on the work. (Ever do that?) This was bad. It was definitely time for a change. But I discovered a very important lesson.

The Right Product/Service + The Right Market = Success.

This formula became the essence of my new business plan.

Out of the blue, a regional director from a professional networking organization contacted me. He was referred to me by a number of people I knew. (It reminded me of the movie *Six Degrees of Separation* or the cult classic board game "Back to [Kevin] Bacon.") He said, "I would love to hire you to be our keynote speaker. We've got this big regional conference with lots of people, and I was wondering if you'd be interested." I said I'd be thrilled. I figured the topic would be leadership. But he said, "I'd like you to speak about networking."

I said, "You know, I'm really flattered, but I have never spoken about networking in front of a group before."

He said, "Well, you seem to know everybody."

Then I asked, "Why networking?" It seemed like a good question, since he represents a networking organization.

He said, "Well, I'm told you have a different philosophy on it that is valuable and fun, and I think we need to hear it." Enough said — booked!

I never delivered a presentation on networking before and didn't know where to start. So I created two lists—a list of things I thought I was really good at with networking and a much longer list of all the areas where I was really bad.

I punched it up with PowerPoint slides and made it very self-effacing with stories to tell. Then I delivered the talk to almost 400 people.

About the third slide in, I forgot that I had slides! I began speaking with the group instead of speaking to my slides. It was July 2, 2003—I remember because the date was printed on my PowerPoint presentation and because it was a critical date in establishing my business. I had the group laughing, I was connecting with them, and I knew some people in the audience to begin with. I was bouncing off the walls. Even my bad jokes (which were most of them) got laughs. It was incredible. And I had an epiphany in front of all those people—this had to become my product/service. I have to talk about networking. I can help so many people. This became my topic, my passion, my purpose.

That meant that I had half of my formula down—the right product/service. I even asked the group if I should do more of these talks. "Yes!" they shouted.

But I needed the second half of my formula—what should my target market be? The group I had spoken to was composed of small-business owners. I didn't want to target them because I felt it was too broad a niche.

I asked myself, who needs to hear this networking message? What market would value my message the most? I realized that the answer was the insurance and financial services industry.

I made a phone call to a professional association that serves general agents and field managers in the insurance and financial services industry. I explained what I was looking to do and I was referred to a former president of the association. I contacted him and he put me in touch with other influential people in the industry.

As my research continued, I realized that no one else was doing what I was venturing to do in this industry, and there was (and still is) a big need. I also learned that the Federal Trade Commission was about to roll out the Do Not Call list (October 2003) which would completely change the way the financial services industry marketed to prospects. It was perfect timing. They needed to learn how to network more than ever because of the phone restrictions being put in place.

So I discovered my target market. And had my formula nailed.

Networking/Referral Techniques + the Financial Services Industry = Success

This became the focus of all of my marketing and Revenue Producing Activities.

That is the benefit of having a target market, provided it's the right market. It may not be something you just discover overnight; it's a process. The whole police and fire department thing was a great experience. I wouldn't change it. It had to happen that way. Plus, I had clients that were paying me. And you go where the money is when you're starting a business. Business owners and sales people know this—you have to start somewhere. So it's OK to make a mistake and realize, "This market isn't for me." But have the inclination to find the right target market for you. It will absolutely pay off!

That is what happens to middle of the road sales people (or base reps in the insurance and financial services industry). They reach an average level and never get beyond that because they just spin their wheels. They have no focus or direction and are always looking for that next piece of business rather than having it find them. These sales people will always struggle or just get by — they represent 80% of any sales force.

The Right Formula

I mentioned the formula—having the right product or service, is half the battle won, and having the right target market, is the other half. If you are not in the right business—if you are not selling the right product or service, you may be in the "This is just what I do" mode. Is this a fulfilling place to be?

I am working with some reps (in *my* target market) right now who I know are not going to be long for their career. They have a great target market—the second half of the formula—but they hate what they do—so the first half of their formula is missing.

I am working with one woman with a brokerage background who says, "I can't believe I'm selling insurance. I'm embarrassed to tell my friends."

I told her, "You're going to fail in this business. Get out. The firm probably doesn't want me to tell you this, but you're not right for the job. You're not going to be successful with it. Unless you can find some aspect of this business that you can get behind, you are going to fail. Maybe your focus shouldn't be life insurance. Maybe long-term care is an area where you can get more passionate. I know people who are very passionate about that for personal reasons. Maybe you should focus on being a financial planner and help people manage their money. But if you can't find some shred of the business that you love (or even like), it's over for you." (She was gone in three months.)

Ways to Find—or Create—Your Target Market

I found my target market because it's an industry that I really like. In fact, if I had it to do over again, I would be a financial advisor, and I would eventually be managing a firm. Without a doubt! I'm not great at too many things, but I believe I'd be great at that. Now, I'd still do what I'm doing now because I love what I do, but I would have walked down a much different path. Today, I have the best of both worlds—I am a professional speaker and consultant, and I work in the insurance and financial services industry, which has been phenomenal.

Do What You Love

If you can do the things that you love in an industry that you could see yourself working in, that's a pretty powerful combination.

Do what you love and love what you do. And work with people who do something that you love.

I work with an advisor named Mike who is a gym rat, a fitness nut. I have had a number of one-on-one meetings with him. The managing director of the firm wanted me to meet with him because he is a good guy, but he is a base rep (middle of the road) who leveled off. He is very focused and disciplined outside of work—a must if he's into fitness like he is—but management felt that he could probably do something more, and they felt that something was wrong.

Since I box and am into weights and fitness, Mike and I had a lot of extracurricular activities to talk about. When we got together, I got the sense that all he wanted to discuss was supplements, weights, boxing and fitness. When I said, "Listen, we have to do work now," he deflated. He didn't want to talk about his work at all. I told him, "You've been working as a financial advisor for three years. I have to be honest with you, Mike—it seems like you hate what you do."

He said, "Well, I don't love it, that's for sure. I'm kind of bored with it. I don't know where to go with it. It's kind of what I do. I know my stuff, but I'm just not excited about it. You're right."

"But you're clearly excited about going to the gym," I replied. "You're excited about fitness. What if you combined the two?"

"What do you mean?"

"What if your target market becomes people who work out, trainers, gym owners, GNC franchises, the companies that make supplements and exercise equipment and professional bodybuilders."

He looked at me in awe and said, "You can do that?"

I said, "Yeah, why not? You could get certified as a trainer. Work at a gym half a day a week just because you love it, and you can create your own target market. Look at it as 'I can help you with your financial fitness.' Position yourself in a way that you get excited about this stuff, and you can talk about all the things that you love."

Mike started landing clients that were into fitness as he continued to niche himself in the industry. He delivers financial seminars at gyms and is raising his level of sales production. He has an understanding of how to spend his marketing time — where to go, what to read, what to say, and who to meet. And he gets to lift weights with his clients — an added bonus!

All Mike did was pick a lane and get focused. You can do the same thing. Turn your vocation into your vacation.

At another firm, I'm working with a woman who is still looking to reach the next level of success. She is an outdoors nut. She is into whitewater rafting, camping, hiking, etc. That's what she does in her down time up in New England. I told her, "Obviously that needs to be your target market." So now she is looking to work with some of the companies that sell outdoor gear and equipment, as well as camps, organizations and resorts that teach whitewater rafting and other outdoors courses. It has opened up a market for her that she can get excited about, and she probably does not have a lot of competition in that marketplace.

I am working with another guy who is an aspiring writer. He is a fanatic about writing. He writes about historical figures just because he likes to. He would love to own a small bookstore. On Saturdays, he and his wife will go to a bookstore and cozy up with a cup of coffee and read books. I asked him, "Shouldn't that be your target market?"

He asked, "How can I do that?"

I said, "Keep writing, get your book written, and at the same time, work with others who have the same interest." Now he's excited about it and his sales production is starting to reflect it.

Discover Who Needs What You Do

Another way of determining your target market is to focus on an industry, profession, demographic, vertical or market segment that needs what you want to do most. So if you are passionate about long-term care, then it's evident that your target market needs to be senior communities, assisted-living communities, estate-planning attorneys, CPAs and folks who are looking to be responsible and put protection in place. Knowing who needs what you do makes your target evident, and the target market is now aligned with the product or service that you are most passionate about.

I know financial advisors who make a great living just focusing on long-term care. They're experts in it. It makes their networking quite easy because they know where they need to go, what they need to say and to whom, and what they need to know, read, write and report on.

Look for an Untapped Opportunity

Another way to go about it is to find a target market that presents an untapped or underserviced opportunity. One of my clients is an Internet marketing company. (If you're paying attention you'll realize this is not my target market.) They have a very niche market right now—people who are in the personal image business. They target hairdressers, gyms, photographers, make-up artists, nail salons, massage facilities, etc. Many of those types of businesses do not have Web sites, or if they do, they don't know how to use them. So this company has identified an opportunity known as the "offline opportunity" because these types of companies typically don't do their business from the Web; it's all word of mouth. They have availed themselves of an opportunity. It hasn't taken off yet, but it probably will because they see that there is a need that nobody else is filling.

Talk to Your Friends and Family

Having a target market is also important because, in financial services and other industries, you realize that your friends and family can be very important in helping you build your business. They can give you ideas and maybe connect you with people who reflect your target market. We're very short-sighted in viewing our family that way. We tend to think that business is one thing, and family is something else. If your friends and family can't help you, who can?

Years ago, I had an interesting conversation with my dad. At the time, I was working with police and fire departments (as I had mentioned earlier). I had said that work was pretty busy. He said, "I have to ask. What the heck do you do?" He had no idea. He knew I put a shirt and tie on and spoke to different groups. But he didn't understand exactly what I did.

"I help police officers and firefighters with their communication and management skills."

He said, "Did you ever consider contacting the New York City Police Department and seeing if you can do that for them? Why don't you contact the police academy? The fact that I'm a retired police officer may do something."

I thought, "What a great idea." I did it, and they became a client. I started running programs in the NYPD's police academy, and I was working with captains and above. It was a great gig. And they were the only client I've ever had who saluted me. (When the cadets are lined up along the hallway and any "suit" comes by, they're going to salute because they don't know who you are. That's my claim to fame.)

But if it weren't for my dad putting that in my mind, and if I hadn't had a target market, that never would have happened. So I was able to reach a level of clarity in explaining what I did. But also, he gave me some really good information that turned profitable.

That's the purpose of having a target market—you just never know. You could be speaking with a friend and say,

"I'm really looking to work with more small-business owners in the area of semi-conductors." You'll bring your conversation up a few notches.

Having a target market is the difference between a chiropractor who says, "A good patient or prospect for me is anyone with a spine" and a savvy chiropractor, who says, "I am looking to help more people who are suffering with lower back pain due to pregnancy or those who are suffering with carpal tunnel because they work with their hands." Those are markets I can think about, and I can think of half a dozen people I would refer to this chiropractor. (Have I convinced you yet?)

Your Background

If you have a background in a particular industry or profession, it might make sense for you to consider that as a target market. After all, you would have experience, knowledge, contacts, and credibility in a previous role on your resume.

You do want to be careful, though. If you hated that line of work or fear becoming too pigeonholed in a particular marketplace, this may not be the best option.

I was in the hospitality industry for almost 20 years. The last thing I wanted to do is have that be my target market. I spent a lot of time running restaurants so I never saw myself working in that industry again (even as an outside resource). It's a great industry, don't get me wrong. I learned skills and have experiences I would never replace but it was time for a change.

Your target market has to excite you and provide personal, emotional, mental, and financial fulfillment otherwise it's a bad business model.

Why Some Professionals Resist Having a Target Market

The biggest pushback I get from many sales people is this: "Well, that's great, but I don't want to turn away business. Won't I lose opportunities if I become too niched? I don't want people to get the wrong idea that all I do is work with police and fire departments." My answer to that is that it gets back to your communication skills—the more you articulate who you're looking to serve, the more other people can help you find clients in that market to serve.

I'm not saying that you should turn away business unless there's a good reason to do it. I work with that Internet marketing company, and they are not in my target market. I also work with a pharmaceutical company and a handful of other firms. I just worked with a CPA firm, and I've worked with law firms and others that are outside of my niche. But I didn't go looking for them; they found me. If it's a good fit and I think that I can add value, I will take it on. If it is not a good fit, I will turn it away.

So I'm not suggesting that a sales rep should turn business away—however, my experience has been that the more targeted you are, the more business will find you. I don't think you're leaving opportunity on the table; rather, I think you are attracting more of it to you by targeting your focus.

Let's say that your specialty is financial planning, and your market is physicians. Some advisors do focus on physicians. So if you're speaking with an attorney—not your target market—you could tell the attorney, "I actually focus on working with physicians. Most of my clients are physicians. I've been doing that for years, and that's what my practice really reflects." The attorney may reply, "That's really good to know, but would you be open to working with an attorney?" You're creating marketing gravity because now he respects what you have accomplished. Obviously you must be good at what you do if you have this type of marketplace. The situation creates a level of attraction. Just work it into your language: "I work mostly with physicians." Or "My market reflects mostly physicians," or police departments, or whatever it is.

I was on a flight to Detroit a couple of years ago. I was seated next to Jim Nantz, the 2008 National Sportscaster of the Year. He has been with CBS since 1985 and has called the play-by-play on more network broadcasts of basketball's Final Four and Championship games than any other announcer in the tournament's history.

Most people who follow sports know who he is. We were chatting, and he said he was going to Detroit for the PGA Tour. He asked what I did. I said, "Funny you ask," and I told him. I used my elevator pitch (covered in more detail in the next chapter). I kept it very light because we weren't at a networking meeting. He thought it was interesting and asked how I got involved in networking.

Then I excused myself and took a stretch. As I got up, a gentleman in a shirt and tie across the aisle got up and introduced himself to me. He said, "I didn't mean to eavesdrop, but that's Jim Nantz there, right?" I said it was. He said, "I heard what you said to him, and I found it really interesting. You run networking programs for financial services companies, right?"

I said yes.

He said, "Well, I am a partner for one of the largest law firms in Detroit. You may not typically work with law firms, but would you be open to helping my attorneys and some of the partners be better at our networking? We're not good at it."

Of course I wasn't going to say no. My conversation with Jim Nantz had created gravity and a marketing opportunity. I wasn't even speaking to the attorney originally but had established credibility with him as a networking expert, and he wondered how that might translate to his people. Scenarios like this sometimes have a way of playing out as business opportunities.

To my knowledge, I have never turned away business that I would have wanted because I have a target market—rather, the opposite has been true. I think new salespeople and certainly new advisors need to hear this. That is often their biggest worry—"I don't want to put all of my eggs in one basket or turn away business." But you won't.

I also find that the most successful advisors and salespeople I know have a niche. Try to avoid getting into the notion of "Everybody needs what I do." Everybody doesn't need what you do, nor do they want what you do. Can your product or service be a fit for almost everybody? Maybe. But if they don't see it that way, it doesn't matter. Again, the whole deal is that you are trying to create marketing gravity. You're trying to be referable. That's the end game. You just make yourself that much more referable by becoming an expert at what you do and helping whom you need to help. And your formula—the right product or service coupled with the right market—has to be in place for that to happen.

Having a target market also tells salespeople—who are notoriously bad organizers—what the best use of their time is at any given moment. When you have down time, you can read about your target market. You can subscribe to industry trade publications and join professional associations. And get involved!

Takeaways

- Your target market is whom you serve best and, therefore, wish to serve most.

- Having a target market enables you to direct your revenue-producing activities, or RPAs.

- To succeed in what you do, you need to figure out both parts of the critical formula—the right product or service and the right target market.

- Do what you love, or work with people who do something that you love.

- You can find or create your target market by doing what you love, finding people who need what you do, looking for an untapped opportunity and letting friends and family members know who your target market is.

- Many professionals fear that they will turn away business if they begin serving a target market. That is not true—having a target market gives you marketing gravity and credibility and makes you more referable. Plus, there is nothing wrong with working for people who are not in your target market if it makes sense to. You never have to turn business away.

- The more targeted you are, the more business will find you. You are attracting more business by targeting your focus.

- Having a target market also tells salespeople—who are notoriously bad organizers—what the best use of their time is at any given moment.

- Everybody doesn't need what you do, nor do they want what you do.

Your Turn

Having a target market makes you a specialist, which gives you credibility and creates marketing gravity. It also makes you more referable. Collect your thoughts about your target market on the following worksheet.

YOUR "CALL TO ACTION" PLAN

Developing a Target Market

1. Whom do you serve best and, therefore, wish to serve most—in other words, who is your target market?

_____

_____

2. Why did you select that market? What makes it a good fit for what you do and people you enjoy working with?

_____

_____

3. How can having a target market enrich your business?

_____

_____

CHAPTER 5:

You and Your Elevator Pitch

"Outstanding people have one thing in common:
an absolute sense of mission."

—Zig Ziglar

P EEC™ (pronounced "peace," as in "peace of mind that this will work every time") is an acronym that I developed to describe a person's elevator pitch, or positioning statement. It stands for Profession, Expertise, Environments and Call to Action.

I have been talking about the PEEC Statement™ for years, and I handle an endless amount of emails a day from sales reps all over the country inquiring about how to write one of their very own. They'll send me their statements and say, "How is this?" I give critiques and say, "This could be richer," or "This is not specific enough." The insurance and financial services industry is getting to know what a PEEC Statement™ is, although I've shared it with reps in many other industries, as well as with job searchers.

I developed it because, even as a professional communicator and someone who is good at networking, I never felt like I did a good enough job at telling people what I did and how they might help me. I was able to do it, but I just felt that I could be better. I wanted to have a powerful way to teach it, too.

I am a big acronym guy, and I thought, if I can boil this down to an acronym—a footprint that everyone can use to take the next step—that would be great! I have found that just the notion that there is such a thing as an elevator pitch that you can learn and master is very attractive to sales professionals and business owners at all levels. And job searchers too.

I want to make it clear that it's not really an elevator pitch. The only reason I call it that is because everybody knows what an elevator pitch is. But it's more of a positioning statement. An elevator *pitch* sounds like you're trying to *pitch* someone or sell them something, and that's not the purpose the PEEC Statement™.

PEEC™ is a positioning statement because what it should do is position you as someone to speak with; as someone interesting and compelling; as somebody who is focused, knows what they want and is basically looking for help in getting it. If your strategy truly is to *pitch*, then it means that you are selling something to someone or making an offer, and again, that is not the intent.

Let's go through the PEEC Statement™ — Profession, Expertise, Environments, Call to Action.

Profession is who you are, what you do and with whom. It should be the best possible thing that you can say to somebody in a business setting when they ask about you. *Profession* should be the most interesting, compelling, different, memorable thing you can come up with. If it's boring, commonplace or ordinary, then it's not serving its purpose, and it's just going to be blah, blah, blah.

Warning, here comes a boxing metaphor. When I box, I'm typically up against somebody who is twice as good as me and half as old (or so I'm told). That is clearly their advantage. So one of the things that has worked for me in boxing is that, when I start in the first round—I come right out with both barrels firing. Rather than working with some combinations and throwing some jabs here and there, I just come out hooking. I'm a 185-pound ball of fury that my opponent (or sparring partner) is going to have to deal with right then. By the time he realizes what's going on, I'm throwing a shoulder, I've got an upper cut, I'm ahead on points and energy, and he is figuring out what's going on.

It's kind of the same thing with your response when somebody asks about your Profession. You don't want to knock them on their haunches or have them have to deal with you in an "Oh, no!" type of way; do it in a positive way. You want them to be really engaged in what you have to say. Unlike boxing, networking should not be adversarial. It should be collaborative.

That said, boxing and networking are both "contact" sports. (Clever, right?) So making a little contact is going to be advantageous in both arenas.

Anyway, your Profession should represent the best possible thing you have to say to somebody at that very moment. Typically, people are engaged with the first few words that are spoken to them, and if it's nothing out of the norm, then it's not going to be very memorable. You could respond with a quote or something funny. It could start off like this: "Well, you know how a teacher develops students to…" or "You know how a magician is able to engage people with sleight of hand? Well, what I do is…." Or it could be a statistic. "Did you know that 76% percent of job searchers that land jobs do so through networking?"

Sometimes I will tell people, "You know who Anthony Robbins is, right?"

They'll say, "Oh, yeah, he's that motivational speaker that I see on the late night infomercials."

"Well, that's exactly what I do, only not nearly as successfully and I'm not nearly as tall." So I get a laugh, but they know where I'm coming from.

Profession is who you are, what you do and with whom. For a financial advisor, it might sound something like, "I am a financial advisor for ABC Financial Group, and I help professionals with their financial management."

There are many ways you could say that in a creative or even a funny way. I suggest being creative and different. The more creative the better!

Just don't be too shticky — "I'm a financial dream maker…" or "I help improve people's lives…" If it sounds too much like shtick or seems too lofty, people will raise their guard as they may think you're getting ready to sell them something, exaggerate, lie to them, pull the wool over their eyes, and rip them off — you know the deal. (Naturally, this is the last thing you want to do.)

Expertise represents the stuff you know. I make a distinction between skills and expertise. A lot of people think skills and expertise are the same thing, but they are not. Expertise is your depth of knowledge on a given topic or a series of topics. *Expertise* simply means knowledge, while *skill* refers to your ability.

You can have expertise in an area but not necessarily have those skills. Yet I find that the opposite is rarely true—usually, if you have the skills, you have the expertise to support them.

Here is another way I like to define expertise: It's what you would have to teach somebody if they were going to have to do your job.

It's important to note that just because you have expertise in an area does not mean you are necessarily an expert, although you might be. A new financial advisor may say that she has expertise in a number of areas, including life insurance, annuities and retirement planning, but that doesn't mean she is an expert in those areas. If you are an expert in a particular area, you can say, "I am considered an expert in the area of long-term care," if, in fact, you are.

Can I really use the word expertise if I've only been in the business for a year?

I get that question from new sales reps (or financial advisors) all the time. New reps have a problem using the term "expertise" because they haven't been doing the work very long. I tell them, "Well, you're licensed, right? You passed your test, and you're learning about it, right? So you do have expertise (more than the average bear, Yogi), and you are going to continue to learn. You are not speaking out of school if you say you have expertise in that area."

You shouldn't list more than three areas of expertise in your PEEC Statement™ because what you're saying may come across as a laundry list and others may stop listening. Pick two or three areas of expertise that you know the most about, like the most, and may have the most interest in, or pick one in particular that you are really focused on. Just make sure your areas of expertise relate directly to what you described as your Profession.

I know a very successful advisor who is an expert in the area of long-term care. Now, of course, she has knowledge about health insurance, life insurance and other products, but her lead (her jab) is long-term care. That's her value proposition, her favorite way of helping people, her door-opener, and she has a story to tell about it. She is comfortable saying, "I am considered an expert in the area of long-term care."

As a result, because her expert status has gained her credibility, what she ends up getting from prospects and even clients is, "Do you think you would be able to help me with retirement planning or investments?" And of course she could.

Environments get back to your target market—whom you serve best and therefore wish to serve most. It's very important to talk about that when you speak to people so that they know where you are looking to take aim because, again, if everyone is your target market, then no one is your target market.

Many times, I'll sit down with a sales rep and ask who their target market is. They'll say, "Individuals, young professionals, small-business owners, corporate executives and those thinking about retirement."

So I look at them and say, "Oh, so you don't have a target market."

They're baffled. "What do you mean?"

I ask, "How do you market to everyone?" From what you described, who aren't you focused on? And I remind them that if everyone is their target market, then no one is their target market. They are not making themselves referable (or as referable as they could).

It's the same thing as saying, "I'm a chiropractor and my target market is anyone with a spine." This is much different than saying, "I like to help those that do work with their hands that suffer from carpal tunnel and women suffering from lower back pain due to pregnancy."

Do you see the difference?

The second approach lends itself to making us think about specific people that could benefit from the service provided by this chiropractor. You have to believe that this chiropractor is someone who has a tremendous body of work in this area, as well as a strong track record since this is a specialty.

How impactful would it be for you to have a specialty?

Think about it. If you are focused on a lot of different areas (which is to say you're not focused at all), you will have a difficult time networking and will struggle with where to go, what to say, and to whom.

Don't try to serve everyone. Or be everything to everyone. It just doesn't work that way. Let your competitors do that. In most cases, the more pinpointed your target market is, the more referable you become.

If you're looking to do business with anyone, someone, and everyone — you'll end up doing business with no one. And it may be a long time before no one becomes someone. By the way, the same thing goes for anybody, somebody and everybody. Catch my drift?

It's amazing the type of information that comes out as soon as you're able to strategize and finally articulate your PEEC Statement™.

Just recently, I was working with a sales rep who has 11 years of experience in the property lines segment of insurance, so now he is focused on life insurance and becoming a financial advisor. He has a wife and family, so he needs to be successful at growing his business. He told me, "I don't have a target market. One of my reasons for sitting down with you is that I need to develop this PEEC Statement™, and I need to discover who my target market is." He had been through my seminar, so he knew about the importance of a target market and establishing a niche.

While asking him a number of questions, I realized that he has a background in housing and property management. He owns rental properties and knows a lot about the housing market. As we discussed his background, I said, "So you don't have a target market, huh?"

He looked at me, put his head in his hands and said, "Oh, my God."

I said, "Duh? You need to connect with property managers and commercial realtors."

He got it then. We brainstormed on a number of ideas and approaches, and he said, "I can't believe I didn't even consider this. And right under my nose!" All of a sudden, he got excited. It became obvious to him how he should spend his marketing time — where to go, what to say, and to whom.

Now, that's a target market!

Call to Action is what you're after, specifically. If you can't articulate what you're after, how is someone going to provide it for you? Most people don't know what they're after. They just think they're after one of those five things—the five reasons why people network—as in "I'm just after more business." (Well, most business people are looking for more business.) But what does that look like? Who do you need to meet, where do you need to go, what do you need to learn? What does more business look like? You have to be specific in your request.

Here is an example of how it can pay off to be specific when articulating your PEEC Statement™. During a recent trip to Connecticut, I was referred to two individuals who are very high-level, successful people. They do not work within financial services, so they are not in my target market. But they were referred to me through a rep with whom I have a great relationship. This guy thought that if I met with these two gentlemen, we would be able to exchange business because we are all kind of like-minded.

So I ended up having lunch with one of the gentlemen and then coffee afterwards with the other. One is an expert in the area of supply-chain management. The other runs a human-resources consulting firm.

I was asking the first guy questions about his business, and we got into a great discussion. And since I liked him, I thought there were some people he should meet whom I know. Then he asked me what I was looking for. I said, "One of my goals for the New Year is that I'm looking to get more involved with helping brokerage houses with their business development."

When I said that, I got an interesting reaction: "Well, it's funny you should say that because I know some really influential people in brokerage." They mentioned some companies I had heard of. One is a Wall Street firm, and the person he knows is the No. 3 person in the firm. He said, "This guy is my best friend. You need to speak with him."

If I hadn't mentioned it, it never would have happened. That is the point of being specific—if you ask for it, you just might get it.

In the spirit of networking, your Call to Action should really be whom you are looking to meet or be introduced to. It should not be a fact find of some sort, "I would like to sit down with you and discuss your financial planning."

And it shouldn't be a sales pitch, as in "I'd like to set up some time, maybe 15 minutes if you have it, to discuss your financial-planning needs." Or, to recap the five reasons people network—your Call to Action should be what you're looking to learn, the problem you're looking to solve, the job you're ultimately looking to land, the company you're looking to work with or the person who will be the love of your life.

The Call to Action is almost always pinned on either a title or the name of a person. So I may say, "I am really looking to meet or be introduced to Donald Trump." Or "I'm looking to meet or be introduced to managing directors in the major financial services firms of the world, such as…."

Remember the index cards from Chapter 1, where I wrote down the names of people I wanted to meet at an event? That is the Call to Action—it doesn't get more targeted than that.

If I'm at a social event, and someone asks me what I do, I will respond with my PEEC Statement™ and then let them know who I'm always looking to meet or be introduced to at business events. I may start out with, "I am a professional speaker."

They will say, "Really? What do you speak on?"

"Well, I speak professionally about networking and referrals — typically to sales reps in the financial services industry." Or "I get hired to help financial advisors generate more referrals."

"So companies hire you?" they'll ask.

"Yes. I'm typically hired and often retained by companies like…, and I'm usually brought in by general agents and managing directors. I'm always interested in suggestions as to how I can connect with more of them." That way, what I'm saying doesn't sound threatening. But I've still covered everything in my PEEC Statement™, including the Call to Action.

People may say, "You know, my friend is the number three person at ABC Financial Services." These things happen all the time.

It really just gets down to thinking like a networker because networking, in my mind, is not a switch that you flip on and off. It's a mindset; it's a lifestyle. Once you understand networking, the switch is always on. And if the switch is always on, you are allowing yourself to be open to more opportunities.

I find that sales professionals, reps, advisors, associates, and account executives alike often have a difficult time understanding and embracing The PEEC Statement™. Why? Because sales professionals are hired and trained to sell, sell, sell. Always be closing! Everyone is a prospect! PEEC™ reflects the opposite of what most sales reps are taught — get the appointment and sell.

In a networking environment, the philosophy is not to sell but to collaborate and help one another. The PEEC Statement™

allows that to happen but it's difficult for an old school sales rep (or those trained to sell the old fashioned way) to accept.

Five Rules for The PEEC Statement™

As I mentioned earlier, I love rules. Well, it's important to have rules for the PEEC Statement™, too; otherwise, you may use it incorrectly. The PEEC Statement™ may seem simple on the surface but there's a lot of moving pieces to it. It often takes people a few go-rounds before they really understand how to create one and ultimately use it. These rules make it so.

Rule No. 1: You Have to Be Asked

If you go around introducing yourself and rattling off your Profession, Expertise, Environments and Call to Action with everyone you meet, imagine the reactions you would get. Think about it. You're meeting people for the first time. It's way too overwhelming—too much too soon. It comes across as pitchy. You have to be asked. But, if it's in response inquiring about what you do, it's a much different story: "I appreciate your asking all of these questions of me. Hey, but enough about me, what about you?"

"Funny you ask!" You might say and then you can respond with your PEEC Statement™.

Of course, there are always exceptions to a rule. Well, almost always. There are three exceptions to this rule—situations in which you don't have to be asked for your PEEC Statement™:

1. **You are the speaker at an event.** In that case, it's the perfect intro. It's also a perfect close. When you are the speaker, you can say almost anything as it

relates to who you are, what you do and with whom. Hey, you're the speaker!

2. **You are directed to give your "elevator pitch" at a networking event.** Sometimes they will give everyone a minute or so to give their "elevator pitches" to others. In that environment and situation, it fits—it's expected.

3. **You already have a relationship with the person you are speaking to.** Obviously, if you're speaking to your dad, you don't have to wait for him to ask what you do.

The PEEC Statement™ is an ideal way to begin talking to friends and family about the work that you do and the types of connections you're looking to make. You could say, "Uncle Joe, let me bounce this off of you." And now the PEEC Statement™ fits the scenario.

You are not pitching Uncle Joe, but after you explain that you're looking to connect with physicians or speakers or whatever your market is, Uncle Joe becomes a resource, not a prospect. Unless Uncle Joe wants to be a prospect — that's a different story.

Now that your uncle has a better understanding of what you do and who you help, he may have no problem pointing you in the right direction and introducing you in all types of situations.

You can actually do business with your family without giving them a hard sell. If you're a financial advisor, you could say, "Look, I don't want to pitch you, sell you or make you uncomfortable. But I'm learning a lot about life insurance, annuities, investments, retirement and that type of stuff. So if I can be a resource to you or help you in any way, it would be my pleasure." And that's it.

And of course, there are those times where you might end up doing business with Uncle Joe after all.

Other than these exceptions, stick to Rule No. 1 — You Have to Be Asked.

Rule No. 2: It Has to Be Short, Sweet and to the Point

Your PEEC Statement™ shouldn't be any longer than 30 seconds or so. Any longer than that, and it may become drawn out and boring. The more you practice, the easier it will be and the smoother it will sound.

Rule No 3: It Has to Be Specific

You remember way back in math, when we were reducing fractions from 4/8 to 2/4 to 1/2? They had an acronym for that called LCD—Least Common Denominator. It's the same with The PEEC Statement™—everything you say within this framework should be reduced to the least common denominator. So if it's small business, what type of small business? What industry? What profession? What vertical? What market segment? What geography? What revenue level? Number of employees? The more specific you are, the more powerful (and memorable) it's going to be.

Rule No. 4: It's All About the AIR Time™

You have to be able to create AIR Time™ with whomever it is you're speaking with. Let me give you three examples.

First, I mean AIR Time™ as in the advertising world, where you pay for 30 seconds or a minute of air time. During the Super

Bowl, a one-minute commercial costs $3.5 million—that's premium air time. Of course you want it to be the best it can be so that you can get the biggest bang for the buck. It's kind of the same thing with your PEEC Statement™—you want to make the most of your 30 seconds (all 3.5 million dollars worth).

Second, you want to generate AIR Time™ in terms of people wanting to know more about you—"Oh, really? So why do you want to work with physicians?" Or "Oh, so you're a speaker?" Now you are having what I call (this is a pretty technical term, so you may want to write it down) a conversation! People actually want to have a conversation with you about this. And now you're "on"!

Third, I mean AIR Time™ as in AIR™—another acronym. It stands for Advice, Insight and Recommendations, and it helps you with your Call to Action. Right after I mention who I am looking to meet or be introduced to, I will say, "Any advice, insight or recommendations you have, please—I would love your suggestions." People love to be asked for advice rather than being on the receiving end of a sales pitch. (Hey, that's my advice!)

Rule No. 5: Your PEEC Statement™ Shouldn't Change Like the Wind

If your target market happens to be physicians, and you're speaking to a manager in the manufacturing industry, that industry does not magically become your target market. Don't suddenly change your focus all of a sudden just because you met someone influential that you think you can "sell". Don't make it "fit" the situation at hand. If you're looking to get into manufacturing, and it's just a coincidence that you met that person, that's one thing. But you shouldn't keep transforming your PEEC Statement™ or tailoring it to your conversations. Remember, if everyone is your target market, then no one is your target market. Stay on target!

Example of a PEEC Statement™

So someone says to me, "Hey, enough about me. What about you?" A textbook PEEC Statement™ that I might present in response sounds something like this: "Funny you ask. I am a professional speaker. I operate a speaking and training company called Building Blocks Consulting. I help sales reps grow their business. My expertise is in networking, referral marketing and recruiting. I work almost exclusively in the financial services industry. What I'm looking to do at this event is meet managing directors or managing partners from companies like…. Any advice, insight or recommendations you might have in helping me make these connections is appreciated."

The most common response that I get when I say something like that is, "Wow, a professional speaker? How'd you get involved with that?"

I'll say, "Funny you should ask," and I'll tell them. I'll have a conversation with them. Now I've got them, right? We've generated AIR Time™, and I have also created marketing gravity.

The second most common response I get is someone saying, "Boy, that's great," and they reintroduce themselves to me, this time using their own PEEC Statement™ because they realize that they left opportunity on the table. They realize that they could have done a much better job of presenting their own PEEC Statement™ to me. Then our level of awareness is much greater and it gives us much more to talk about.

I have heard and researched many philosophies and approaches as it relates to the elevator pitch. Mine is just the best (kidding). Seriously, take whatever approach you use and apply it to your own style and industry. Make sure your communication is clear, precise, interesting and engaging. I created The PEEC Statement™ formula to insure all of these things. And it works!

Once you get really good at presenting your PEEC Statement™, you might discover that it's really not a script at all. It starts off as a script because you need to learn it a certain way. After that, your PEEC Statement™ should become an easy way for you to discuss what you do and who you help. It should simply be a guide to keep you prepared, focused, and on track.

Takeaways

- PEEC™ is an acronym that you can use to come up with your personal elevator pitch, or positioning statement. It stands for Profession, Expertise, Environments and Call to Action.

- Having an abbreviated version of your PEEC Statement™ helps you drop it into more conversations.

- Even though everyone calls it an elevator pitch and thinks of it as such, it is actually a positioning statement because it positions you as a professional and as an expert in a given area. It helps you explore opportunities to gain more momentum, traction and contacts related to the type of business that you're looking to do in a non-confrontational but direct sort of way.

- The first rule about your PEEC Statement™ is that you have to be asked for it. This rule does not apply, though, if you are a speaker at an event, if you are at a networking event where everyone is instructed to give their "elevator pitches" to one another, or if you already have a relationship with the person you are talking to.

- The other four rules about your PEEC Statement™ are as follows: It has to be short (30 seconds or so), sweet and to the point; it has to be specific; it's all about the AIR time™ (advice, insight and recommendations); and it shouldn't change like the wind.

- My PEEC Statement™—given only when someone asks me about myself, of course—is: "I am a professional speaker. I operate a speaking and training company called Building Blocks Consulting. I help financial advisors grow their practice. My expertise is in networking, referral marketing and recruiting. I work almost exclusively in the financial services industry. And what I'm looking to do here is meet managing directors or managing partners from companies like... Any advice, insight or recommendations you might have in helping me make these connections is appreciated."

Your Turn

You need to know who your market is before you can develop your PEEC Statement™. Then, once you have your PEEC Statement™ written, you will need to practice it—almost to the point of using it as a script—but eventually, it will become second nature to you. Develop your own PEEC Statement™, and an abbreviated version of it, below.

YOUR "CALL TO ACTION" PLAN

You and Your Elevator Pitch

1. First, review this sample PEEC Statement™: "I am a <u>financial advisor</u> who works for <u>ABC Financial Services</u>. I help people <u>build wealth and protect their assets</u>. **(Profession).** My expertise is in a number of areas, including <u>annuities, retirement and 401(k) accounts</u>. **(Expertise)** I work almost exclusively with <u>physicians</u> **(Environments).** What I'm looking to do here is meet <u>established physicians who are looking to diversity their portfolios</u>. Do you have any advice, insight or recommendations for me? I'm open to your suggestions." **(Call to Action)**

2. Fill in the blanks to build your own PEEC Statement™: "I am a _____ who works for _____. I help people_____ _____. My expertise is in a number of areas, including _____. I work almost exclusively with _____. What I'm looking to do here is meet _____ _____ who _____. Do you have any advice, insight or recommendations for me? I'm open to your suggestions."

3. Now write an abbreviated form of your PEEC Statement™ to use in quick conversations: "Well, actually, I'm a _____. I provide _____ _____ to _____. If I can connect with _____ who can help me do more of that, that would be great."

CHAPTER 6:

Networking with the Right People

*"Consider how hard it is to change yourself and
you'll understand what little chance you have
in trying to change others."*

—Jacob M. Braude, American Humorist and Writer

As I mentioned in Chapter 2, no matter how great an event is, we probably won't like about two-thirds of the people we meet there. Maybe we should consider ourselves lucky when we do meet someone we hit it off with. Think about when you first met the people who are still in your life today. Usually there's a great story behind how you met the people that you now have a lasting relationship. (How did you meet the love of *your* life?) Did you know at the time that you would be friends or BFF's (that's best friends forever if you're out of touch) or whatever? Or did the relationship go through phases?

It works the same way with the connections you make through networking. You meet people at events and given your initial contact and the behavior that follows, you develop a relationship. But at networking events (as in life) you meet all kinds of people and greet many different faces. Everybody is different. Different interests, agendas, and motives. As a networker, you have to be prepared to deal with all of these new faces in new places. Which one are you?

The Faces of Networking

It's important to note that these names that I've given the faces of networking are not intended to be sexist in any way, even though I've given some of them female names and some of them male names (think girl—boy, girl—boy—duck—duck-goose.). In real life, there are male and female versions of each of the eight faces. You just have to know them when you see them.

Negative Nelly

There's always someone in the crowd who's negative. They're negative about the economy, health-care reform, the political climate, job search—"Nobody's hiring." They're negative about their business, the industry that they're in, their profession. They're negative about the event and everyone they meet and everyone else's products. They're negative about companies they've worked for.

Negative people love company and attract more negative people.

Now, some people are determined to be negative, no matter what you say. I will not work with those people, the true Negative Nellies. I refuse. I have turned away business from negative people. Nobody wins in that deal because when they don't do their part, they will blame you. And that's a negative perspective—it's always the other person's fault.

So choose to work with positive people. Even positive people sometimes have valid complaints, and that's normal. But Negative Nellies complain just because they're not happy unless they are miserable. That's cool—they give me my next story to tell, but I don't need to work with them! Or network with them. It's just as simple as that.

I tell sales people all the time that negative prospects will turn into negative clients. I understand that reps that are new in their business need clients, but they should look to get to the point where they don't need to work with negative people or others who aren't helping them take their practice to the next level.

> **Quick tip:** Try to only hang out with positive people. Positive people equals positive prospects which equals positive clients. Get it? I'm positive of that!

Hard-Sell Harry

Remember Dave, from our trade show in Chapter 2? Hard-Sell Harry is basically Dave. All he cares about is selling to everyone that he can. He only wants to talk about his products and services. He is sizing you up as a prospect, trying to identify pain you might be suffering as it relates to your business and looking to shake you down for your money.

Hard-Sell Harry knows exactly what he's doing. In some cases, he may not realize the purpose of a networking event. Way back when, I didn't know, either. When I first started going to networking events, my mindset was, "Anybody need training and consulting services?" I don't think I actually said that, but that's where I was mentally, and it was completely wrong, of course. So in some cases, people in this category may just not know—no one has taught them the difference between selling and networking. But in most cases, I think they know.

Recently, I did a talk for a networking organization near my home town as a favor to somebody who started the group to build their business. He wanted me to be the kick-off speaker and set a positive tone for the meeting. My talk was about 15 minutes, and it was on the PEEC Statement™. I went through my talk, the reaction was great and the meeting continued. At the end, wouldn't you know it, a woman came over to me and started to pitch me on printer services, graphic design, advertising media, and all this stuff—a really hard sell: "You know what you need is…" and "In fact, what you ought to do is…" and "What I can do is…."

I just looked at her and said, "Look, respectfully, weren't you listening to me when I was speaking? You are completely hard-selling me on something that I don't need, don't want and really don't want to be speaking about with you."

She kind of caught herself but didn't know what to say.

I said, "Look, no harm, no foul. I didn't mean to make you feel uncomfortable, but that was one of the major points of my presentation — networking is not selling." And I left it at that.

But in most cases, Hard Sell Harry knows exactly what he's doing. He's preying on people who may be new to a group, new to their own business, or just don't know what they're up to. Buyer…err networker beware!

Self-Centered Sally

It's a similar situation with Self-Centered Sally, but it's not so much that she's pitching her wares; she just wants to talk about how wonderful she is—how great she is at what she does, how everybody loves her, how much money she makes. "I'm so successful. I've been published here, and I've been reviewed there, and I've been in business here, and I know this person."

I work with a seasoned sales rep that is new in her current role. She worked in brokerage and some other places previously. She loves to tell you all the important people she knows and how successful she has been. People say she is a know-it-all. I guess she needs to say all of these things to feel good about herself. It's only a matter of time before she fails out of her current business.

Nobody benefits from those conversations other than her. And really, at the end of the day, does she?

Ravenous Rick

Ravenous Rick is just there for the buffet and the booze. That's it. He basically wants to kibitz (as they say in the trade) a little bit, get some drinks and nibbles, and he's happy. Yes, it's all about the food. The ball game is on anyway, and he can fill his belly. If he can chat with people for company, that's fine.

But Rick doesn't really want to be bothered about talking about work—his or anybody else's. He will make small talk because he knows he should. But at the end of the day, Rick really couldn't care less. It's a place to go, something to do, what the heck. If business comes out of it, cool. If it doesn't, that's OK—he had a good meal. Pass the pretzels!

Blackjack Betty

All that Blackjack Betty really cares about is business cards. Throwing cards at people and collecting them. She thinks she's in Atlantic City. So when Betty is at an event, she wants to talk to a lot of people, but not for too long. It's really just about handing a business card to everybody she can. It's barely a conversation. She may say, "I'm Betty, a Mary Kay lady, and this is what I have. Here's my card, and do you have a card?" In Betty's world, that's networking.

The name of the game for Blackjack Betty is whoever has the most cards at the end of the event wins. In fact, Blackjack Betty is so caught up in playing cards that she has forgotten to count them or recount them. She'll circle the room again and meet you a second time because she does not remember that she has already met you. Have you ever had anyone do that to you?

A successful event for Blackjack Betty is, "Look, I got almost everybody's card. I win." Betty rarely does business with any of these people anyway because she doesn't know enough about them. And what to do with all those cards? She may be crafty or rude enough to put them in her database or to add them to her newsletter mailing list. But other than that, she doesn't really know what to do with them.

There is no concept or focus to her strategy, no target market. It's a shotgun approach: Ready, fire, aim.

> **Important note:** It's considered spamming if you collect business cards at an event and add those contacts to your mailing list without permission. That's not networking.

Silent Sam

Silent Sam is someone who doesn't want to be there, but on some level, he knows he needs to be. He's the guy who's hanging around at the coffee station. He is shy or at least reluctant to get out there to shake a hand and kiss a baby because he doesn't want to come across as pitchy or salesy. He hopes that the other person comes to him. But even if that happens, then what?

Silent Sam is there under false pretenses. He is there because he needs to be there. Or he's told he needs to be there. He just figures, "If I'm here, maybe something good will happen.

Maybe if I collect a card or two, that's good. If I meet somebody, that's good too. Just let the time go by—please."

In fact, Silent Sam is happiest when no one bothers him. He thinks, "You know, this networking stuff is not for me. It's just not my thing. I'm quiet. I don't really like to be around people like this." He knows that it's wrong, and he feels a little down because of it, but again, the way he thinks is that, "I've escaped one. I've cheated the claws of death."

Another way Silent Sam thinks is, "There has got to be a better way, and maybe if I come here, I'll figure out what that better way is."

> **Another important note:** Introverts can be great networkers too. I find that those that are introverted, introspective or downright shy may have a more difficult time greeting people initially but have a much easier time following up and developing a relationship moving forward. I'm an introvert too (really!). Don't let this prevent you from growing your business, landing that job or meeting your dreamboat. That's why you're reading this book!

Social Susie

All that Social Susie wants to do is hang out with people she already knows and have a good time. Yes, it's all about socializing. And that isn't all bad. If you want to just go and have coffee with a few pals, there's nothing wrong with that. But the flip side of that is, why are you going to this networking event in the first place? Go to Dunkin' Donuts for coffee-talk with friends.

Of course you should have a good time at any networking event—the final Pool Rule is to have fun, so that should be part of it—but that is Social Susie's only reason for being there. There has to be more to networking than just socializing.

Now, there's a lot to Social Susie. It's not that she just wants to have a good time—she may not know how to have a good business conversation. Susie may feel that she'll compromise friendships if she brings business into the discussion. It's not that she wants to appear mysterious; she just doesn't want to come across as salesy and potentially ruin a friendship. Susie doesn't understand that networking is a way to foster those relationships. It's almost as if she is hiding the fact that she is there for business reasons, and she gets caught up in the hubbub of having fun without knowing how to turn a fun conversation into a business conversation. Can't a business conversation be fun?

Now the common phenomenon that I see with salespeople who are typically outgoing is that they like to hang out with other people and have a drink. That's all good, but not all of them know how to turn those conversations into business. Don't misunderstand. I don't think you should be selling those you are socializing your products and services. But you can talk about your business and ask about theirs. The PEEC Statement™ would work well here. Funny you ask!

I have met Social Susie at events. She is looking for a nice, young, single guy. She is looking for her second husband. She is looking for somebody to vent about love and life. The male version of Social Susie, Social Sal, wants to find a couple of guys and talk about sports. Or meet other Social Susie's.

Networking Nick

Networking Nick knows The Pool Rules™. He has a PEEC Statement™. He knows exactly why he's at an event or in a conversation and what the outcome ought to be. Networking Nick is out to meet people and help them. He is out there to learn something. He is looking for his next venue so that he can do more of the same type of work that he is so good at. Networking Nick is cool!

Nick actually loves to network. He sees the value. The networking "switch" is always on for him. And he is typically very successful at what he does. In fact, Nick seems to know everybody, has the connections, has the ability and loves nothing more than pointing people in the right direction for relationships. He's a natural connector.

Networking Nick knows that other people like him, and he chooses to hang out only with other Networking Nicks.

You can see that people are so different — complete with varying styles, approaches and mindsets. They come in the form of both genders too — Social Susie can just as easily be Social Sal. And it is not up to us to change those mindsets—nor can we, really.

I'm not saying that Hard Sell Harry, Social Susie, or any of the cast of characters are necessarily bad people. But they are bad networkers. And they will make it more difficult for you to network.

Uncomfortable moment! Do you wear any of these faces?

If so, what are you going to do about it? What will you change? How can you find out if you do in fact act like one of these bad networkers?

Answer — ask others you know and trust those that network with you. Then work on changing those behaviors. Simple! But not always easy.

People Seldom Change

Sounds horrible, huh?

One of my favorite Aesop's Fables is about the scorpion and the frog. An oldie but goodie.

A frog is hopping along its merry way, and a scorpion jumps into its path. The frog jumps back. The scorpion says, "Why did you jump back? Why are you so afraid?"

The frog answers, "Because you're a scorpion. You can kill me."

"Well, that might be so, but I won't kill you, on one condition," the scorpion says.

"Of course. What do you need me to" the frog asks.

"I need to get across this river. You can swim—I can't. Let me jump on your back, swim me across the river, and I promise I won't kill you."

The frog thinks a minute and says, "But you could sting me at any time."

The scorpion says, "That might be so. But I can't swim, so I won't make it the rest of the length of the river, so that would make no sense. I would never do that."

The frog thinks about it and realizes he doesn't have much of a choice, so they kind of shake on it.

So the scorpion jumps on the frog's back, the frog submerges himself in the water, and there they go, swimming along. Halfway across the river, the scorpion stings the frog. The frog looks up and says, "You stung me. I can't believe you've done that. Now we're both going to die." And they both did.

The moral of the story is that you can't change someone's nature. A scorpion is supposed to sting. It is in its nature to sting. So asking it not to sting would be asking it to do something that goes against its nature.

If you come across people who are, in fact, scorpions—in the form of Hard-Sell Harry, Self-Centered Sally, Ravenous Rick, Blackjack Betty, Silent Sam and Social Susie, your job should not be to correct or change them. It may just be their nature.

I know it's crass, but often, people are who they are. The good news is a small percentage of these networking "characters" can be changed. Taught the error in their ways. They're probably not aware of their behavior and have never been taught how to network. Or never told that their approach to networking is incorrect.

Most people simply don't care how they come across and they just do what they do. Se la vie.

So what's your approach in dealing with these characters?

Remember, you are not in the business of teaching other people how to network. You are there for one of the five reasons I mentioned earlier. So be polite and respectful, and excuse yourself. "Susie, it's been great speaking with you. Thank you for keeping me company and hope to see you soon. Good luck tonight!"

You want to be Networking Nick, who fishes in the right ponds, and who seeks out other Networking Nicks (or Nicoles). You want to go to places where you're going to meet with good people so that you can focus on The Pool Rules™, PEEC Statements™, asking great questions, and doing all the things you should be doing to create marketing gravity. It's all about learning and helping people. When you meet others that are like minded, you know it immediately.

Once you become more familiar with The Faces of Networking, it won't take you long to recognize them at a networking event. And then you can gravitate toward the Networking Nicks and Nicoles—or as we say in the trade, the ones who "get it".

Takeaways

- At most networking events, you will meet the usual cast of characters—the faces of networking. They include Hard-Sell Harry, Self-Centered Sally, Ravenous Rick, Blackjack Betty, Silent Sam, Social Susie and Networking Nick. Of those, Networking Nick is the only one you should really spend time getting to know.

- Here is an overview of the eight faces of networking:

  › Negative Nelly is happy only when she's miserable, and she wants everyone else to know how much she hates everything and everyone.

  › Hard-Sell Harry only wants to talk about his products and services.

  › Self-Centered Sally just wants to talk about how wonderful she is.

  › Ravenous Rick is just there for the buffet and the booze.

› Blackjack Betty is "playing cards"—for her, It's about handing a business card to everybody she can.

› Silent Sam is shy or at least reluctant to get out there because he doesn't want to come across a pitchy or salesy.

› Social Susie is all about socializing, and she does not know how to have a good business conversation.

› Networking Nick gets it—he seems to know everybody, has the connections, has the ability and loves nothing more than pointing people in the right direction for relationships

• Don't think that you have to be in the business of teaching other people how to network. Your job is not to correct or change them, but rather to be a Networking Nick and to gravitate toward other Networking Nicks (or Nicoles).

Your Turn

Our goal as networkers is to personify the ideal—Networking Nick. Think about the Faces of Networking, and try to identify behaviors that would make you less like the first seven faces of networking and more like Networking Nick.

YOUR "CALL TO ACTION" PLAN

Networking with the Right People

1. Which of the members of the networking cast of characters have you encountered? Do you see yourself in any of these characters?

   - ❑ Negative Nelly
   - ❑ Hard-Sell Harry
   - ❑ Self-Centered Sally
   - ❑ Ravenous Rick
   - ❑ Blackjack Betty
   - ❑ Silent Sam
   - ❑ Social Susie
   - ❑ Networking Nick

2. Do you consider yourself to be a Networking Nick? If so, why? If not, what could you do to better in terms of networking? _____

   _____

   _____

   _____

   _____

CHAPTER 7:

It's All About Communication

"Listening is not hearing."
—Stephen Covey

The ability to communicate is the most important thing we can ever learn. What's ironic is that even though it is the skill (or set of skills) that people practice most often, it is the thing we are worst at. In part, this is because we take it for granted—we communicate (or try to communicate) so often that we don't think there is anything to it. Other than getting the language correct and learning the basics, we lose sight of how important communication is. It is a myth that effective communication comes naturally.

What does communication have to do with networking?

Everything! Without great communication, there can be no networking. Being purposeful about articulating who you are, what you do, and with whom is all about communicating well. Communication isn't just about saying stuff—that's roughly 20 percent of it. The other 80 percent is having someone listen and understand what you are saying. So understanding is not about the other person just thinking they have it; it means that they really are on the same page as you — so to speak. This is vital in having the contacts you make refer you the type of business you may be looking for — and of course, helping those contacts right back.

Webster's dictionary defines communication as a process by which information is exchanged and understood by individuals through a common system of symbols, signs and behavior. The key word is "understood." If a message is not understood, you have not communicated.

I consider myself a professional communicator, and as a friend of mine says, every day I am reminded of how stupid I was just two weeks ago. I will think later that I shouldn't have said what I did, or I should have been clearer about something—and I do this for a living! According to the Carnegie Institute of Technology (CIT), 75 percent of communication is ignored, misunderstood or completely forgotten. So three-quarters of what we should know, we don't. If we had just half of that information back, imagine how smart we would be. How often do we say "Yes, you did tell me that," or "No, I don't remember that"?

Also, according to CIT, 85 percent of personal relationships fail because of a breakdown in communication. You think you're in one place but you're not, or you just don't speak about certain things with one another. Just look at the divorce rate and the number of unhappy marriages. It boils down to a breakdown in communication. We think our spouse or friend wants one thing, but they want something else.

CIT also estimates that the average person speaks 125 to 150 words per minute, yet the human brain absorbs more than four times that information. I'm told that people in the Northeast (typically New York) may speak faster than the average person, but the human brain still can absorb so much more. This means that we all have extra time and brain capacity.

Imagine that! So if a conversation doesn't grab us, then our minds will wander off to other topics. This extra "brain space" prevents us from listening as closely as we should be.

(Are you even paying attention now?)

If you have good communication skills, listen well, speak well and articulate on purpose and with purpose, then it is much easier to network. One of the biggest compliments I get from people is when they say that I am a great listener. It gets back to one of The Pool Rules™: to talk less and listen more. And when I do speak, I ask what I think are good questions.

Here are some basic concepts as they relate to communication theory. I warn you it's a bit heavy. It's so important to be reminded of these concepts because without effective communication there is no effective networking. Relate these concepts to how you communicate everyday with prospects, clients, referrals sources, bosses, associates, hiring managers, and interns. If you're really brave, try to relate these concepts to your personal relationships. Good luck!

The Sender

There are two parties in any communication exchange: the sender and the receiver. The sender expresses their message (in face to face communication anyway) through *words, tone of voice* and *body language.* For any good communication to take place there has to be *intent.* The *intent* needs to be to get the message out clearly and effectively with the purpose of the other person (or other people) understanding it. Simple, right?

Words

In front of an audience, I am very particular about my words because my   is not just to entertain people with what I hope is a good presentation but to also educate them. I need them to know what I am talking about. If they don't know what I'm talking about, then it is my fault, not theirs. I will ask, "Am I making sense?" not "Did that make sense?" I put the clarity part on me, not on them.

In fact, in our everyday communication, as a speaker or sender of a message, how much better would we be if we put the clarity part on ourselves rather than on the other person? That should be the *intent*.

It's important to use words that people understand—don't talk down to them as though they were fifth graders, but think about your audience (one person or many people).

The best practice is to use words that people understand. I can think of examples where people may as well be speaking a foreign language because they're using jargon that may be understood by some people but not others. To me that is a breakdown in communication. A lot of people won't say, "Tell me what you meant by that." They don't want to look silly for not understanding, so they let it go. That gets back to the three-quarters of communication that is misunderstood because it is not clarified. Have you ever been in a lecture or at a presentation when someone asked a question, and you were glad because you were wondering about that, too? If you were wondering, why didn't you ask? Because you felt that you should understand but you didn't, and you didn't want to embarrass yourself.

For example, if I'm at an insurance industry event, obviously I don't know as much about their business as they do, so I am not shy about asking questions for clarification. I'll say, "Tell me more about where you think health care is going right now. What do you think is going to happen? I know what's in the papers, but tell me from an industry perspective."

Or, if I'm speaking to somebody and I think I might have an upper hand in terms of what's going on, and I know that the person I'm speaking with doesn't, I'm going to consider that, and I'm going to want to use the appropriate language and come across in a way that doesn't make them feel badly about it. Instead, I will create a positive air about it. That's good communication, and that's considering your words when you're sending a message. You are increasing the chances that you will be liked, engaged and understood.

Tone of Voice

Your tone of voice, or tonality, is very important, also. Tone is how you increase the volume and pitch of your voice. If you speak in a monotone, you may appear disinterested, just going through the motions. Generally, if you're really excited about something, your tone of voice reflects that.

Part of my job as a public speaking instructor (my college teaching gig — I teach one class) is that I have to assess the students' public speaking skills. I also have the entire class assess each student's presentation. We all weigh in on the things that went really well and the things that could be improved. One of the things that we focus on is tonality. During one class, there was a student who was presenting to the class. Her speaking was fine in terms of what she was saying, but she was very even in her tone. She said, with no inflection, things like, "I find that really amazing." "That's really incredible." "That really blew me away." "That was very surprising." I jumped all over that when she was done because it didn't come across as being genuine—her tonality did not fit her words. I see that at cocktail parties and networking meetings. People are just not engaged, not genuine, or simply don't care. (Not good traits by the way.)

Tonality can actually have more of an impact on how you communicate than words. That student's words were fine, but her tonality was missing — as was her message.

Body Language

Body language brings it all together. This is a case in which pictures certainly speak more loudly than words. When you see how somebody reacts—their facial expressions, their gestures—that reflects what's in the soul, how people are really thinking and feeling.

The student I mentioned had almost no body language other than making occasional eye contact. Now, you don't need to be theatrical or channel Hamlet to communicate well. But when you have everyday conversation, your mannerisms certainly follow your sentiments.

The student who had no tonality had almost no body language, either. I ended up giving her a grade of "B" because of what was missing—the effective body language and tonality. Otherwise, she would have gotten an "A" because the content that she presented was fine.

You can see that there is an order of things. Words have the least impact, and body language has the most impact on your communication. There is a statistic for all of this, again according to the Carnegie Institute of Technology. They estimate that words contribute to only about 7 percent of how impactful your message is. Your tonality or tone of voice contributes about 38 percent of the clarity of your message. Your body language contributes about 55 percent. You need all three of those components to communicate the most effectively, statistically speaking.

So, in essence, you can give a presentation and say almost nothing, right? So can a mime. A group can typically follow a really good mime. He uses no tonality and no words—it's 100 percent body language. Yet he can still get his message across — like in a good game of charades.

It's the same sort of thing when you are networking. I am drawn to people who are somewhat expressive and are clearly passionate about their life and the work they are doing. You can usually tell that by their tonality and body language.

On the flip side, I know people who are very dramatic and overly theatrical, and it's almost like turning the volume up too high—it's as if you can't hear the music even though the volume is on full-blast. So it's possible to have overkill, too. It's not to say there is such a thing as over communicating—I don't think there is. But there is such a thing as over pronouncing yourself and going over the top. And I think that compromises communication, likeability and, therefore, networking.

The Listener

The listener (or receiver of a message) will receive the communicated message with varying levels of success based on how they are listening. (Naturally, the listener then becomes the speaker or sender as they respond to the message.)

Of course, there are all of those barriers that prevent us from listening as we should in the first place. Other than actual sound, what are some of those barriers?

Emotions, preconceived notions, prejudices, experiences and overall attitudes just to name a few.

In communication workshops, I will have people position themselves face-to-face, nose-to-nose, belly-to-belly with one another and have them come up with controversial topics to discuss. They might be topics about gun control, politics, health-care reform, Afghanistan—issues that are pretty charged and for which there is no right or wrong answer; it's just that everyone has a different perspective. What ends up happening is that the people in the activity become passionate and emotional about their position and they stop listening (or at least listen differently). Doesn't this happen all too often in real life?

There are many different types of listening. Without listening, there is no communication, in a face-to-face scenario. And without communication there is no networking.

Ignoring

It's as if we are playing different roles, and ignoring is one of those roles. In some cases, you ignore someone and it is inappropriate to do so.

In other cases, ignoring someone (or a comment they may make) can be the right thing to do. If you are in a conversation with three or four people and what is being said does not pertain to you, it is appropriate for you to ignore the conversation or excuse yourself. So ignoring isn't always bad. You shouldn't be on full throttle with every conversation that you're in anyway because every conversation isn't a good one, and there are ways of dealing with those scenarios. Just don't get caught if you *should* be paying attention (like now!).

Pretending to Listen

When I speak to an audience, I will often get positive nods, but I know that sometimes those people who are nodding haven't a clue what I'm talking about, even though they're portraying the body language of somebody who might be really listening. Again, we do this sometimes without meaning to be disrespectful, but maybe we've gotten distracted, or that extra brain time gets in the way. I catch people doing that in the classroom. (So maybe it's me.)

Selective Listening

With selective listening, people choose the part of the communication that is of greatest interest to them.

Cognitive Listening

This is the type of listening that you engage in with the intent of learning, as in, "This isn't that interesting to me, but I need to know this for the test," or "I need to know this to get my designation or license."

Critical Listening

The purpose of this type of listening is to give feedback — both positive and negative, as well as suggestions.

Appreciative Listening

This is when people listen for pleasure—to music, to a speaker or to the sounds of silence. (Props to Simon and Garfunkel.)

Attentive Listening

With attentive listening, you are trying really hard to under-stand the message. You are trying to pay attention, be present, and in the moment, but because of the intricate nature of the conversation or because it's a fast pace or because you don't want to show that you don't know something, you refrain from asking a question. Your heart is in the right place, but you don't engage and try to get more. It's the kind of listen-ing done by that student who did not raise his hand in class to ask a question. He thinks, "I'll get whatever I can, and hopefully I'll figure the rest out later."

Active Listening

Active Listening is listening on steroids. Active listening is absorbing someone's message like a sponge absorbs water. I think that the best form of active listening is done by somebody who is listening to something that they are going to have to teach. I showcase that in my public-speaking class. I tell my students, "OK, you are going to have to speak about this." Then all of a sudden, they are paying attention. They don't want to get up in front of a group and not know what they are talking about.

Of course, you shouldn't be actively listening all the time. It's not necessary or possible. But in most networking scenarios, especially with the one-thirders (the one-third of all people who you will like), you really need to be as engaged as you can. The better you are at listening, the better you are going to be at communicating overall. And again, great listening equates to great networking.

Whenever I am working with top sales producers, I ask them the same question. I will say, "Before we get started, and before I get an understanding of how I can help you, clearly you're very successful. You're doing a lot of things right. If you had to pick one skill or one thing that you do really well that has gotten you where you are today, what is that skill?" The most common response I get is "listening." (Not sales skills!) These successful producers say, "I just ask people questions, then I shut up and listen to what they have to say. And because I listen, I'm able to solve their problems because I understand where they're coming from."

What gets in the way of our listening? Often it's hard to stay focused on one thing, and our minds wander. Also, because it's human nature, we often get caught up in a "me" mentality. And we have that extra brain time when our brains just kind of wander.

We put so much pressure on ourselves to do so many things at once that it's hard for us to down-shift and focus. That will prevent us from listening while networking or trying to engage with a prospect during a sales appointment. Also, a lot of people think that networking is about *talking*—they forget that there is a primary *listening* component to it.

In face-to-face communication, we tend to speak 80 percent of the time and listen only 20 percent of the time. What would happen in our day to day chatter if we reverse that— speak only 20 percent of the time and listen 80 percent of the time? Even though I am a speaker, I am not known as a Chatty Cathy. I am not a small-talker at events. If something is interesting to me, I can talk about it. I'm not shy, but I'm not the guy who is going to talk your ear off. I will ask what I think are good questions and listen to the answers. That is how I try to be engaging.

Sales producers often talk themselves out of a sale. How many times have you *talked* yourself out of a sale? A conversation? A better deal? Or a relationship? People simply talk too much and don't listen enough. Especially in sales.

There is a four-step process you can employ to become better listeners or to force yourself to become more of an active listener. Listening is a skill. Typically, we all have the capacity to hear (recognize sound), as well as the capacity to listen (recognize understanding). It just requires *intent* and practice to become better at listening.

A Four-Step Process for Active Listening

The four steps of Active Listening are restating, reflecting, summarizing and asking questions.

Restating

When I'm networking with people, I put everything into trying to understand what they are saying, as best I can. So I will restate—repeat—what they have said and paraphrase it into my own words. It would sound like parroting to state it back to them in their exact words. So I will say, "What I hear you saying is that…" and then paraphrase what they said. "Oh, you spent the weekend at a party. That sounds great. You must have had a lot of fun." Then they know that I am listening.

Reflecting

Reflecting, or adding your own insight to what someone has said, shows someone that you are trying to relate to what they have said. I will say something like, "Man, that must have been a great party. It sounds like there were a lot of great people there. Not only did you probably have a lot of fun; I'll bet it was a great opportunity to talk about business, too." With that kind of interaction, the person definitely gets the sense that I was listening. I have now restated and reflected on what was going on.

Reflecting forces us to listen, and it convinces the other person that we are interested, which makes us come across as interesting.

Think about when you have a problem in life. Don't you tend to go to the same person or people and confide in them—a family member or friend? We tend to gravitate to the same people because they are the few people in our lives who listen to us and who truly get it. They remember what you say and ask you about it a couple of days later—"How did you end up handling that speeding ticket? Will it cost you points on your license?"

Those are the people who are *actively* listening to you, and it makes you feel comfortable and important. Not enough people offer us the gift of listening. When was the last time you felt that someone was truly listening to you? When was the last time you offered the gift of listening to someone? Remember, people don't care how much you know until they know how much you care. The best way to show that you care is by truly listening.

Summarizing

To summarize is to clarify specific points made during a conversation. Break the conversation down into chunks so that you understand it. In essence, you are attempting to summarize parts of the conversation.

The more complex the topic is, or the less knowledgeable you are about the content, the more focused you need to be on summarizing. If you can follow the conversation easily, you don't have to try as hard to be focused.

For example, I recently had dinner with a couple of business connections that have become friends. They are just brilliant when it comes to politics. I love listening to them debate back and forth. One conversation they got into was about the John F. Kennedy conspiracy theory, the assassination, who did what, the Mafia's involvement, etc. I am not as knowledgeable about the topic as I'd like to be—I've seen the movies, and I'm interested. But these guys knew all the players, all the circumstances, and they knew what happened in courtrooms. It was amazing to listen to them. They have read many books on the conspiracy theories and have followed it closely through the years.

In my defense, they have a few years on me, so they were around when JFK was assassinated, and they lived through it. But I had to keep chiming in like I was a three-year-old: "You guys have to fill in some of the gaps so that I can follow you." I was interested, and I was trying to listen. But I had to keep asking questions just to keep up. Otherwise, I would have been lost, and it would have been like a tennis match, watching the two of them volley back and forth. I walked out of that conversation not only more interested in what they were saying, but much more knowledgeable.

Asking Questions

If you don't know what something means or are unfamiliar with anything throughout the course of a conversation, just ask. "What is hydrochloric acid?" "Who is Steve working for?" "Where were you?" "What's the value of having a target market?" "How will that product help my clients?" People will tell you what you need to know, and you will walk away from that conversation smarter than you were before.

As mentioned earlier, I define networking as *a proactive approach to meeting people to learn, with the prospect of helping them.* So the best way to learn is to try to listen more (and better) and ask questions. The result? You might sell something and build a relationship. Or two!

The Four Communication Styles

I have an assessment that I use with clients that is a variation of the Myers-Briggs Type Indicator profile. It is a psychological assessment that Carl Jung created. He made the argument that we behave in different ways for a multitude of reasons and that, as we try to relate to one another, we come from different places. He believed that the better we are at understanding those various places and how we come across, the more likely we will be able to relate to other people.

Once I assess a sale rep's style, it reveals their comfort level in terms of communication and interpersonal skills, and it gives me a baseline to coach them on their target market, who they need to be working with, where they need to be hanging out, the paths they need to take and the language they might want to use.

Before reading the rest of this chapter, take the assessment on the following pages to determine your communication style. (If you read the analysis first, it could skew the scoring and the results of the assessment.)

Communication Styles Questionnaire

This questionnaire provides you with pairs of statements describing your behavior or thinking. For each set of statements, circle the response—either "A" or "B"—that is more characteristic of you. In some instances, neither the "A" nor the "B" may be typical for you. If this is the case, please select the response which would be *more* like you.

1.	A.	I get right to the point.
	B.	I like to analyze the facts before I answer.
2.	A.	I like to propose original ideas.
	B.	I like working with people.
3.	A.	I like to deal with practical people.
	B.	I get excited about new concepts.
4.	A.	My feelings often guide my actions.
	B.	I usually evaluate things before I act.
5.	A.	I am a no-nonsense kind of person.
	B.	I like having some fun at work.
6.	A.	I use lots of data to help make decisions.
	B.	I can be very creative.
7.	A.	I like colleagues who are sincere.
	B.	My ideas are a little far out.
8.	A.	I use step-by-step analysis to make decisions.
	B.	I think long-range planning is a waste of time.
9.	A.	My intuition is often pretty accurate.
	B.	I appreciate fully documented procedures.
10.	A.	I am pretty sensitive to the feelings of others.
	B.	I usually focus on immediate needs.

11.	A.	I am usually logical and consistent in my actions.
	B.	I often help friends solve their problems.
12.	A.	I like to deal with abstract ideas.
	B.	I like to get things done.
13.	A.	I am concerned with getting the work out.
	B.	I like to assess all the alternatives before acting.
14.	A.	I can be too intellectual for some people.
	B.	I try to analyze why people do things.
15.	A.	I am a practical and realistic person.
	B.	I am a "big picture" person.
16.	A.	I can be too quick to express my feelings.
	B.	I can be impersonal and detached.
17.	A.	I like short meetings with solid objectives.
	B.	I like to socialize during meetings.
18.	A.	I'm known as being level-headed.
	B.	I sometimes base a decision on a strong hunch.
19.	A.	I sometimes get too emotional.
	B.	I'm great at ideas, but poor at implementation.
20.	A.	I like to read reports backed up by analysis.
	B.	I get bored reading reports.
21.	A.	I like brainstorming sessions.
	B.	I dislike people with "half-baked" ideas.
22.	A.	I base my thinking on how I feel at the moment.
	B.	I like to take immediate action on problems.
23.	A.	I don't like to change my proven methods.
	B.	I'm concerned about changes that affect morale.
24.	A.	I daydream about the future.
	B.	I'm concerned about today's problems.

25.	A.	I accomplish much in a given amount of time.
	B.	I like to take my time and get all the facts.
26.	A.	My imagination sometimes gets carried away.
	B.	I'm known as a good problem solver.
27.	A.	I'm impressed by results.
	B.	I'm impressed by the potential of ideas.
28.	A.	I'm impressed by people who have good social skills.
	B.	I'm impressed by people who are well organized.
29.	A.	I'm primarily concerned about today.
	B.	I often reflect upon my past experiences.
30.	A.	I'm concerned about the past, present, and future.
	B.	I often think about future events.
31.	A.	I'm occasionally seen as too sensitive.
	B.	I'm occasionally seen as being "out in left field."
32.	A.	I like facts rather than theories.
	B.	I like to complete projects that I start.

Based on C.G. Jung's Theory of Psychological Types

To manage and ultimately communicate with teams effectively, it is important that a leader be aware of the personal styles of each team member. This profile is designed to provide you with a simple psychological framework of four styles that might be encountered interacting with another individual or within a team. This instrument is only designed to be suggestive, rather than predictive, of actual behavior.

Communication Styles Scoring Sheet

Circle the letters that reflect your statement selections. Score carefully.

	Sensor	Thinker	Intuitor	Feeler
1.	A	B		
2.			A	B
3.	A		B	
4.		B		A
5.	A			B
6.		A	B	
7.			B	A
8.	B	A		
9.		B	A	
10.	B			A
11.		A		B
12.	B		A	
13.	A	B		
14.			A	B
15.	A		B	
16.		B		A
17.	A			B
18.		A	B	
19.			B	A
20.	B	A		
21.		B	A	
22.	B			A
23.		A		B
24.	B		A	
25.	A	B		
26.			A	B
Total Circled Per Column				

	Sensor	Thinker	Intuitor	Feeler
27.	A		B	
28.		B		A
29.	A			B
30.		A	B	
31.			B	A
32.	B	A		
Total Circled Per Column				

The assessment you just completed compiles four different numbers — one in each column, and the column that ends up with the highest number, reflects the style that corresponds with your greatest comfort level. The numbers in the four columns must add up to 32 because there are 32 scenarios. (It would be unusual for a person to score an 8 in all four columns — although it could happen.) Most people score high on one or two columns and lower in the other two columns.

In referring to the Communication Styles Scoring Sheet and reading from left to right — if you scored 14 points in the first column, 9 points in the second, 6 points in the third and 3 points in the fourth, your primary communication style is Sensor, and your secondary style is Thinker. The highest number shows where your comfort level is and how you will most likely behave in situations, especially when feeling stress or pressure.

You might have two numbers that are the same or very close, and that indicates that you gravitate back and forth between those comfort zones.

We all exhibit these four styles to some extent—rarely would anyone score zero points in any of the four columns. Here is a basic breakdown of each of the four communication styles.

Sensor

A Sensor is someone who tends to gravitate toward process. They are action-oriented. They do stuff. They are busy, busy, busy. If you're in Los Angeles on Rodeo Drive, everyone has a cell phone to their ear. They are doing many things at once—they're on the phone, texting, Tweeting, friending, walking, and shopping. That's a Sensor mentality.

Sensors are very action-oriented. They tend to make quick decisions, typically without hesitation—seemingly out of fear of not doing anything. Sensors often come across as impulsive. Sometimes the decisions a Sensor makes doesn't consider the consequences of the actions. My father-in-law is a textbook Sensor (I'm guessing). He is a newly retired real estate attorney, and he is one of these guys who has a cell phone—sometimes two cell phones—attached to his ear(s) at all times. Even though he has retired, he hasn't stopped. Sometimes I think he is busy just for busy's sake.

But I think there is a lot of good in that because I might be at a ball game with him, chatting about something, and he'll say, "I know who you need to talk to." Then he'll dial a number and hand me the phone. He does not wait for anything. He is a man of lists, and he is not a guy who will say, "I will get to it." He just does it. (Not a bad thing, by the way.)

This is a great guy (and therefore a great style) to have on your team, but there can be a down side to that communication style. Each style has what is called "Suggested

Limitations"—the perceived shortcomings of that style from the perception of someone who is not that style. (So a Thinker — one of the other communication styles, may not see the Sensor approach as a great thing.)

Given this, the "Suggested Limitations" of Sensors are that they may not plan well or necessarily think things through. They react and make decisions without considering the consequences. They are seen as impulsive or obsessed with making a decision just for the sake of making one. This is not to say that those things are true, but they are true from the perspective of some of the other styles, from people who cannot relate to that style. Follow me?

A Sensor is all about right now—live for today. Sensors thrive on recognition. Their offices may display a lot of trophies, plaques and other awards — the ego wall. Their offices are usually neat and organized, simply because everything that needs to be done has been done. Everything is filed, completed, shredded — done. It's not to say they're not busy, but they typically don't touch the same piece of paper twice. It's all about getting it done, then next, next, next.

So if you want to start a conversation with someone you know is a Sensor, start off by saying something like, "I will only take a few minutes of your time" or "Let me get right to the point" or "I might be able to help you expedite this." They tend to be very bottom-line, especially the higher the number in their Sensor column. Sensors are famous for making lists, and then if they do something that wasn't on the list, they add it just so it can be checked off. (Ever do that?)

Now if you approach a very high Sensor and you are not making the best use of their time and "bottom-lining" things, they're going to have a hard time listening closely, if at all because their mind is on all the stuff they have to do. So you're not feeding into the way their brain typically works.

There are professions that lend themselves to the various styles. I come from a food-service background. There is a sense of urgency in working in a kitchen, so Sensors are well-suited to a career in that area. And writers, who face constant deadlines, are often Sensors. Also, managers who are on the front lines with a lot of plates spinning (so to speak) are often Sensors. Certainly, many sales professionals fall into this category.

Here is a quick overview of the Sensor personality type (for all of you Sensors):

Sensor

Suggested Strengths:

- Action-oriented—Acts quickly, is a doer.
- Decisive—Makes quick decisions without hesitation.
- Impulsive—Can make decisions out of impulse without thinking about the consequences or chooses to deal with the consequences later.

Suggested Limitations:

- Poor planner—Often does not take the time to sit and plan.
- Compulsive—May be prompted to act by a compulsion or obsession.

Time Frame:

Now. Lives for today.

Thinker

The Thinker is all about analysis, introspection and attention to detail. Remember Mr. Spock from Star Trek? (The original Star Trek that is.) He was always considering the logical thing to do. That's a Thinker mentality. (This is not to suggest that the other styles don't *think*.) Thinkers are very objective—"Prove it." "Where did that statistic come from?" "Did you measure that?" "How do you know that?" Thinkers are very focused on detail. The little things equate to the big things. They're very rational. They like things to be based on logic, research or theory. They make decisions based on facts. Feelings rarely come into play in a Thinker's decisions.

"Suggested Limitations"—from the perspective of non-Thinkers are that Thinkers are nitpicky, unemotional and insensitive to other people's styles. Non-Thinkers may think that time frames mean nothing to Thinkers and that the only thing that matters to them is proof of facts.

A good way of approaching a Thinker is to say, "I would love to meet with you. I am in the process of preparing myself for that meeting," or "I would love to talk to you about some of the research I engaged in," or "I would like to get your analysis on something," or "I would like to review some spreadsheets that I've compiled," or "I want to talk about the budget."

Professions that Thinkers would do well in are analytical and focused on detail, such as accounting, engineering, programming, graphic design, IT and pharmaceuticals.

Here is an overview of the Thinker personality type (Detailed enough for you?):

Thinker

Suggested Strengths:

- Detail-oriented—The small things matter and are noticed.

- Rational—Likes things that are based on reason or logic; needs to know the facts and consequences.

- Objective—Makes decisions based objectively on fact, not based subjectively on feelings.

Suggested Limitations:

- Nitpicky—Picks up on every minute detail.

- Unemotional—May be seen as insensitive by other styles.

Time Frame:

All times. Balances past, present and future.

Intuitor

Intuitors are creative. They are typically very big-picture people and are usually a click or two ahead of everybody when it comes to vision. Intuitors are visionaries, and they often see things differently or before others do. They are not necessarily the best executors, but they will say, "Here's the idea. Go get it done." I know managers like this—they see things and have very good executors around them who will get the tasks done.

Intuitors generate ideas and have visions that affect the future. They are conceptual and create new things from their imagination. They dream things up, often on a whim. They are very creative. They have an artistic nature and see the world differently than other people do.

Their "Suggested Limitations" are that they may come across as dreamers, unrealistic and trendy—the one who wears the skinny tie or the funky shoes, and then the next year, you see that more people are wearing them, so it was as if they were ahead of the curve.

Intuitors basically like to look into the crystal ball and think about what tomorrow might bring. The future is bright (better wear shades).

Steve Jobs just introduced the iPad to the world (which might be outdated by the time you read this). Jobs says, "It's the perfect middle ground between the laptop and the cell phone." Until he creates another middle ground. Next will be all the products and software that supports the iPad. And of course, there's the next gadget and technological advancement by Apple. That's an Intuitor mentality.

Years ago, I was doing a workshop with the kitchen staff in a hotel in Peru. The staff was mostly Spanish-speaking. I had to work with a translator who was in a sound booth in the back of the room. Everyone in the room had a headset on so that they could hear the translator. I would speak, and then stop. The translator would repeat what I said in Spanish, and then I would get a reaction to what I had said, and then I would continue. So it took me twice as long to get done. I would say something that I thought was funny, and I would have to wait to see if it really was, and then 3-2-1—laughter (or not).

The hospitality industry seems to attract people who are Feelers and Sensors. That was certainly clear among this staff. I had gone through this assessment with them and was debriefing about our findings. I was talking about Intuitors, and this young guy named Leonardo was the only Intuitor in the room. He was only about 16 years old. He ranked very high as an Intuitor—maybe a 14 or a 15. The others, not so much, and they were razzing him, giving him a hard time. They were telling him in Spanish, "You're different than everyone else here. You don't fit in. You're not like us." Leonardo wanted to fit in, and you could see that he was sad about this.

I said to the group, "Since Leonardo is the only Intuitor here, on some level, that kind of makes him the most important person here. He is the only person here who can look at things with a creative flair that maybe nobody else here can do, or at least not as well as Leonardo. He can do things that you guys can't do. He may see things that you don't. You all fit together because you're all very similar. He's going to stand out and perhaps do great things."

I looked back at Leonardo, and he had a big grin on his face. I said, "It's important to have a team with guys like Leonardo because they see things that other people don't see." Two months later, Leonardo got promoted and became a pastry chef given his eye for creativity. He may have had the last laugh.

Web design and cartooning would be obvious industries where Intuitors would do well. But is there a place for creativity in pretty much every field? I would say yes. Very often CEO's of large companies are great visionaries and therefore may score high as Intuitors. (Learn more about this on your iPad.)

So how do you start a conversation with an Intuitor? Say, "I want to bounce a few ideas off of you," or "I want to brainstorm with you," or "I want to feed into your creativity," or "I'm interested in your perspective," or "I would love your thoughts."

The following is an overview of the Intuitor personality type (Get the idea?):

Intuitor

Suggested Strengths:

- Idea generator—Has visions that affect the future.
- Conceptual—Creates new things out of imagination.
- Creative—Has an artistic nature.

Suggested Limitations:

- Dreamer—Has visions of great things to come, but they may be unrealistic.
- Trendy—Tends to like the latest fashion, technology, etc.

Time Frame:

The future. Lives for tomorrow.

Feeler

Feelers love to socialize and be around people. When they network, it's kind of like a politician shaking hands and kissing babies (or shaking babies and kissing hands). They're very perceptive; they can read between the lines. Feelers relate to people easily. They sense when someone is having a great time or when someone has an issue. They can be persuasive because they can relate to people so well. Typically, Feelers are upbeat, positive, and great motivators.

Feelers like to dwell on the past because they tend to be very nostalgic in reflecting on the "good old days". (I feel this way when I get back to my home town and visit old friends and go back to the same old places.) Feelers like to talk about the way it used to be and good times gone by. They can relate to other people's stories and are sensitive to them.

But the flip side of that coin is the "Suggested Limitations". Feelers may come across as poor listeners because others may interpret Feelers as working the room but not really listening or engaging. Or they can come across as being manipulative because they know how to relate to people and therefore can really influence them.

There are industries in which Feelers do well. Certainly a lot of Feelers are in the financial services industry because it's a people-oriented business. Also, Feelers do well in the hospitality industry and in customer service.

To communicate well with a Feeler, you might want to say, "Happy Monday! How was the weekend? What did you do? How are the kids?" Get them emotionally involved in what you're saying and the Feeler may be a fan forever.

The following is an overview of the Feeler personality type (I love you, man.):

Feeler

Suggested Strengths:

- People oriented—A total people person.
- Perceptive—Exhibits perception (feeling, anticipating and reading between the lines.)
- Persuasive—Knows how to persuade people how to do things.

Suggested Limitations:

- Poor listener—They think they already have all the answers; they are seen as asking questions they don't wait to get answers for. They work the room.
- Manipulative—Knows how to make people do what they may not normally do.

Time Frame:

The past. Likes the security of days gone by, and nostalgia.

Let's say we are throwing a party. Each personality type will play a different role in making the party happen.

A Sensor wants to make a list and decide who will find the venue, who will go shopping, who will decorate, who will invite the guests, and determine how to get things done as soon as possible. They're very much into action and getting everything done quickly and efficiently.

A Thinker will worry about how much it will cost, if there will be enough space and parking, what food and drinks will be served, how food will be served, what needs to be purchased, and of course the down side of any decision.

An Intuitor will try to come up with a theme—should we make it a costume party? Let's make this party unique. How can this be the best party ever?

And a Feeler will focus on who's going to be there and what to do for fun.

As you can see, each communication style has a much different perspective and can cause major conflicts. Think about the last party you organized.

The same types of conflicts can also happen in the business world. Think again about the iPad. Engineers and techies (Thinkers?) are focused on functionality, distribution and logistics (Sensors?) want to get the product to market seamlessly, graphic designers and other creative types (Intuitors?) want it to look cool, and sales teams (Feelers) want to sell it. All perspectives are important but some may get in the way of others.

How does all of this relate to networking? The key to networking is to realize that people do come from different perspectives. Our job as networkers is not to change the way others communicate but rather to relate to how they communicate. If you can do that, you'll listen better to one another, understand more, and ultimately connect.

The bottom line with this assessment is not just to relate to people better but to relate to yourself better too! It's important to understand how you come across, for better or for worse. If you are speaking to someone at a chamber mixer that you can't relate to right off the bat (you're a Sensor and he's a Thinker), you can try to shift your conversation where you're more focused on details and theory (them) rather than

process (you). In being familiar with the four communication styles, you can be almost like a chameleon — you can
shift a bit and tailor your conversation accordingly. Keep in
mind that you're not looking to manipulate people, you're
simply looking to relate to them the best you can. Naturally,
these styles apply to your personal life too!

One of my best friends, Keith, never went to college. He is
now 38 years old and looking to go back to school. He has
been in trades, works for a manufacturing company and is
very bright. He reads all the time and is very knowledgeable about a lot of varied topics. His dad is actually a Hell's
Angel. Keith grew up the only child in a very tough environment. His parents were divorced very early on, and his dad
is as tough as they come.

Bikers were always in his back yard, and they would make
fun of him because he would come home with his school
books. Keith grew up very quickly. He's a tough guy and
very driven. One of the things that I really love about him is
that he can relate to anyone.

If he were to take the assessment, his numbers across all
four columns would probably be very similar—he is rare in
that respect. (His numbers are highest — not by much in the
Sensor and Thinker columns.) Keith is able to shift gears
easily. He is very easygoing, and doesn't get too caught up
in any one style. He doesn't get too excited about anything,
yet he doesn't go the other way, either. So he can relate well
to a biker, a boxer, a corporate executive, a job searcher, an
at home mom (or dad)—anyone. Because Keith is so well-
balanced, he has an easy time relating to more people and
more often. And he's not in sales. Imagine if he was?

Takeaways

- It is a myth that effective communication comes naturally.

- According to the Carnegie Institute of Technology (CIT), 75 percent of communication is ignored, misunderstood or completely forgotten.

- Also according to CIT, 85 percent of personal relationships fail because of a breakdown in communication.

- CIT also estimates that the average person speaks 125 to 150 words per minute, yet the human brain absorbs more than four times that information. This means that if a conversation doesn't grab us, then our minds will wander off to other topics.

- If we listen well, speak well and articulate on purpose, then it is much easier to network.

- There are two parties in any communication: the sender and the receiver.

- The sender focuses on words, tone of voice and body language and you must have an intent (your intention) to get his or her message out.

- CIT estimates that words contribute to only about 7 percent of how impactful your message is. Your tonality or tone of voice contributes about 38 percent of the clarity of your message, and your body language contributes about 55 percent.

- Use words that people can understand; avoid jargon. Most people won't ask for clarification about something you say because they're embarrassed to reveal that they didn't understand you.

- Vary the tone/inflection of your voice. If you speak in a monotone, you may appear disinterested.

- The listener has varying levels of listening, some more effective than others: ignoring, pretending to listen, selective listening, cognitive listening, critical listening, appreciative listening, attentive listening and—ideally—active listening.

- The best form of active listening is done by somebody who is listening to something that they are going to have to teach.

- The better you are at listening, the better you are going to be at communicating overall. Great listening equates to great networking.

- We tend to speak 80 percent of the time and listen only 20 percent of the time. I like to suggest that we reverse that—speak only 20 percent of the time and listen 80 percent of the time.

- There are four steps to communicating more effectively: restating, reflecting, summarizing and asking questions.

- The psychological assessment that Carl Jung created categorizes people into four personality types: Sensor, Thinker, Intuitor and Feeler. Most people have primary and secondary styles and score lower on the other two styles. Very few people exhibit all four styles to a similar degree.

- The Sensor is action-oriented, decisive and impulsive but can be perceived as being a poor planner and compulsive.

- The Thinker is detail-oriented, rational and objective but can be perceived as nitpicky and unemotional.

- The Intuitor is an idea generator, conceptual and creative but can be perceived as being a dreamer and swayed by trends.

- The Feeler is people-oriented, perceptive and persuasive but can be perceived as a poor listener and manipulative.

- Taking the assessment will help you learn more about others so that you can communicate better with them. It also will help you learn more about yourself and your perceived strengths and limitations.

Your Turn

Knowing which style you are—and which style important people in your life are—can help you become a more effective communicator and networker. With practice, you will get to the point where you can identify someone's style by knowing just a little about them.

YOUR "CALL TO ACTION" PLAN

It's All About Communication

1. What prevents you from listening during a sales appointment or when networking? _____

_____

_____

2. Complete the personality styles assessment. What are your primary and secondary communication styles? _____

_____

_____

3. How can your communication style(s) benefit you in your profession? _____

_____

_____

4. How can your communication style(s) hinder you in your profession, and what can you do about that, other than being aware of it? _____

_____

_____

5. Which people in your life will you ask to take this assessment so that you can communicate with them more effectively? _____

_____

_____

CHAPTER 8:

Places to Network — *Ponds to Fish In*

"Location, location, location."
—William Dillard, Founder, Dillard's Department Stores

In real estate, they say that the prime selling point is "location, location, location." The places where you network—i.e., the ponds you fish in—are real estate, in a sense. They are the places where you want to leave an impression, create visibility and showcase credibility. Then people will start to associate you with those locations.

As we discussed in Chapter 4, having a target market helps you become specialized, become an expert and become knowledgeable about a specific industry, profession, vertical or marketplace. It also helps you determine what ponds to fish in and where to go. So if my target market is the financial services industry, that tells me exactly where I need to go—maybe to an association meeting or to a cocktail party that is sponsored by a company in my target industry. It makes where and how I need to spend my time pretty obvious.

Remember, the quality of people you meet (Faces of Networking) is in direct proportion to the quality of the event attended. So rinky dink event — rinky dink people. I know this sounds awful but it's true.

There are a lot of different types of organizations out there. Some are good, some — not so much. How do you separate the good from the bad? Ask yourself these questions.

Do you like the people you meet at the event? Do they have similar business interests? Do they know how to network? Can they help you with your goals (to get more business, land a job, learn something specific, solve a problem or socialize)? Can you help them with their goals? Are the people that attend at least as successful as you? Do you learn something when you attend? Is the event worth the investment of time and money? Can you build effective business (and perhaps personal) relationships? And a stretch — do you have fun?

If the answer is yes to *all* of these, great! If not, the search continues.

I hate to sound cynical, but there are too many people out there that are bad networkers or that are simply out to rip you off. Be careful! Remember the definition of networking — learning and helping people. If the networking group has this or something like this as its mission, that's a great start.

Worth repeating — the quality of people you meet (Faces of Networking) is in direct proportion to the quality of the event attended. So be selfish with your time and spend it wisely.

These are some of the categories of networking groups that I think work really well. I'm the first to say that you shouldn't join everything. You have to pick and choose because you need time to do your actual work (remember that?) and generate sales.

Hard-Contact Meetings

Like boxing, networking is a "contact sport." The more contacts you make, the more effective you will be.

Imagine having 20 to 25 people (sometimes more) who you meet with once a week (not once a month) for an hour and a half, usually from 7 to 8:30 a.m. Each person in the meeting represents a different profession. You might have a financial planner, an insurance agent, a property and casualty rep, an estate-planning attorney, a chiropractor, a mortgage banker, a title closer, a real estate attorney, a home inspector and a CPA. That's one of the things the membership committee will look at—how your profession fits in with those who are already members, and is there a conflict of interest? There has to be a symbiotic relationship (the professions complement one another), and there can be no conflict or repetition of professions.

In a hard-contact meeting there is a president, a vice president, a treasurer, a membership committee—a whole board. They are not paid employees; they're part of the group. The president typically calls the meeting to order and runs it, after offering housekeeping and other group business. Then they go around the table and give everyone an opportunity to do a one-minute commercial on who they are, what they do and with whom. Everybody else takes notes about each commercial (or they should) so they can work on generating referrals (specific names of people looking to do business).

At the end, after everyone delivers their commercials, referral slips are written out and placed into a jar, a hat, or whatever. Then you go around the table and talk about the specific referrals you wrote slips for in the meeting—"I have a referral for Michael. Please call my colleague — he is expecting your call. He needs a speaker for his sales meeting." And ultimately you can potentially close business.

The hard-contact format is a powerful model that works for most professions. It tends to be more of a business-to-consumer model rather than business-to-business, but there are exceptions. I find that the groups that are based within cities or close to cities tend to be more business-to-business, while those that are suburban tend to be more business-to-consumer. If you participate, do a good job of presenting yourself, are interesting and do good work, you will become referable very quickly.

Some groups are better than others, but the hard-contact format is a great model, and it's certainly great for sales-people, especially if you're promoting and selling services that we all know about and use. We all need to insure our cars and homes, buy a home, sell a home, book a trip, and plan a wedding. So it's not all that difficult to generate referrals for the members of the group.

Sounds fun, right? It is, but groups that follow the hard-contact model have rules (they have to or it doesn't work), and if you play by them—and by The Pool Rules™—it's a great way to spend your time.

For example, there is typically an attendance policy which is great because it helps you build networking into your schedule. You know that every Tuesday from 7 to 8:30 a.m., this is where you have to be. Many of the groups do very well. Others are struggling because they're not good at upholding the rules.

Hard-contact meetings are a no-brainer if you are a financial advisor, CPA, mortgage person, property and casualty specialist, health insurance agent—we all need these services. But for that very reason, it may be difficult for you to find a group if you're in one of those professions. People in those professions typically start these groups from scratch because they understand the value.

The key to joining a hard-contact group is to find a group or chapter that does not already have a member who does what you do. (This may simply be a quick online search.) Even if you know of only one group but there is a competitor there, I recommend that you attend the group meeting anyway. You can't be a member of it, (or deliver your commercial) but you can visit, and potentially get referred to another group that needs you.

I tell salespeople this all the time, and they will come back from a meeting and tell me, "You know what? There was a seat open because the financial advisor was getting the boot." Or the financial advisor was moving on. Be in the right place at the right time, and it may work out for you.

Hard-contact meetings are one of the biggest lost opportunities for people who don't know about them or disregard them.

The best example of a hard-contact organization is Business Networking International or BNI (www.bni.com). I'm a big fan of BNI, because they're very organized and do an excellent job at developing chapters and maintaining high standards.

Some groups have higher standards than others, but the bottom line is that if you're interested in joining a group, they have to see something in you—that you can add value and that you are more about giving than getting.

Quick Tip — Just follow The Pool Rules™!

Soft-Contact Meetings

Soft-contact meetings are venues that are organized, but there is typically no structure or infrastructure. When you go to a hard-contact meeting like BNI, you don't have to figure out what to do. The plays are already drawn out—you just have to run them. It's different with a soft-contact group. You show up, and the venue is there, and you sign in, but then it's up to you where to go. You have to come up with your own set of plays.

Examples of soft-contact meetings are Chambers of Commerce, cocktail parties and alumni meetings at schools.

Chambers of Commerce

I like chambers because they are usually very organized, they're often fun, there's typically a theme—maybe a holiday theme—and the events are usually well-run and very well-attended. And I like the fact that there is an emphasis on networking. It's clear that it's a business meeting and that people are looking to trade connections and ultimately do business.

The flip side of a chamber—and it's not that they're bad; it's just that it's the pure nature of it—is that it serves a generalist population. So you don't know who you will run into. You might run into another financial advisor or another mortgage person. It doesn't have the exclusivity that a hard-contact meeting has. It's friendly competition, and it's all good, provided that you accept that and do not feel threatened by other people in your own profession. The way you can benefit from a chamber is to become active in it. Become visible. Get on a committee, go to meetings, practice the spirit of giving, get involved, get to know the executive director and all the community people, and become helpful to them. Help build the chamber, and by doing that, they are going to refer business to you.

You do not have to be a member of the Chamber of Commerce to go to these events, although they encourage you to. You would pay an annual fee to be a member. Or you can just go to the meetings and pay a fee at the door. They typically have a very high turnover because people will go to a few meetings and then quit, thinking they didn't get any business out of it. Well, the chamber is not in business to give you business. You have to work at it, get known and give, just like anywhere else.

There are certainly benefits of joining a chamber. You can go to extra meetings and other events they offer. You can probably get published in their newsletter.

Also, chambers attract local professionals—the local mortgage person, the local realtor. So if you are trying to create a local presence with your business, it is a good idea to consider becoming part of your local Chamber of Commerce.

Again, networking is a contact sport so you have to get involved.

> **Quick Tip** — Go to a chamber event and introduce yourself (or get introduced) to the Executive Director of that chamber. Ask them how you can get involved!

Cocktail Parties

Cocktail parties tend to have more of a relaxed feel to them than chamber events—more of a social flair. But it's still the same type of event, especially if it's a cocktail party that's sponsored by an organization for business reasons. In that case, networking is expected, but it is lighter fare.

Alumni Organizations

This is another hugely untapped resource. Alumni organization meetings could be framed as a cocktail party or a business event, too. They are an excellent place to network because everyone shares a common bond. You're all wearing the same colors; you went to the same school. It's important to leverage those associations. At alumni meetings people trade business ideas, and very often you will have job searchers there who are looking to get back on their feet. You can network directly with all of your fellow alum, as well as directly with the college or university you attended.

The alumni concept doesn't just apply to schools — you could be fellow alum of a certification program, a fitness program, Weight Watchers, boot camp, a book club, a bicycle touring group, whatever.

> **Quick Tip** — Reach out to people that you have an association with through a group or organization. Initiate a meeting to learn about one another and to explore how you can stay in touch and be of mutual help.

Conferences and Conventions

What's really good about conferences and conventions is that you typically have to spend money to travel there, so it ensures that the people who attend are serious about the event. Players, baby! It weeds out those who are not. (Again, I'm just saying.) There is usually a fee to register, and often there are additional fees for a la carte events. The people who go to conferences and conventions are there on purpose and often with purpose.

The people who are active at conferences and conventions are active in general—they're either making it happen in their own business, or they're looking to make it happen. Those are good people to be around!

When you attend a conference or convention, you go because you either serve that market (they are your customers) or you are in that industry or profession (you are one of them). Both are important.

For example, because I am a speaker, I am active in the National Speakers Association (NSA). My reason for joining this association is not to prospect; fellow speakers are not my target market, although I have done business because of them. My purpose is to keep up with the latest business trends, learn something specific I can incorporate into my business, and help people who are learning the ropes. Of course, there are social reasons too.

There are also conferences I attend in the financial services industry for a completely different reason. I am looking to continue learning about the industry that I serve, keep up with the latest trends and ultimately to get business.

Either way, it's important to be active at conferences or conventions whether they represent your industry or your target market.

One of the benefits of attending conferences and conventions is that they usually span a few days. It gives you plenty of opportunities to speak to people who do what you do but are doing it differently or better. Or you can make connections with the intention of doing business. As mentioned in The Pool Rules™, it's important to go there with a set agenda of what you are looking to accomplish and who you're looking to meet.

Quick Tip — When attending a large venue like a conference, bring index cards with you. Have one card that lists the people you're looking to meet or reconnect with, and have another that lists the questions that you need to ask or the things you need to get accomplished there. It's like a road map. The index cards help keep you focused because you can very easily be overwhelmed at a conference. There are so many things going on. You can't be everywhere; you can't speak to everyone. But if you can at least get those things on your list done at minimum, it is worth the price of admission. And the price of those index cards!

Trade Shows

Trade shows often have the look and feel of a conference or convention. Sometimes there is a trade-show (or an exhibit center) component to a conference or a convention. At trade shows, you can network with people who come to your table or booth and with other exhibitors.

If you are an exhibitor, you will pay to have a table or booth, and you're there to talk about your products or services and to answer questions, make friends, collect business cards and conduct demos (if appropriate). I have found that there is too much selling going on when people exhibit and not enough networking. I find that people are looking to throw the pitch on you and get you to take this and sign up for that. I don't think that is the purpose of a trade show at all.

I think the purpose is to meet as many people as you can; to answer as many questions as you can; to be nice, helpful, engaging and memorable; to be helpful to other exhibitors;

to collect contact information and ask permission to follow up and stay in touch.

When you are networking and not exhibiting (not paying for a booth)—you are just an attendee. In that case, you are there to meet people, to make a good impression, to be helpful, to learn and to point people in the right direction.

You can do that with people who are exhibiting, but here is the caution: Some exhibitors get offended by that. If someone is paying money to have a booth at the trade show, and you're networking with him to help yourself, he may take offense to that. Many people won't; they get the whole framework of networking. But others get offended by it. It is something to be wary of.

The easy part of the trade show is collecting business cards. Business cards breed business! Most people have no problem with leaving you their card — even if it's just to end the conversation. (You've done this. Don't lie.) The hard part (other than shipping materials and setting up and breaking down the booth) is following up after the event. If you don't have any intention of following up (getting back in touch with prospects) then what's the point of exhibiting?

We'll discuss following up in more detail in Chapter 10.

Community Service Groups

Service groups are not networking groups. Their mission is to do a common good, to help the common man. These groups usually meet every other week over lunch to listen to a speaker, socialize a bit, and to get behind an important cause.

What's great about service groups is that they attract great people. Like in the movie Spiderman, "With great power comes great responsibility"—well, in service groups, with great causes come great people. These groups might focus on funding to help with post-Katrina clean-up, the disaster in Haiti, or to establish a college fund. With such important causes, influential people often come out of the woodwork. This might include top executives of large corporations, superintendents of schools, and local politicians.

Examples of service groups include Rotary, Kiwanis, Elks, Lions (tigers, bears, oh my!)—name your animal. These groups are not for everybody — either you love them or you don't.

The members of these groups (or clubs) don't want to be pitched or sold to (they're big on this Pool Rule). In fact, your purpose there is really not supposed to be networking (per se) but when you put interesting people in a room, interesting things happen. Certainly, you can network but you need to be light about it. You don't want to be there to "work the room" otherwise you may be asked to leave the club. In fact, they don't want the speakers pitching and selling products and services either.

Of course, people do business as a result of these organizations, but again, it is done very subtly. Service groups operate at a very high level of integrity and are very protective of their members. And rightfully so!

Women's Organizations

Women's groups are excellent places to network because women tend to network very well (better than men!) and to do business with one another very effectively—and in many cases, prefer to. I have spoken in front of women's groups, and I tell them that. They certainly agree with me.

Women in business want to help other women in business, especially in fields like financial services, because women face challenges that men do not face, and women can identify with, speak to and relate to these challenges. There is common ground. (Never underestimate the power of common ground.) As a result, there are more and more women's business groups emerging.

In fact, in some of the client firms I work for, there are women's alliances groups put in place to help support women sales reps and give them a sounding board to express their challenges.

Professional Association Meetings

Association meetings are similar to conferences and conventions but on a much smaller scale. Their meetings are local to a region, state, or county and usually meet monthly. The conferences and conventions tend to represent an association on a national level and meet annually. (For example, National Speakers Association (NSA) has local chapters globally but also has a national conference that meets once a year. There are also winter, spring, and summer conferences.)

Associations are perhaps my favorite places to network — on both national and local levels. Why? Because associations represent a specialist population (as opposed to a generalist population at a chamber) so you have an idea of who you're going to meet, what they do, and what you might ask. This gets back to the benefits of having a target market — knowing where to go, what to say, and to whom.

Remember, every industry and profession has an association. How do you find them? (Just visit Google and press the buttons.)

Another thing that I love about associations is that there is a definite emphasis on networking. They really encourage it. They get it. They understand the big picture, and they know that it's a big reason why people join in the first place.

I work with an association in the construction industry. You can be active with them on the national, regional, and state levels. The organization is great about hiring speakers and keeping up with the latest trends. They do a great job cultivating a networking attitude. Half of its members represent very large construction companies and manufacturers in the construction industry. The rest of its members are architects, specification writers and design professionals. You might also find an attorney and other professionals that work in the construction and design field. When a construction company gets a contract, they can hire architects, spec writers and other contractors to work on the project. The architect can also lead a project and bring some of the other businesses in the fold. There's a strong cross pollination effect happening within this association which explains why retention of its membership remains high. Now that's networking!

Associations tend to be very good about calling you back, backing you up, helping you out and following through on things that you need, especially at the local chapter level. The good associations pride themselves on serving their members. Remember, associations are trying to grow their business too — through added membership, affiliations, and involvement on the board (which is usually a non-paid voluntary position).

Speed-Networking Organizations

From a fun standpoint, this is one of my favorite types of networking venues. It's based on the format of speed dating (talk about fun!). I used to facilitate and run speed-networking events. And even that was fun!

These networking groups are very selective about the people who sign up for their events. They don't want to have 14 financial advisors attending; that would defeat the purpose. There are usually 20 to 22 participants. If there are more attendees, they will be split into two groups.

Everyone there is in a different profession. You start off face to face, nose to nose, belly to belly with somebody. A bell rings, and you have five minutes to spend with each person—that's two and a half minutes each—to talk about who you are, what you do and with whom, and to collaborate, if there is a fit and if you can help one another. You are not pitching people on your services. You're informing them about what you do and with whom you are looking to work. If there is a great connection there, you exchange cards. After the five minutes are up, the bell sounds, and the inside row circles to the right. Now you are face-to-face with somebody else. And so it goes.

Within an hour and a half, you have connected with 13 to 15 people. Sometimes food and drinks are served. The time flies by, but by the end of the event, you are exhausted because you are "on" each time you meet a new person. It's like you're doing 15 takes of the same commercial. (Remember the movie Groundhog Day?) But you can walk away with 15 business cards which can equate to 15 follow ups, meetings, conversations, and who knows how many prospects. Beats cold calling!

Speed networking events are a missed opportunity for a lot of networkers. Again, it's an untapped resource. You meet a lot of people, and you never know where it's going to lead you. You could end up with a date!

Seminars

Seminars that you *attend* belong in a marketing or education category of networking venues, but I believe that *conducting* seminars is one of the best ways there is to network because you are the authority on a given topic. Instead of having to connect with several people one at a time, you are in front of everybody. If you put on a great program, everyone wants to come over and talk to you because you are the speaker and the resident expert.

You can certainly network at seminars that you attend, but when you are actually conducting the seminar yourself, it's like you're pumping up the opportunity with steroids. But you can't be there to do a sales presentation or infomercial. You have to give content and value, and that's the beginning of a great networking opportunity.

Joe, a financial advisor at one of my client firms is a perennial conference qualifier (means he's always the top in sales), is a Certified Financial Planner and has a lot of credentials. He runs four seminars a week through local community colleges as part of their adult education, or continuing education, program. He's a great teacher and delivers a lot of value. Joe works with two groups a week, two seminars each, for four hours a week. On Monday and Wednesday he might have Group A, and on Tuesday and Thursday he might have Group B. People register for the seminar and they get a three-ring binder containing materials along with some marketing collateral. Joe brings a

CPA and another advisor from his team and fills the room to about 20 people. He provides coffee and doughnuts, thanks everyone for being there and then tells a story.

Joe says, "One of the reasons I do this is because I've always wanted to be a teacher. But there is a lifestyle that I want to maintain as well, and being a teacher full-time, I may not be able to do so. This is my way of being a financial planner, which I love, and also to teach, so I get the best of everything. The other reason I do this is that I would ultimately love to have you as clients.

I am going to give the best possible seminar that I can here, with as much content as I can offer. You can ask me any questions and I'll do my best to answer them. At the end of the program, if you think I can help you and you potentially want to work with me and have me be your financial planner, I would be flattered and thrilled. If that is not the case, but you get great value from this program and can refer other people who can learn from the program as well, that's OK, too."

And that's it. Joe's sales pitch is over, and then he goes into the seminar. At the end of his seminars, out of 20 people, he typically has 18 people—nine couples—who sign up with him for an appointment (sales meeting). He'll close almost all of them. Joe is successful partly because of the way he positions himself. Also, he is very knowledgeable and has no problem showcasing it. He networks throughout his seminars and continues to fill his classrooms, as well as his database due to the referrals. During the day, he or someone on his team is making those appointments. At night, Joe is conducting the seminars. On Fridays, he plays golf. Not the worst business model in the world.

The networking comes in when you collect contact information and follow up. Your purpose for following up is to see if the people that attended your seminar have any additional questions, help them in any way, if they're interested in learning more about how you can be a resource to them, and if there are others they know that should attend your next seminar. Also, ask permission to stay in touch and promise to do so. (And do so.)

One thing that I really want to emphasize about delivering seminars is to be very light on the sales pitch (if at all) and heavy on the value. (Often your value becomes your sales pitch.) You don't want to get a reputation for delivering infomercials. Remember, no matter what business you're in, your focus should be on helping people.

Going to another speaker's seminar is great, too. You will meet people who have something in common with you because they are looking to learn the same thing that you are. It is not as powerful as conducting the seminar, obviously, but you are there with people you might end up talking to and developing a relationship with.

Delivering seminars is absolutely one of the best ways to market your business and network with people that are interested in learning more. But organizing, promoting, and delivering a seminar is not easy. It takes a lot of time, persistence, organization, marketing, and coordination. After this, the speaking part is easy. Or is it?

I mentioned in Chapter 1 that a fear of public speaking prevents a lot of people from making networking a part of their marketing campaign. Well that same fear prevents salespeople from becoming better speakers and offering as much value as they should. Delivering seminars is the best way to be the center of attention and offer great value to many people at once. In essence, you're networking with many people than with just one.

If you're looking to overcome your fear of public speaking or if you're already good and simply want to improve your skills, *Toastmasters International* is a great resource. Visit www.toastmasters.org for more information.

Online Networking

Social media is the new buzz! If you do a quick search on "social media" you'll discover lots of seminars, webinars and experts (they're just learning this stuff too!) out there offering information on how to utilize social media and how to monetize your efforts.

At this time, the top four social media platforms that people are using are *LinkedIn, Twitter, YouTube,* and *Facebook.* You can buy software programs like TweetDeck and Ping.fm that allows you to interface with all three at the same time.

I heard somebody in a conversation recently say that *Facebook* is what happens at happy hour, *Twitter* is what happens at the water cooler and *LinkedIn* is what happens in the boardroom. Not bad! Maybe *YouTube* is what happens at the audition.

What the social-media experts tell me is that you should be active with your social media for at least one hour a day—updating your *LinkedIn* profile, participating in chats and discussion groups, responding to your inbox, and expanding your database.

If you own a business, are in sales or engaged in job search, it's important that you do something as it relates to your online presence. Learn everything you can about social media — the best practices, the benefits and how to make your efforts profitable.

Here's the danger. A lot of people get so caught up with social-media activity that they believe that's all there is to networking. Social media is a great way to connect and reconnect with people on a global platform, no question about it. But don't forget that there's more to networking than spending hours online. You have to do some of the offline stuff too. Use social networking as part of your networking campaign; it shouldn't be your networking campaign.

Very often, *Facebook, LinkedIn, Twitter*, and some of the others serve as a safety net or even a deterrent from building relationships "the old fashioned" way that still work. You know, adding that personal touch. These days, how nice is it when you get a phone call or a hand written card rather than an email or a post on *Facebook*? (lol)

This all goes back to what your purpose is — more business, land a job, learn something, solve a problem, or social. If your time spent with social media is serving your purpose, fine. Remember, at the end of the day, people still get clients and jobs through face to face meetings and interviews.

I donate a lot of time speaking to groups of job searchers about resume writing, interviewing skills, and of course, networking. I once had a job searcher at the beginning of my seminar ask, "Oh, your topic is networking? That's great. I network all the time!"

I said, "Really? Tell me about your networking. Where are some of the places that you go? I'd love to hear stories."

He said, "Just yesterday, I spent eleven hours on *LinkedIn*."

I stared at him in horror. Turns out he's been looking for a job for 14 months.

If these online tools are not used wisely, smartly and correctly, I look at them as networking Kryptonite because it's very easy to hide behind your computer screen. It's very passive. It takes more effort to get out there (as in out of the house) and meet people. But you can use these tools to *cultivate* or *initiate* those relationships and connections. Then what?

You Can't Just Show Up

Like everything else, all the information in the world (just knowing about these types of organizations and platforms) means nothing unless you go and get involved. You can't just show up and expect people to walk by and give you business (that's online and offline). You have to get involved with leadership, bring referrals in, help with membership, help other people, join or start a committee, brainstorm and volunteer.

The perception of those who get involved in organizations is that if they are shakers and movers here (the chamber, a networking group), they are probably shakers and movers in their own businesses, too.

Focus on meeting and helping like-minded people because you and they will help one another meet more like-minded people. Don't look to meet everybody, help everybody or get to know everybody. None of us has enough time to do that. (You can't "friend" everyone on *Facebook*.)

No matter how good an organization is, there are always the good guys and the bad guys. There's always that person who's just out for themselves or the person who says one thing and does another.

Those are just the "usual suspects" we mentioned earlier—Hard-Sell Harry, Self-Centered Sally, Ravenous Rick, Blackjack Betty, Silent Sam and Social Susie—you are always going to find some of those people (again, both online and offline). I'm not saying that it's bad or that you can change it. You can't. Just be aware. Always look for people who you can help and who can help you right back—the Networking Nicks and Nicoles of the world. Maybe they'll find you too!

Takeaways

- Having a target market helps you determine what ponds to fish in and where to go to network.

- The quality of the venue you attend is in direct proportion to the quality of the type of people you will meet.

- Organizations that have helping people as part of their mission are probably going to be very good. Steer clear of the ones that don't.

- BNI is an example of a hard-contact organization that can put you directly in contact with like-minded professionals.

- Soft-contact meetings—which include Chambers of Commerce, cocktail parties and alumni meetings at schools—are venues that are organized, but there is typically no structure or infrastructure. You show up and sign in, but then you have to decide where to go and who to speak with next.

- Conferences and conventions are valuable networking forums because people who travel to them are serious about their business. And because they usually span a few days, they give you plenty of opportunities to speak to people who do what you do but are doing it differently or better.

- At trade shows, you can network aisle-in (with people who come to your table or booth) and aisle-out (with other exhibitors).

- Community service groups like the Rotary, Kiwanis or Lions Club exist to further causes, and they attract influential and good people. If you network with them, keep it subtle and light because these groups are very sensitive about protecting their members from sales pitches.

- Women are better networkers than men, typically, and women's groups are an untapped resource. They are also a great target market for female salespeople. If you are a male, you can serve as a speaker, supplier or vendor to these groups.

- Local association meetings are powerful venues if you're seeking local exposure. Just as a chamber provides a generalist population, an association provides a specialist population. Plus, local chapters are very responsive to your needs and are open to networking because they are looking to build their membership.

- Conducting seminars is a powerful way to network if you are delivering value and if you keep your focus on helping people, not on a sales pitch.

- *Facebook* is what happens at happy hour, *Twitter* is what happens at the water cooler and LinkedIn is what happens in the boardroom. These tools are great for cultivating relationships that you generate in person. But don't rely solely on social media exclusively to build your business; it can actually be a networking deterrent because it could prevent you from making the face to face connections you should.

- Wherever you network, get involved and help others. A general perception that people have of those who get involved in organizations is that if they are shakers and movers here, they are probably shakers and movers in their own business, too.

Your Turn

The places where you network—the ponds you fish in—are the places where you want to leave an impression, create visibility and showcase credibility. Use the following worksheet to formulate a plan for where to go.

YOUR "CALL TO ACTION" PLAN

Places to Network — *Ponds to Fish In*

1. Place a checkmark next to the following networking venues you have "fished" in. Color in the box next to each venue that you would like to get involved with for the first time or to a greater extent.

   ❑ Hard-contact meetings such as BNI and LeTip

   ❑ Soft-contact meetings such as Chambers of Commerce, cocktail parties and alumni organizations

   ❑ Conferences or conventions

   ❑ Trade shows

   ❑ Community service groups

   ❑ Women's organizations

   ❑ Entrepreneurial organizations

   ❑ Association meetings

   ❑ Speed-networking organizations

   ❑ Seminars

   ❑ Online networking

   ❑ Other organizations

   List: _____

   _____

   _____

   _____

   _____

CHAPTER 9:

How to Start Your Own Networking Group

"Never doubt that a small group of thoughtful,
committed people can change the world.
Indeed. It is the only thing that ever has."

—Margaret Mead

I have wanted to start my own networking organization for quite some time. About six years ago, I wrote a business plan for this endeavor. I made a list of all of the things that I thought were—and still think are—awesome about networking organizations and the things that I think work best. Then I compiled a separate list about these same organizations that I think don't work well or at all, should be eliminated or need to be improved upon. My business plan focuses on all the positive attributes of these organizations. But I never did anything with it because I had business partners at the time who I later decided were not the right business partners, and I pulled the plug.

But I am holding onto the business plan because one day I am going to start that business. I'm going to have a networking organization. I want to be known as not just somebody who speaks about networking but as someone who is actively engaged in networking processes. It's because of this vision that I encourage sales professionals to start their own networking groups if they're entrepreneurial and have the desire to do so.

Jay, a financial advisor and a friend of mine, wanted to start a networking group. He heard me speak about networking, and it inspired him. He understood the value of networking, but he was never able to make networking groups work for him. He just couldn't see eye-to-eye with people who were in the groups and couldn't cope with all the politics that some of them lent themselves to. He had no success in these groups and ultimately quit. So my conversation with him became, "Why don't you start your own group? Do it your way—just make sure you have a plan consistent with The Pool Rules™." So he did. Jay is a Thinker and a Sensor. The details are important to him, and he is a brilliant executor.

So Jay started a networking organization called the Lunch Bunch, and it is still in place today. He put together a handful of professionals who were like-minded, who he liked, who were in professions that complemented one another, and who were game for building an organization.

Jay has had a lot of success with this. Not only did he start writing business as a result of starting this group, but he became friends with the members. And the Lunch Bunch turned into having dinner with people, holiday parties, getting to know people's spouses—it truly became something bigger than they imagined. It became so successful that he started a second group. One group meets the first and third weeks of the month, and the other meets the second and fourth weeks. The groups are composed of different individuals—22 people in one and 15 in the other—but they've all gotten to know one another, and they cross network together.

Not only did Jay's business continue to improve as a result of starting this second group; his confidence did, too. He put his own branding on it. And he was able to relate to the group members because most of them were people he knew or knew of previously. And it changed his perspective of networking—it encouraged him to get involved again with different networking groups. He's involved with at least two other groups that I know of, and his practice has really reflected this. It has completely changed him.

I have visited one of his groups twice, and I saw the fruits of his labor. The quality of the people was evident; they weren't just any business owner off the street.

There are a number of reasons this is working for Jay, and this chapter outlines some of the components necessary to create a successful networking group.

I have created small networking organizations like this over the years—nothing that required a big financial investment, just small organizations—and some of these groups are still together. Because of that, I have seen what works well. I've also made a lot of mistakes over the years, so I also know what doesn't work so well.

I believe that networking groups work for only one reason: they add value. If they don't add value, then they are going to disband or get a bad rap.

Here are some battle-tested suggestions for starting a networking group.

Establish the Purpose of the Group

Is the purpose of your group about doing more business? Most networking groups are. Or is it about helping job searchers land employment? The down side of that purpose is that once a member finds a job, he or she will leave the group.

Is the purpose of the group about brainstorming and business strategy? There are mastermind groups whose purpose is to brainstorm; in the insurance industry, they are called study groups. A mastermind is a group of like-minded people in different businesses (or it could be the same business if the group is industry specific like in a study group) who meet to brainstorm about how to make their businesses better.

They're not there for the purpose of getting referrals, although they might get referrals anyway. Their purpose is to improve the processes related to their businesses. There is a facilitator, and the members talk about their businesses and establish trust among one another. They discuss what's going well and the issues they're facing—what could be better—and they open it up to the group to brainstorm about what they can do to resolve their issues. Each person with an issue is held accountable (to themselves and perhaps to an "accountability partner" in the group) to choose a solution and implement it.

The purpose of the group should be established up-front so that no one has false or misguided expectations. (I have seen this happen.) In Jay's case, he wanted to generate business referrals with a specific group of people. And he wanted people in his group who wanted the same thing.

Get "Buy-In" from the Charter Members

I call the charter, or founding, members of a group the Board of Action.

Jay asked three people of the same mindset to be on his board. They discussed what the parameters of the group should be—the rules, how often to meet, if there would be a formal agenda, the desired outcome, what to do if someone misbehaved, etc. He had to collaborate with the board and come to agreement on all discussions rather than making it the Jay show.

Once the members of the Board of Action have "buy in", they will all be that much more engaged in seeing the process through. This is very important. The group should not be about any one person's agenda. If it is, the group will fail.

Get the Best Candidates

You have to get the best candidates to join your group—quality rather than quantity. I have started groups before just to get as many people in a group as I could. Years ago, I did a really good job of putting a lot of people in a room, but there was a lot of conflict because there were people who were in different phases of their careers. People had different expectations, personalities, goals, professions, geography, levels of success—and it turned into a big mess because there were people in the group who didn't know how to play by the rules. Actually, there weren't really any rules to speak of at all. It was anarchy—chaos.

Some organizations, like Chambers of Commerce, do well with no established rules of engagement (or at least not many). But at least an expectation is set with a Chamber. Going into a situation like that, you know that it's like survival of the fittest, and you are on your own. It's up to you to meet people that you like with the intention of establishing a business relationship.

But if you're forming your own group, you want the percentages to be in your favor. You want to look for quality, not quantity. In Jay's case, he was very particular about the people who joined his group, and his charter members had to approve each member. They looked at a lot of things. They looked at personality and chemistry—each member had to be somebody the board liked. If they didn't like them, there was no point in having them come into the group. The members must have the type of personality that will be consistent with the overall vision of the group. If not, there will be conflict down the road.

Discuss Individual Goals

The goals of each individual are important, too. The obvious goal might be to land the job or get more referrals but often there is an underlying goal. You may want to establish a specific niche market, roll out a new product, or develop a skill. I've had people overcome their fear of public speaking because of being in a networking group—that was one of their goals. They figured it would force them to be around business-people, learn how to speak better and give them an opportunity to practice. Find candidates who have similar goals.

As the group gets more familiar with individual goals, it can establish better relationships while adding a lot more value. (That's a good thing.)

Set Proper Expectations

In one of the groups I created years ago, there was a member who I am still friends with today. At every single meeting, he expected someone to connect him with a would-be client—he wanted a qualified referral from every meeting. That was an unrealistic expectation, especially since he didn't know very many people in the group. Business happens at the speed of trust. It takes time for people to gel, understand where you're coming from and become comfortable with one another's level of competence and compatibility. Each member's expectations should be realistic and consistent with the purpose of the group.

Consider the Profession

If somebody has an unusual or hard-to-refer profession, that will compromise the group's effort to help that person, and vice versa. If a guy is looking to join your business group and he sells a specific type of cement for buildings in the Southwest, and your group is in the Northeast, he may be hard to refer. You might want to think twice about accepting him as part of the group. (This really happened in one of my networking groups. You can't make this stuff up.) On the other hand, don't be too short sighted either. You never know who somebody knows or may come in contact with. That cement guy may close one piece of business in your group that makes his whole year. Heck, he may provide a lot of great referrals to the dismay of some of the members. Never underestimate the "you never know" factor.

Geography

If members of this group have to travel far and wide, it will be one more reason for them to be late or not show up at all. Make it as easy as possible; select a convenient location. If people do travel from all ends of the earth, you could alternate meeting locations to try to accommodate them.

Level of Success

You want to have people in your group who are successful or want to be successful—not people who are looking for a quick win or a quick pot of gold. Look at potential members' levels of success, body or work, and business potential. You don't want to be arrogant about it — we all started somewhere, but networking should always be win-win. If it's not a win-win situation, nobody wins.

Level of Commitment

Obviously, you want to have people that are highly committed to the group. But what does that mean? Members should view the meetings the same way they view a scheduled sales appointment with a prospect. Unless a business opportunity falls from the sky, you are keeping the appointment. Also, when members of the group call one another, those calls should be viewed the same way that a prospect or client call may be viewed — return it promptly. A member's level of commitment is measured in their attendance of the meetings, preparation for the meetings, and participation in the meetings. Also, there's all the follow through after the meetings and an overall level of respect of the process and of fellow members. Now that's commitment! Yes, it's asking a lot but think about the outcomes and the overall vision of the group. And the type of people you want to spend your time with in business meetings.

Phase of a Member's Career

If everyone is equally or similarly successful, but you have some people who are looking to retire and downshift their business, they are in a different phase of their lives and career than the other members. They may not be a great fit for the group because their vision and purpose is different.

You also want people to be "equally needy." You don't want to have one member who is in great need and the others not as much. You will end up favoring that one person more, or that one person is going to ask to be favored more, and that's not going to lend itself to a good fit (win-win) with the group.

I also think that you want members in your group who *get* networking—they understand The Pool Rules of Networking™. They have a giver's mentality. People who are all about giving will probably be great networkers.

Fee or Not a Fee — That is the Question

I could make an argument either way. If there is a fee to join the group, then everybody has "skin in the game", and it could be an incentive for people to be active and participative because they have made a financial investment. Often, a high fee structure attracts a high level candidate. The flip side of that coin is that there doesn't need to be a fee structure, which means that you have to create incentive in a different way. How? You do that by adding value. Some people prefer a fee structure because they feel that if they are not paying to be a member of the group, they will not be as engaged and not see the group as having much value.

Ultimately, the board will decide what is best for the group. There is no right or wrong format. The right way is always the way that works. If the group continues to grow, attracts top flight talent, produces a great return on investment, and is fun, well, then that's the right way.

Establish the Scope of the Group

To grow or not to grow—that is the question. If it is a for-profit group, and there is a fee to join, are you going to limit the group to 20 or 40 members? Is there a ceiling, or are you looking to grow it because it is a profit center? I had a group that was limited to eight members because that's what the majority wanted. Most of the people in the group were very wary about having anyone else come in. They figured that we had worked together for so long, and a lot of personal things got shared. So there was a certain level of trust that could be compromised by a new member coming in, and it would completely change the dynamics of the group. This is an important component to consider.

Decide on a Location

Geographically, does the location make it easy for members to get there?

Also, think about the image you want to portray, the type of atmosphere you want to create for your meeting. I've had meetings that were held in a boardroom. That speaks to a high level of business and creates a certain ambiance. I've had other meetings that were held at a café, a much more informal setting. And in some cases, some people didn't take it as seriously because of that. One meeting that someone else created was held in a think tank, a technology company. It really lent itself to brainstorming and heavy thought, being in the war room. That ended up being a good venue for them.

Maybe it's different each time—you could switch offices. One month the meeting is held in your office, and the next month it's in my office. And the person who is hosting brings in the doughnuts and coffee.

Formulate an Agenda

It's really important to have an agenda. I know of groups that don't have one. If you don't have an agenda, it's very easy for discussions to become social and for people to get off topic and go off on tangents, and you end up compromising the whole goal of adding value.

I'm not saying that you shouldn't be social and that everybody shouldn't like one another, but there is a time and a place for socializing, and people's time is valuable. If it becomes too much of a coffee clutch, it's just not going to last.

The agenda will consist of whatever the charter members think it should consist of. It has to lend itself to referring one another more business (if that's the purpose), and you have to stick to that agenda during your meetings.

It may or may not be the same agenda at each meeting. That depends on if the same person runs the meeting each time, if the agenda works, or if you want to add variety to the meetings to make them more interesting. All of this is fine, but it's ultimately what the Board of Action determines works best for the group. Remember, it's all about adding value.

Some groups have the same person lead all of the meetings. Others pass the baton, and a different person leads the meeting each time. I believe that everybody should have a chance. It gives everyone that much more respect for what it takes to run a meeting—everyone gets a taste of it. But again, it's all about what works for the group. It needs to be discussed and explored. You can't just throw this together, put a bunch of people in a room and think it's going to work. As you can see, there's much more to it than that.

Establish the Rules of Engagement

You have to have rules. Rules of Fight Club! What gets measured gets done. If there are no rules, you allow more problems to happen. What happens if someone is late, doesn't show up, breaches integrity, does bad work, has a conflict or doesn't give referrals? The Board of Action should decide what would work best. And, as different circumstances creep up, you might have to develop more rules.

I believe there should be an attendance rule dictating how many absences are allowed. If someone exceeds their limit, what happens next? There should be a performance rule—what is expected of members. There should be rules about tardiness, behavior, integrity and conflicts of interest. Without rules, measures to follow them, and consequences if the rules are broken, there will be chaos. Standards will be lowered, exceptions will be made, favoritism will take place, credibility will be compromised, rights will be wronged, and value will be lowered. Again, the board has to make decisions about all of these factors ahead of time.

Believe it or not, people actually like rules and like to be held accountable — they may not always admit it but they do. Establish the Rules of Engagement that work best for the group and that produce the most positive results.

Have a Sergeant-at-Arms

You need a Sergeant-at-Arms who is in charge of tracking attendance and making sure that people are on time for meetings. If they're not, this person holds them accountable, has the tough conversations with them and ultimately launches them from the group, if necessary. He or she also tracks referrals. This person has to be a "model citizen" and a good example of following the rules of engagement first hand.

Establish Consequences

Your Board of Action needs to decide what happens when rules are broken—is it three strikes and you're out, 20 push-ups, or what? Decide on specific consequences for specific breaches of conduct. Whatever decisions are made, make sure to always show professionalism and respect the dignity of everyone involved. It's not always easy but keep all matters as business decisions, nothing personal.

Schedule Meetings in Advance

Meetings have to be scheduled in way in advance. It's important to have your meetings at the same time and same day of the week throughout the year, such as every Thursday morning between 8 and 10 a.m. (Again, whatever works best for the group.) Now it's on everyone's calendar, and it can be managed to avoid any scheduling conflicts. Again, the meeting has to have a high level of urgency, equal to a sales appointment. It can't be perceived as something that can get bumped if something better comes along. If it's always getting bumped, it means the meeting is not adding value, it's not a good fit, and there's a low level of commitment.

Get Everyone Involved

The entire meeting shouldn't be one person lecturing. People should be able to give commercials (a 30 second or one minute spot to deliver your elevator pitch) and to talk about their businesses and what they're looking for. And all members have to be equally involved.

Try to Keep Politics Out of It

This one is tough because when you get a group of people together, politics will always get in the way at some point. But if you do the right thing, you've got nothing to worry about. If you stick to the task at hand and make sure that it's all about giving and helping people do more business, fewer politics will be involved. Politics are actually a cover-up for doing something your own way versus doing something the right way.

Track One-on-One Meetings

Encourage and track one-on-one meetings or smaller group meetings that convene in addition to the regular meeting. If members meet one on one, they will get the opportunity to know each other better and ultimately do a better job referring business to one another. These meetings will also make the group meetings more effective.

One-on-one meetings are important. They should be encouraged and tracked. An agenda item of every group meeting can be to have members report on one-on-one meetings that they may have had and share what they learned or what happened as a result of those meetings. (And a round of golf counts!)

Highlight Your Members

Find creative ways to highlight each of the respective members. The group has to be about showcasing one another in positive ways. And, if you avoid shameless self-promotion, it may be appropriate for you to take the opportunity to speak about some of the great things you are doing in your work. If everyone is doing the same thing in the spirit of creating a positive atmosphere and educating the other members on how they are all helping the cause, I think there's value in that.

It's even more powerful to give testimonials about others in the group. Talk about how you referred them and how overjoyed the recipient of their services is with their work. Third party endorsements go a long way. This might be another component to build into your meeting agenda.

Ruthlessly Add Value to the Group

Be ruthless about figuring out how you can make the group bigger, badder and better. Does it mean bringing somebody from outside to speak to the group from time to time? Always ask for suggestions. Look to have each meeting be better than the last. And one of the best ways to do that is to constantly ask people for their suggestions and even bring in suggestions from outside the group.

Be Creative

See if there's a way to vary the meeting so that people don't know what to expect next. So maybe you'll use the same agenda you always use, only do it backwards! Or instead of everybody giving their PEEC Statements™ to the entire group, you're going to give the PEEC Statement™ of your neighbor on your left. Or, in your PEEC Statement™, you have to mention a Star Trek character, or you have to use a James Bond-ism. Or everyone's presentation has to use the word "magical" in it. Or build in some Shakespeare. Infuse some fun into it! Get people out of their norms. It's great when you can keep people guessing about what will happen at the next meeting. Stay tuned…

Resolve Conflicts Quickly

Here's the part that is not so much fun. There will always be conflicts. No matter how many rules you put into place, people sometimes will not see eye-to-eye. If that's the case, then you (or the convener) have to resolve those issues quickly. Don't let them linger! If an issue lingers, politics and rumors will take over, and the group will become fractured. Try to be fair, and do what's right and what's best for the group. Always keep the benefit of the group in mind and take a very objective perspective. Otherwise there will be other issues to deal with.

Get Personal

Doing business is certainly one of the main goals of a networking group, but it shouldn't be just about business. It's interesting to find out about people's kids, their lives, where they went on vacation—nothing too personal. But work represents only one-third of people's lives. In theory, it represents only eight hours of the day. What about the other two-thirds? The two-thirds often drive the one-third.

One of the networking meetings I started years ago is still going; I had to eventually quit going because of my travel schedule.

It's a great group of people that I stay in close contact with. The meetings always start with great things that are happening in the members' personal lives. Everyone weighs in with something positive and fun, and it's a nice way to start the meeting.

As the level of trust increases, often personal problems emerge. If the group is open to dealing with some personal issues, fine. It may help increase the relationship of everyone in the group. Just make sure everyone has the benefit of getting a bit personal and it doesn't derail the purpose of the group — to do more business or whatever. The meetings should not become group therapy sessions — unless that's the purpose.

Track Success

When people give referrals, mark them down (or have your Sergeant-at-Arms track them). Some groups even track revenues that have been realized based on referrals. In quantifying revenues you can calculate exactly what your seat at the table is worth. You can set financial goals with other members of the group and talk about ways to hit your targets.

I know a top producing financial planner who is part of a networking group. He doesn't really need the networking group anymore financially but remains because he is one of the founders and enjoys the meetings. He estimated that his seat was worth $20,000 a year. He can pass that seat along to someone else in his firm (with the approval of the group), but he's thinking, "Why do I want to put that money in someone else's pocket?" And now he is trying to see what he can do to raise the value of that seat to $25,000. It's a measure now, a target. Maybe if he has more one-on-one meetings, gets better with his commercials, gave more referrals to different members, or invited a CPA that shares his marketplace into the group, he could make it a $25,000 seat — or more. Of course, I know people that earn a lot more money from their "seat at the table" and through their networking efforts but it all depends on the type of business you are in and how referable you become. The referability factor comes from your ability to follow The Pool Rules™ while helping key people along the way.

Strive to Improve Yourself

With every meeting you go to, strive to be better at what you do—not just professionally, but in terms of the group. How can you provide more value to the group? How can you be a better resource and get more involved?

Starting your own networking organization is a lot of work. It is not easy. It takes a lot of time up-front, and in some cases it might take an investment of money. But if you follow these rules (and maybe a few of your own), you'll have a great experience and enjoy the satisfaction of building something from scratch. And who knows, it might even become your next business!

There are networking organizations that are franchised. If you don't want to do all of the groundwork, consider investing in one. All of the processes are in place; all you have to do is go through the training, develop a great networking group based on your training (and many of the guidelines in this chapter), and it's yours! Still hard work but at least this way you have a footprint to follow.

It all comes down to what works best for you and your existing business model.

Takeaways

- Networking groups work for only one reason: they add value. If they don't add value, then they are going to disband or get a bad rap.

- The purpose of your networking group should be established up-front so that no one has false or misguided expectations.

- The charter, or founding, members of a group—your Board of Action—need to decide on the purpose of the group, rules for the group, consequences for breaking the rules, how often to meet, if there should be an agenda and the desired outcome. This Board of Action should also approve each member who wishes to join the group.

- Select group members who are similar in their goals, expectations, professions, geography, level of success and phase of career.

- Decide, with your Board of Action, whether there will be a fee structure to the group. Charging a fee to participate can provide an incentive for people to be active and participative because they have made a financial investment in the group. If there is no fee structure, you must provide value in other ways.

- Decide, with your Board of Action, if you want the group to grow or if you prefer to keep the membership at a certain number.

- When deciding on a location for your meetings, select a geographically convenient location. Also consider the image you want to portray—the type of atmosphere you want to create for your meeting—and select a venue that is congruent with that image and atmosphere.

- Set and follow an agenda for each meeting. What ends up happening if you don't have an agenda is that it's very easy for it to become social and for people to get off topic and go off on tangents, and you end up compromising the whole goal of adding value.

- You have to have rules. What gets measured gets done. If there are no rules, you allow problems to evolve. Decide, with your Board of Action, what should happen if someone is late, doesn't show up, breaches integrity, does bad work, has a conflict or consistently fails to give referrals.

- Assign a Sergeant-at-Arms to be in charge of tracking attendance, making sure that people are on time for meetings and tracking referrals. This is the person who holds people accountable, has the tough conversations with them and launches them from the group, if necessary.

- Establish, with your Board of Action, specific consequences for specific breaches of conduct.

- Schedule all meetings in advance, and have them at the same time and same day of the week throughout the year. This will increase the chances that people will attend.

- Encourage all members to be involved equally.

- Try to keep politics out of your group by reminding members that it's all about giving and helping people do more business.

- Encourage members to meet with one another in addition to the regular meeting, and track these one-on-one meetings.

- Say something positive about various members at each meeting—showcase something they are doing well at work or in their personal lives.

- Ask your members how you can make the group better and how to make every meeting better than the last. Find creative ways to conduct your meetings so that people don't become bored with the routine.

- Resolve conflicts quickly. If you let an issue linger, politics and rumors will take over, and the group will become fractured.

- Encourage members to get to know more about one another's families and personal lives, if appropriate. It doesn't have to be just about work.

- Consider having your Sergeant-at-Arms track referrals that members give one another and the revenues represented by those referrals.

- Always strive to provide better value to the group.

Your Turn

Starting your own networking group requires a lot of planning, but it could become one of the most rewarding things you have ever done. The checklist on the next page will help you get started.

YOUR "CALL TO ACTION" PLAN

How to Start Your Own Networking Group

1. What will be the purpose of your networking group?

2. Who will you ask to be on your Board of Action?

3. Where will you find potential members?

4. Will you charge a fee for participation? If so, how much?

5. Will you limit the number of members? If so, what is the maximum number of members the group will have at any given time?

6. Where would you like to hold your meetings?

_____

_____

_____

7. Who will be your Sergeant-at-Arms?

_____

_____

_____

CHAPTER 10:

The "Building Blocks to Networking" System™

*"Everyone has a plan until they get
punched in the mouth."*

—Mike Tyson

The best networkers have a system in place so that they can stay focused while systematically building their database—and ultimately establishing great relationships. A lot of what I've been talking about so far has dealt with what to do, where to do it and with whom. In this chapter, a lot of the jigsaw puzzle pieces start to come together regarding *how* to network. I developed a four-step system to help sales professionals, business owners and job searchers navigate their way through The Pool Rules™, the PEEC Statement™, and the other concepts discussed.

The "Building Blocks to Networking" System™ is a battle-tested footprint that I created years ago. I have been using it myself and teaching it, and the results have been pretty incredible. It is a great process for ensuring that your networking game plan makes sense and remains focused. I have found it to be the best way to get to the right places, say the right things and meet the right people on a consistent basis.

The components of the "Building Blocks to Networking" System™ are simple. It comes down to these four steps: Preparation, Presentation, Follow-Up and Maintenance.

Preparation

There's an old saying, "If you fail to plan, you plan to fail." This is true in job interviews, business meetings, presentations, sports, pretty much everything. Well, planning is required in networking too. The planning or Preparation phase is the research piece of the networking puzzle. You need to consider a number of things before attending a meeting, conference, trade show, cocktail party, golf outing or other event. Other than being equipped with business cards and a few throw-away pens, what else should you do to be best prepared?

Know Your PEEC Statement™

Just thought I'd mention again that it's important to know your PEEC Statement™ cold. Role-play it in a mirror if you have to. Practice using it on friends, prospects, clients, vendors, and strangers on the street. Remember, at this point, your PEEC Statement™ shouldn't necessarily be a word for word script. What it *should be* is a mind-set — a visual PowerPoint slide triggering you to articulate your Profession, Expertise, Environment (target market that is) and Call to Action at the drop of a hat.

Review The Pool Rules of Networking™

Yes, review your list and check it twice. Make sure you are clear about all the things you should and *should not* be doing. Rules are put in place for a reason so make sure you bone up on yours. By reviewing The Pool Rules™ in Chapter 2, you will refresh your memory, formulate a strategy and build your confidence. Some of you may need this confidence booster to overcome a fear or two and maybe — to get you to the event in the first place. Don't delay! Hold your breath and just go!

Learn About the Event

How cool would it be if you could learn about an event ahead of time? Well, you can. Most people just don't take the time to do a little homework. With some ingenuity you can learn about an event and decide if it's right for you. If it's not, fine, you can save yourself a trip while also saving time and maybe a few bucks. But if it is a fit, you'll have enough background information to plan accordingly and make it a valuable use of time.

Let's just say you plan on going to an event for a marketing association. It's on your calendar and you prepaid so you have every intention of going. You can simply do a search of the event and quickly find the homepage. Once you're there, you can track down the board members or the "big cigars" for that particular association. You'll discover the names of the president, vice president, treasurer, membership committee, education coordinator, etc. etc. Chances are you'll also find their contact information. This is a great resource! Now, call (not email) the president with the intention of introducing yourself and learning about the event. It's better to make a call rather than to send an email because you're also looking to build rapport and to get to know them.

If you get a voicemail greeting, leave a detailed message stating that you will be attending their event and look forward to meeting them. Also mention that you're anxious to connect with them personally so you can be best prepared to participate in the meeting. Most organizations (not all) are very receptive to calls like this and will respond quickly because they're looking to promote their organization and build membership. A win-win!

When you finally connect, be prepared with written questions to insure you get the most out of the call. In answering these questions and perhaps some others, you can determine whether attending a particular venue is a good use of your time. (Remember to offer your PEEC Statement™ to set up your questions.) These are the questions I would ask a board member after getting them on the phone.

- *Is the location and time of the meeting correct on the website? (This information is notoriously incorrect so it's a good question to ask upfront.)*

- *Who will be in attendance? (Find out about the professions of the attendees, companies they represent and if most are members. You might also want to consider how many represent your target market.)*

- *What type of turnout do you expect?*

- *Which of your meetings have the highest attendance?*

- *What is the nature of the meeting? (Is it a regular monthly or quarterly meeting, a kickoff, year ending, special event, fundraiser, or networking event?)*

- *What is the appropriate attire? (You never know!)*

- *Is the fee to participate correct on the website? (If you prepaid, make sure you paid the correct amount.)*

- *After attending, is there an opportunity to become a member?*

- *This seems like it will be a great meeting! Once I'm there, is there anything I can do to help you? (Registration desk, hand out paperwork, whatever. Why not be of help to the board?)*

Of course, tailor your questions as appropriate.

Also, ask the exact same questions to the vice president and perhaps the treasurer and see if you get similar responses. If the answers to your questions tell you that you could meet potential prospects or referral sources you may be targeting (or if the meeting seems it would be valuable in some other way), it is very much worth your time. It may also be a good place to go if you can get more information about the next event or meeting you should attend or the next contact you should be making. If not, continue your research to find the venues (and contacts) that may be more worthwhile.

You can follow up with hand written cards expressing your thanks for the time on the phone and that you look forward to meeting them.

When you arrive at the event, who might be the first people that greet you at the door? Or the first few people you may look to track down? The president, vice president and treasurer! Hey, you already have a connection with them. Cool, right?

By the way, preparing for an event doesn't cost you anything but a few minutes of Google searches, phone calls, and an email or two.

You may recall in Chapter 2 that I mentioned how you should be looking to make two or three quality contacts, not 10 or 20. Well, in meeting the top brass at this event, haven't you accomplished your goal of meeting two or three quality contacts (the president, vice president and treasurer)? And you may be barely in the door!

Now you have some friendly faces greeting you when you arrive. They have a lot of influence in the group, probably know everyone, and are more than happy to introduce you to others at the event. (Your PEEC Statement™ would come in handy right about now!)

On a number of occasions, I have used this approach to prepare myself for an event and upon my arrival; I'm told that the speaker for the event had to cancel last minute. So when the "big cigars" greet me at the door, what do you think they have in mind?

"You said that you speak about networking and referrals, right? We think our group would find a lot of value learning about networking. Look, we hate to do this to you. We know you're not prepared. We know you haven't thought about this. But would you mind bailing us out and being our speaker?"

Well, I wouldn't have the heart to say no.

So there I am in front of the room with no notes or materials but naturally, being the consummate professional, I do a bang up job. How do you think the organization feels about me now?

That's the value of Preparation!

It's all in the Cards

Index cards that is. Once I have done my research, I will often prepare two index cards to help keep me focused. One card has a list of the people I want to meet (if I happen to know them by name) and the other has a list of questions I plan on asking them. When I'm at an event and meeting people, I'll show them my index card with the list of names on it (usually during the Call to Action part of my PEEC Statement™) and see if they know any of them. I'll mention that I'm looking to meet these people to make the connection and also for the opportunity to ask them questions (enter the other index card). Often enough, the people I'm speaking with at the event will know some of the people on the card. Now I have an opportunity to request an introduction to them. There is nothing like being prepared and focused.

What's funny is that the people I'm showing my index cards to think my approach is so good that they ask if I have blank cards to give them so they can make their own list of people they need to meet.

Presentation

OK, you've made it to the event. Now what? Approaching complete strangers is a daunting task for many—even to outgoing sales reps!

This is your opportunity to practice The Pool Rules™, your PEEC Statement™ and your prepared questions (or conversation starters).

There's no sure thing when meeting new people because everyone is so different, and we all tend to have our own agendas. When in doubt, always remember the definition of networking: *learning about and helping others.* When your objective is to learn something about your target market (culture, trends, initiatives, upcoming conferences, product information, challenges, related articles and publications, further contacts) you can't lose. Helping someone in your target market is even better. Givers always gain and favors get returned, especially when the appropriate time comes to ask for them.

Remember, you're looking to start a relationship and potentially meet influential people that you can call on for information and guidance. (Not to sell!) Choose your attitude before arriving at the meeting. Be genuine and have fun!

The best way to start a conversation is to introduce yourself, extend a firm handshake and ask questions (the questions you prepared). Again, it's all about *them*.

If there is a good connection and you think you can help one another, exchange cards, commit to following up, put some follow-up notes on the back of the business card you collected, shake hands and say your goodbyes. If you're really brave, ask for an introduction to someone they know at the event that you want to know. And remember, this should all take place in no more than six to eight minutes (without peeking at your watch).

There are a number of different ways you can approach people at a networking event. I know it can be intimidating to approach a total stranger but if you get accustomed to doing it, you will come across as engaging and confident.

The Registration Table

Most people don't realize the importance of the registration table (where you sign in and "pay at the door" for the event). The registration table is equivalent to mission control.

The people that are working the registration table are usually members of the organization or part of the venue in some way. They will typically know most of the attendees at the event. After all, they have the list of attendees and know who has arrived, paid and pre-paid. They also know who is a member, non-member, potential member, former member and everything in between. Basically, they know it all!

Why not have the greeters at the registration table introduce you to someone that you might be interested in meeting? After all, they are greeters!

When checking in at the registration table, introduce yourself to the one or two people who are there. Shake their hands (with a 7-to-8 handshake) and present your PEEC Statement™. Let them know that you're a first-timer if, in fact, you are.

I would say something like, "I am looking to meet some more people at XYZ Company, especially those connected to the sales department. Who would be good to talk to? Can you point me in the right direction?" They might say, "Oh, you've got to speak to Gilda, she used to work for XYZ Company." I'll say, "I know you're busy here, but would you mind offering me an introduction to Gilda? I'd be thrilled to meet her. And they will wave her over and say, "Gilda, I'd like to introduce you to Michael Goldberg. He's attending our meeting for the first time, and he speaks about networking. He wanted to talk to somebody who's connected with XYZ Company so I thought you might be a good connection for him."

Knock, knock, wink, wink—I just got connected! And I'm barely in the room. Talk about efficient! Also, I've just met three quality people (my goal)—the two greeters at the registration table, and the introduction to Gilda, who may not only work in my target industry but has a connection to my target company.

"Very nice to meet you!" and she says, "So you're a first-timer here, and you speak about networking?"

I'll say, "Yes, I speak professionally about networking and referrals. How long have you been with your firm? Do you like what you do?"

I get into my prepared questions as appropriate. See how I took the focus off of me and directed it toward Gilda?

This has the potential to be a great conversation. Gilda has a direct connection with a company that I want to learn more about and potentially have as a client. And now she can potentially introduce me to other people in her firm. And I could be a resource to her too—I will ask her, "How can I help you? What is it that you're looking for here?"

Going Cold

Sometimes I'll go to an event and walk in the room without leveraging an introduction from the greeters at the registration table. I check in and just simply walk in cold. I may do my research to learn about the event ahead of time so I'm focused and feel prepared but I'll walk up to someone without being introduced. (I'll do this if they're very busy at the registration table and have no time to help me or if I want to make a strong impression by approaching people with the moxie to deliver a strong introduction. This usually makes a great first impression!)

Introducing Yourself to Groups

Usually, groups of people assemble — both large and small. They may be cliques of people that know each other or end up together for some other reason. When sizing up the group, I like to approach the person in the group that appears to be the most important person there. It could be the person who is dominating the conversation. In some cases, it's the boss of everyone who works for the same organization. It could be the person who seems the most outgoing. In some cases, it might be the person who has the most physical presence.

Whatever it is, I will very politely interrupt that person and say, "I'm sorry to interrupt. I just wanted to take an opportunity to introduce myself. I'm a first-timer here. My name is Michael Goldberg," and I'll offer my hand to the person who seems the most dominant. They may say, "Oh, very nice to meet you," and then everybody else will introduce themselves to me. (A great return on just one introduction!)

I will ask, "So what do you all do? Do you work together?" And now it's back and forth, and I've nudged my way into the biggest group.

If you're a little nervous about greeting people, this is a great way to start to come out of your shell. You can build your confidence with this approach. What's the worst thing that can happen? Even if you're an introvert, you have to start somewhere.

When you approach a group of people, they're going to do most of the talking anyway—look at it that way. They might ask *you* questions—"What do you do? How did you find out about the group?" Speaking to a big group in this way may actually be easier because you have more people speaking with you and taking up time in the conversation.

Here is something to be cautious about: If it looks like the largest group is having very light conversation, cocktail party-ish, kind of fun, or at least not cone-of-silence serious, I'll stay because now I'm part of the discussion. "Catch me up—what did I miss?" And I'm kind of in. But if it looks like they were having a proprietary, important or heated discussion, I will either not interrupt or circle back later, or I'll interrupt anyway and excuse myself quickly. I may be able to break up whatever is happening there in a very positive way. I might introduce myself, and say, "Well, very nice to meet you, but I do see that you're in the middle of something here, and I didn't mean to be rude, but I wanted to take an opportunity to meet you and potentially some of the people here. Let me excuse myself. Would it be OK if I circled back?"

Usually, the main person is appreciative of that and will say, "That would be really great. I appreciate that. In fact, I'll track *you* down." Now it becomes impressive because I've demonstrated proper etiquette. I've shown a sense of empathy and courtesy, but I also didn't let any of that stuff stop me from at least trying to make a good impression. I've now showcased some social grace and some charm. And of course, it's always important to mind your manners.

Still another approach is to address a smaller group (maybe a party of two or three). It's the same type of introduction as with a larger group. But approaching a smaller group can seem less daunting than heading for the biggest group in the room. Also, you may have to be a bigger part of that conversation since there are less people. Of course, this will depend on the group.

(Again, introverts, have no fear. Once you've practiced this a few times it will become easier and less daunting. There's always a first time to jump in the pool or climb into the ring.)

Standing by the Coffee

My favorite of starting conversations with people is to look for the one person who is standing by the bar, under a clock, by the coffee, in some spot by themselves because they're terrified and they probably don't want to be at the event in the first place. They may be there because they were told by someone (their sales manager?) that they should go or because, they realize that they should network more to achieve their goal. Can you relate?

This poor person that is standing alone is terrified of two things: that no one will come up to them, or that *someone* will come up to them.

See the dilemma? Think about that for a minute! Yes, a no win situation.

I like to approach these stranded people and bail them out (so to speak). I can be somewhat outgoing, so I might dial it down a little bit and introduce myself. Then I will ask, "What brings you here? What type of work do you do?" And then I will ask, "What would make this event a success for you?" Often, they don't know! They know they'd like to do more business, land a job or whatever — but they may not know the specifics or have a strong Call to Action.

I don't want to make them feel foolish, but I'm interested in hearing what they have to say. And hopefully, if I'm *interested*, that will make me appear more *interesting*. If they say they want more business, I will say, "Tell me what that looks like. What is an ideal piece of business for you? If I were going to meet a prospect for you—the perfect client—how would I know that I had met them? Who is your target market? Who is an ideal client for you?"

So I try to ask the right questions. But many times, people that are new to networking (or not that good at it) don't know the answers to "networking based questions". But once you start making them think about it by asking the right questions they'll come up with the right answers. They'll say something, like, "I'd like to focus on the manufacturing industry."

Then I try to help them find the perfect-case scenario. "Let's see if we can find someone here that does a lot of work within the manufacturing industry. It may be a consultant, product manager, human resources generalist, or attorney."

Now, not only is this person more confident; they are appreciative that I helped them think it through. So then, as I meet new people, I will introduce my new-found friend, and I will give her elevator pitch (PEEC Statement™) for her. I'll say, "I just met Jennifer. She's a recruiter with expertise in the areas of career development, selection, and human resources. She has a niche market within manufacturing and is looking to connect with an attorney, CPA, whomever — that might have a similar niche." Jennifer is relieved because I've helped her crystallize her goal, which she may not have considered before.

The ability to speak to people with the genuine desire to learn about and help them quickly creates marketing gravity. People will be drawn to you. You'll find people coming up to you and introducing themselves. They will become interested in who you are and what you do. Over time, you will become more comfortable speaking to those you don't know and get better at following up with those you do.

Follow-Up

First and foremost, your follow up strategy begins in the Presentation phase. In other words, when your conversation with a networking contact is coming to an end, you may want to explore if it makes sense to continue your conversation at a different time.

"I don't want to hold you up here but it seems there is a lot to discuss and we can probably help one another. Do you want to exchange cards and I'll follow up with you in a day or so to continue our conversation?" Then make a note on the back of their business card (with their permission of course) so you'll be clear as to why you're getting back in touch.

Second, you don't have to follow up with everyone you meet. You won't even like everyone you meet. But you *do* have to follow up if you feel you have established rapport, there is a clear cut reason and you made a promise to do so. As long as there is a mutual understanding, there should be no issues or disconnect.

Third, not following up with those good connections you made is equivalent to not showing up to the event at all. You'll get home or back to the office, neatly arrange all the business cards you collected on your desk and say, "Hmmm…what now? I don't remember most of these people."

You may find yourself throwing the business cards away and muttering about what a waste of time the event was. You'll say that networking doesn't work for you. And you would be right!

Most people at networking events do a horrible job following up afterward. Why? They either don't know how to follow up or don't understand why they should be following up in the first place.

Naturally, if someone you met at a chamber mixer became a legitimate prospect, you would have absolutely no problem getting back in touch with them to do business. Not even a question!

For example, if you're a realtor and someone you meet is trying to sell their house and they want your help, aren't you going to follow up with them almost immediately?

Unfortunately, prospects don't usually fall out of the sky like that. In most cases, people have to get to know you and develop trust before they can become your prospect or be willing to refer you to prospects in their network. It's just the way the world works. Especially if your service requires a large price tag — like a commission earned from selling a house for a homeowner.

If you are going to follow up with someone you have met at a chamber, association meeting or networking group, do so promptly. Keep in mind that most connections we make have a limited shelf life, so it's a good practice to get back in touch within 24 hours or the next business day if possible (it's a Pool Rule). When you follow up immediately with those you have bonded with, it always makes a great second impression.

Review the business cards you've collected at the meeting. Remember the follow-up notes you made on the back? Refer to them — then send an email or even better, a handwritten note with a call to action:

Tim,

It was great meeting you at the trade show yesterday. I really enjoyed our chat and thought we could continue our conversation either by phone or over coffee. What does your schedule look like over the next couple of weeks? Look forward to reconnecting!

Warm regards,

Michael

More often than not, I'll send a handwritten note and then make a phone call because it seems warmer to me. My goal is to establish trust and ultimately develop a relationship. (When was the last time you received a handwritten note?)

Make good on promises or commitments you may have made. There will be some business cards you have collected that do not reflect strong business or personal connections. You may want to discard these. (It's OK, don't feel badly. There's someone throwing your business card away right now. Feel better?)

If there are notes on the back of the card you collected, it either means you made a promise to someone, they made a promise to you or there's a good connection—you like them, you can help them, they can help you, or all of the above.

Keep in mind that following up can simply mean sending an article you mentioned, making an introduction on someone's behalf or providing information. Just as it's important to follow *up* quickly, it's important to follow *through* quickly. If I promise to get somebody an article or to connect them to somebody, I will do that within 24 hours, too.

Here's a follow-up checklist to guide you in the process:

Follow-Up Checklist

- Did you meet with the contact within or close to 24 hours ago?
- Was a promise made to follow up?
- Did you exchange PEEC Statements™?
- Do they have your business card?
- Do you have their business card?
- Did you take notes on the back of their business card?
- Did you determine the best way of getting back in touch?
- Is there a clear understanding of your purpose?
- Is there a clear understanding of their purpose?
- Do you know your desired outcome?
- Do you know their desired outcome?
- Is the connection a prospect, client or referral source?

Never rely on other people to follow up with you because they almost never will. You have to take the initiative and be the one to make the phone call, write the note or whatever. That's why follow up is a Pool Rule.

The more often you follow up with legitimate prospects, the more likely it is that you will make the sale and gain the client. But again, it is easier just to give up. Let's put this in perspective:

- 58% of all salespeople quit completely after a single call to a prospect.
- 20% make two calls before giving up.
- 7% make three calls.
- 15% make five calls or more.
- The 15% of the salespeople who make five calls or more produce about 75% of all the business.

Still want to give up?

Maintenance (OOSIOOM)

Maintenance is having a system in place so that you can use your database and various lists of names as tools to follow up with people and keep them on your radar. Hey, Out Of Sight Is Out Of Mind (OOSIOOM).

You have to keep your prospects, clients and other important people in front of you so that they are top of mind. Keeping their names available in the form of lists helps you reconnect with them and maintain your relationship with them actively.

I make 10 to 20 phone calls a day just in the spirit of OOSIOOM, or Maintenance. That's in addition to returning people's calls within 24 hours and to all of the follow-up that I do. I am constantly on the phone. During a break at a speaking event, I'm on the phone. I love being on the phone talking to my clients and prospects. To me, it's fun and very productive.

When I call people in the Maintenance phase, it's to stay in touch, catch up, see how I can be a resource to them, provide them information or give them a referral. In fact giving business referrals is one of my favorite things to do.

Why? When you give you get. That's the way it works! And it's the glue that holds your Maintenance strategy together.

As part of my strategy, I write five postcards or handwritten notes a day (that's 100 a month if you're keeping track). I go right down my list of my prospects, clients, and others in my database. It takes me all of ten minutes first thing in the morning. It's always a warm note that never gets into anything too heavy.

It could be something as simple as:

> *Hello, Paul—*
>
> *I hope this note finds you well. It's been a while since we've spoken. Interested in how your team did this year. I'm looking forward to catching up soon to discuss!*
>
> *Warm regards,*
>
> *Michael*

Try this strategy for a month. It's amazing what happens!

There are different types of lists that I use to help keep me organized and on track. This is in addition to a regular contact management program. As an aside, it's important to keep your database updated and refreshed. It's not a bad practice to review your database once a quarter to insure recent contacts are posted, others deleted, while still others may need updates due to changes in address, contact information, and work assignment.

Keep in mind that a regular Outlook program will suffice for storing names and contact information, although I have used Act and other CRM (customer relations management) programs. I know that some organizations use Lotus Notes, and some have proprietary programs, while some people just use Excel spreadsheets or simply toss business cards in a Rolodex. It doesn't matter which program or system you use as long as you use **something** — and it's effective.

I'm a fanatic about making lists. Daily lists, weekly, monthly. My daily to-do lists are written in a composition notebook (the kind you probably used in grade school). These daily lists are developed through the use of larger lists that are simply Word documents that get printed out every month. These lists, along with the composition notebook, go everywhere with me. The lists contain all of my scribbles and notes about the things that have happened in the course of the month. This way, I'm really organized. It's right there, and it becomes an update for the next month. (Very high tech I know.)

Here are the types of lists that I maintain.

Prospect List

It's very important to reiterate my definition of a prospect: *someone who knows you or knows of you, understands what you do, sees value in it and is open to learning more to potentially work with you (or hire you) now or sometime in the future.* My prospect list is made up of people who have seen me speak somewhere, who have contacted me at some point or who I was referred to. They all know me. And it's not really a question of *if*; it's a question of *when* we will do business together. Otherwise, they're just not a prospect.

Typically, I don't let a prospect get more than 30 days away without staying in touch with them. My Prospect List is of course backed up in my main database, as well as in my phone. But I like to make my notes on the Word version and update everything electronically on a monthly basis.

When I'm calling prospects, I'm checking in to see how they're doing because I did speak to them or at least tried to speak to them last month—to find out how their year is going, and if I can be a resource in any way, even informally.

Client List

Clients are people who are your economic buyers—they're paying you to do the work that you do. These are people who you are probably already in touch with anyway. It's really important for salespeople to stay in touch with their clients on a regular basis. You should be doing all kinds of creative things to get your clients involved with your world, whether it's a cocktail party that you're sponsoring, a ball game you're taking people to—it doesn't have to be something expensive. Just get them involved in something you're doing.

A financial advisor I know went to an art show sponsored by one of his clients who happens to be the owner of the art gallery. It didn't cost the advisor anything; all he did was invite more of his clients to come see an art show. His client provided the wine and some cheese and light fare. The gallery owner got an opportunity to showcase great art and probably sold a few pieces, and the advisor looked good because he was inviting everybody to come to this very nice event. He wasn't even looking to talk business, but people did. And it turned into something. Be creative when staying in touch with your clients; add value to your relationships.

Consider what model works for you. Bottom line — you have to stay in touch with your clients somehow. All my clients get my blog, and some of my prospects do, too.

In addition, I try to find creative ways to spend time with clients and get to know them better. Becoming friends with clients isn't the worst thing in the world either.

(As far as blogging and newsletters go, it's important to have on your list only those people who subscribe, or opt in. You don't want to be known for spamming.)

Advocate List

My last list, which may be my favorite, is my Advocate List. I define an advocate as somebody who would take a bullet for you, thinks the world of you, and is powerful enough to help you in your business.

That's not to suggest that advocates can't be friends. They could and perhaps should be. Many of mine are. They become friends over time. My goal is for all these people to be friends. I go to happy hours and ball games with them, and it all becomes fun. Some are clients, some are prospects, some are referral sources/chickens—many serve the same market that I do but do something completely different. I think it's really difficult to come up with an Advocate List, and I always challenge people to try to come up with at least five advocates — not that easy to do.

I don't let my advocates get more than 30 days away from me, either. They get a phone call or a postcard. They're all getting my blog. But remember, out of sight is out of mind. You have to keep their names in front of you to keep in touch with them.

Here is the most important part of using your Advocate List: You can't sell them. You can't be pitching business to them. They'll say, "OK, Goldberg, what do you want now?" It has to be, "Hey, Ron, what's going on? How did the kickoff conference go? Great! How did that speaker do that I referred you to? When's the next time you're going to be in New York? We've got to hook up."

But I'll tell you what happens in the spirit of OOSOOM—I'll call one of my advocates, and Ron may say, "It's funny you called. We have our big conference coming up in October, and we haven't booked a speaker yet. Are you available?" Naturally, my first thought is why didn't you think of me in the first place? If I didn't call Ron, he never would have presented me with the opportunity. But people just aren't always like that. Knowing this, I've just become ruthless about staying in touch regularly. It's fun staying in touch with the people that you like and want to work with. You never know!

Most people don't have a networking system at all. They just act and react—but the top salespeople I know have a system. What we've just covered is my iron-clad system. Consider what aspects of it might work for you.

Takeaways

- The best networkers have a system in place so that they can stay focused while systematically building their database—and ultimately establishing great relationships.

- There are four components to the "Building Blocks to Networking" System™: Preparation, Presentation, Follow-Up and Maintenance.

- Preparation involves having a list of questions handy that can determine if the networking venue is a good use of your time—and theirs.

- There are a number of different ways you can approach people at a networking event: ask the people at the registration table to introduce you to a specific person or group of people; introduce yourself to the biggest group in the room or to a smaller group; or engage the "lone ranger" at the coffee station in conversation and help him or her find value in the event.

- Not following up with those good connections you made is the same thing as not showing up to the event at all.

- As a general rule, most people won't follow up, unless you are a prospect for them, so it's up to you to do so.

- Most connections we make have a limited shelf life, so it's a good practice to get back in touch within 24 hours.

- Review the business cards you've collected at the meeting. Refer to the follow-up notes you made on the back of each card, then make a call or send an email or handwritten note with a call to action.

- Remember—it's a Pool Rule that you have to have follow-up already in mind as you're meeting people. So follow-up always starts in the Presentation phase.

- Just as it's important to follow *up* quickly, it's important to follow *through* quickly. If you promise to get somebody an article or to connect them to somebody, do so within 24 hours.

- Persistence pays off. More than half—58 percent—of all salespeople quit completely after a single call to a prospect. And the 15% of the

salespeople who make five calls or more produce
about 75% of all the business.

- There are many components involved in following up: create a strategy, find out each prospect's ideal means of contact, be a valued resource, give referrals, make a no-risk offer and never give up.

- Maintenance is having a system in place so that you can use your various lists of names as tools to follow up with people and keep them on your radar. Out of sight is out of mind, so keep these important people's names in sight.

- Maintain lists of key groups of people—for example, have a client list, a prospect list, a media list, an advocate list and a playing-hard-to-get list.

- Try to keep in touch with the people on your lists every 30 days.

Your Turn

The "Building Blocks to Networking" System™ involves four main steps: Preparation, Presentation, Follow-Up and Maintenance. Use the following checklist to help you build your own networking system.

YOUR "CALL TO ACTION" PLAN

The "Building Blocks to Networking" System™

1. Name a new networking event or meeting that you could attend, either locally or in a city you will be traveling to soon. _____

   _____

2. **Preparation:** To prepare for the meeting, write out a list of questions that you will ask once you arrive at that meeting or event. _____

   _____

   _____

3. **Presentation:** Think about the event you will be attending soon, and answer these questions:

   Who should you talk to? _____

   What's the best way to start a conversation?

   _____

   What should the focus of the discussion be?

   _____

   How many business cards should you collect?

   _____

   What if those you meet don't like you? How do you end the conversation gracefully? _____

   _____

4. **Follow-Up:** After the event, fill in this checklist:

Did you meet with the contact about 24 hours ago?

_____

Did you promise to follow up?

_____

Did you exchange PEEC Statements™?

_____

Do they have your business card?

_____

Do you have their business card?

_____

Did you take notes on the back of their business card?

_____

Did you determine best way of getting back in touch?

_____

Is there a clear understanding of your purpose?

_____

Is there a clear understanding of their purpose?

_____

Do you know your desired outcome?

_____

Do you know their desired outcome?

Is the connection a prospect, client or referral source?

5. **Maintenance:** Develop lists of key people who help you generate business, and keep in touch with them every 30 days. Which lists do you have already or are you developing?

❑ A client list

❑ A prospect list

❑ An advocate list

❑ A list of hard-to-reach referrals or prospects to call persistently

❑ Other lists: _____

CHAPTER 11:

Sure-Fire Ways to Generate More Referrals

"Remember, cold calls are God's punishment for not getting referrals!"
—Rick Grosso

It's important to understand the differences between contacts, leads and referrals. Very often, the terms are used interchangeably. I know we discussed this as part of The Pool Rules™ but it's worth repeating.

A referral is a name and contact information that someone has given you. It is simply someone who is expecting your call or email with the prospect of speaking about doing business together — as in hiring you. As it relates to job search, a referral is someone who is expecting your call or email with the prospect of speaking about a career opportunity. The point is that it's not "cold." It's not an out-of-the-blue contact. You are entering a discussion or a meeting through a bona fide endorsement with an expectation already set.

I spoke recently at a meeting for top sales producers. I had 40 to 45 conference qualifiers at all levels in the room, and a lot of those reps didn't even know the true definition of a referral. They are very successful financial advisors, despite not knowing what a referral is. Imagine if they did!

In looking at it another way, an ideal referral is what you think it ought to be. "A good referral for me is an introduction to a managing director at a financial services firm interested in creating a referral culture." In having a clear cut idea about what a good referral is for you, you are in a great position to let other people know. If they don't know what type of referral you're seeking, how can they possibly help you?

Reasons You're Not Getting Referrals

You're Afraid to Ask

I think this is the No. 1 reason people don't get referrals—they simply don't ask out of fear. And they don't ask because they're afraid that:

- They will look needy.
- It will appear to be all about them.
- Whoever they're asking, such as a client or prospect, will say no or feel compromised or uncomfortable, or it will hinder the relationship.

I absolutely get it. There is validity to all of this. Nobody wants to appear pushy or salesy. (Then again, some people do.) Bottom line is this — if you offer great value in your products, services or whatever, you should be asking for referrals. But there is a right way of doing it. And the right way will not make you a nuisance.

You Don't Know or Communicate Who Your Best Prospects Are

You want referral business, but you want the right type of referral business. I find that the more specific I am in explaining what a good referral is for me (to the right people), the more likely I am to get good referrals. If people have tried to refer you business, and it's just not a good fit or not what you're looking for, it may boil down to how well (or not so well) you're communicating your message. This gets back to PEEC Statements™ and fishing in the right ponds.

You Don't Have a Mechanism in Place to Ask for Referrals

In sales training programs at many large firms, reps are taught that as soon as you close the business, you ask for a referral. It's like a rite to passage. That is the wrong approach in many cases. If you have a good relationship and a good connection with your client or customer (brand new client or customer by the way), you can say, "You know what… if you feel that I've done right by you and you know others who would find value in what I do, I would be thrilled to be a resource to them as well," and leave it at that. Of course, if you can share details about your target market and what ideal business looks like for you, even better!

Here's another perspective. Once you have been successful closing business with a new customer or client, why make it about you? Shouldn't it be about them? When you buy that new car, don't you want to show it off?

It doesn't matter if the product is a new car, a long-term-care policy, life insurance, credit card processing, or a time share, that is the time for the new client to feel good about what they bought or in their investment. It's also the time that they begin to feel better about you and your relationship with them. Why on earth would you compromise that? Why take that moment that should be theirs and make it yours?

Important Note: I don't care how important your product or service is, this is the time for your new client to celebrate and for you to live up to your promises. At this point, always focus on the relationship and doing great work for the client. There's a time and place to ask for a referral and this ain't it!

In this case, the proper time to ask for referrals should be in your follow-up or at some other time in the future. There is a time and place to ask for referrals, and if you have a good mechanism that responds to all of these different components, you will be successful. If you don't have a mechanism in place, and you're just shooting from the hip and wondering if it's the right time, you're not going to do it anyway.

You Don't Give Enough Referrals Yourself

The best way to get referrals is to give referrals. If you're thinking about you all the time (see how you are?), not only will you not get in the habit of giving referrals to others, you won't give the right type of referrals to others in your network. You may not give them to the right people, and perhaps you don't give them in the right way. You get quality referrals as a result of giving quality referrals. That's how it works and it makes the whole asking for referrals thing quite easy. If you're not sure how to refer someone else business — just ask them! I think they would appreciate it.

You're "Selling" Your Referral Sources Rather than Networking with Them

In a networking scenario, it's inappropriate to look at people as potential prospects rather than potential referral sources.

I was part of a networking group years ago. Scott was the president of the group and he had a number of people on his board. I joined the group and wanted to meet one by one with the board members. In the spirit of networking, I thought this would be the best way to learn about the group and their respective businesses and to see if, over time, I could help them in any way.

I scheduled a one-on-one meeting with Scott and clearly outlined that the purpose of the meeting was to discuss networking. We sat down and he started laying paperwork out on the table. I was thinking, "Okay, this guy is very organized." Next thing you know, he pulls out brochures and paperwork and starts to sell me on all of his products and services — complete with sales pitch! This was supposed to be a networking meeting set up to talk about our respective businesses, talk about where we wanted to go, see how we might help one another and talk about the group. Instead, Scott made the meeting about Scott.

I had to end the meeting and I assertively told him, "Look, Scott, I have to be honest with you. I thought it was clear that this was supposed to be a networking meeting. I thought we would talk about our respective businesses and see how we might help one another. The appointment was not made for you to try to sell me stuff I don't need or want. Not only is what you did a waste of my time; it is inappropriate." He reacted as if he didn't think anything was wrong.

Ironically, sometime thereafter, the board asked me if I would give an educational talk to the group. They knew me as a public speaker and someone who knows a thing or two about networking. So, what do you think I talked about? I didn't speak about Scott specifically, but I talked about what the purpose of the group is, what networking is and the mistakes that are made, and his mistake was what I focused on. I think other people in the group knew what I was referring to as they may have experienced the same scenario.

You Don't Network Enough

Or you don't network with the right people in the right places and with those serving the same markets as you. Of course, if you're a bad networker, that doesn't help the cause either.

You Don't Spend Enough Time Planning for Your Business Meetings

I don't necessarily mean networking meetings. But when you're sitting down one-on-one with someone, you won't reap referrals if you're not prepared for that meeting.

A couple of weeks ago, I met with a fellow speaker from the speaker's association, we both knew a lot about one another (Google is amazing). Since we both had notes, it took our conversation to a different level. I had his website printed and the pages laid out in front of me, with handwritten notes made in red ink. Ironically, he did something similar and he had a lot of notes and questions written down. Obviously, we were both really prepared for this meeting, and it created the proper setting — to learn and potentially generate referrals! Unfortunately, too few people prepare themselves to make the impression they should.

You Don't Take the Time to Thank Referral Sources Properly

Or at all! I pride myself on thanking people in creative and fun ways. It's the right thing to do. I think that if somebody is nice enough to refer you business, you have to say thank you. I think it's important to do something creative and memorable. As mentioned, I'm a big believer in handwritten cards:

Dear Tim,

Thank you so much for taking the time to refer me that piece of business. It's exactly the type of work that I'm looking to do. I would love to be able to meet with you or continue our conversation to figure out how we can further help one another. I can't thank you enough.

Warm regards,

Michael

I put about five handwritten cards in the mail every day, and some of them are thank-you cards. It takes me only five to 10 minutes in the morning. That's it. I find that people hang them up in their offices, or I get a quick email (or sometimes a handwritten card) back and I've gotten business because of it.

Also, I like to put my annual thank-you gifts in the mail around Thanksgiving because everybody else shoots for Christmas or New Year's. I want mine to always be the first that people receive. The personal touch often doesn't cost much money. It's the thought that counts and people will remember thoughtful, creative, and personal gestures forever.

There are all kinds of creative ways to say thank you. Certainly; giving somebody a referral in return is a nice way to say thank you, but the more creative you get, the more memorable you will be.

You Don't Pay It Forward

Be a resource to other people. Help them without expecting anything in return. Refer business to somebody. They may not immediately, be in a position to refer you. But do it anyway if you like them, you think it's a good fit and you think that they would do good work. It's all about paying it forward. I'm at meetings all the time, and if there's somebody I take a liking to who is an up-and-comer, or somebody I think I can help, I will do it.

All of these different reasons why we don't get more referral business may sound like common sense, but becoming more aware of them (or at least reminded of them) helps you stay focused. Having a keen awareness of these referral pitfalls is important, especially in networking meetings, in business circles and how you carry yourself and speak to clients.

Sure-Fire Ways to Generate More Referrals

Now let's talk about the flip side—generating more referrals. If you focus on doing these things, you will find yourself in a better position to receive quality referrals from the people around you.

Be Referable

Initially, you need to be liked. If you're not liked, nothing else matters. I'm not going to refer someone I don't like, even if they're great at what they do, unless it's a brain surgeon—I may not like him, but if he's the best in the business, he gets the referral. That might be the exception. But other than that, we just don't tend to refer people we don't like.

Be good at what you do. Be compatible to the type of business that you're looking for. Add extra value. Do all the things that make the person who is referring you look good. (It's all about looking good after all!)

When a colleague gives me referred business, I go a little above and beyond, even more so than I might normally, because I want to make that person look great. I want people to go back to them and say, "What a great referral. Thank you so much for putting us in touch with Michael Goldberg." If you make your referral source look good, they will keep referring you.

Use Your PEEC Statement™

We talked about the PEEC Statement™ in-depth in Chapter 5. Get good at giving yours. Practice it on your friends and family. Practice it with your clients, prospects and centers of influence. One of the things that I see in working with sales reps on a regular basis is that they don't use their PEEC Statement™ nearly enough, even though I've already taught it to them. They say, "Yeah, you're right. I should use it more." And I will reply, "Why have I gone to all this trouble to teach it to you and to coach you on it if you're not using it?"

I was on a conference call recently with a focus group composed of top sales producers in one firm. There were 10 people on the call. I asked, "How often are you using your PEEC Statements™? How many calls did you make last week, and how many of those people did you share your PEEC Statement™ with? How many meetings did you go to? How many potential referrals did you lose?" Not enough activity and way too much opportunity cost.

You know it. Use it. Practice it and get better. Rinse and repeat.

Follow Up on All Referrals Immediately

I'm pretty good at this, but I wasn't always. I often have a pile of business cards on my desk that I have collected in various meetings with people, and my goal is always to follow up within 24 hours of meeting that person or, if I have met them on a Friday or before a holiday, I will follow up the next business day.

If you handle referrals in a very timely, responsible way, you will get more of them. If you don't get around to handling them, it won't happen. And you'll solve that problem fast!

A couple of years ago, I helped a friend of mine who was in job search. I connected her with a great client of mine, Paul. It was a referral, so I told her to call him and that he was expecting her call, for the prospect of potentially getting an interview. I had helped her with her résumé and other areas of job search. I followed up with her the very next week and asked, "Did you get a chance to contact Paul?"

She said, "I haven't had a chance to do that. I got busy." The position had already been filled. And Paul said to me, "I never heard from your friend", and I was embarrassed.

I really let her have it! I said, "I'm a little disappointed. I set you up with a friend and very good client who was going to give you a shoe-in type of interview. I was a little embarrassed and disappointed that you never spoke with him."

She let me have it right back: "Look, I've been busy."

I said, "I apologize for even getting involved with this. I can't in good faith help you anymore because you have compromised me with a client." She remained out of work for the next 6 months. How many referrals sources have you disappointed by simply not following up? How much money or how many career opportunities has it cost you?

Keep Your Referral Sources in the Loop

Keep your friends close and keep your referral sources closer. As different situations are percolating, circle back from time to time with the person who has referred you, for several reasons—to let them know where things are, to take another opportunity to thank them, to create another touch point with them and to ask how you can help them. You can say, "I will keep you up-to-date with this.

Thank you once again. This is the type of business I'm looking for—no question about it. Tell me what you're focused on right now and how I might be able to help you." It's an opportunity to do all those different things while keeping your referral source in the loop. They'll always appreciate that.

Spend More Time in All the Right Places

Where do those in the best position to refer you hang out? Go there. This gets back to fishing in the right ponds. I'm always looking to go to places that attract those that work with my target audience. Speakers, trainers, coaches, consultants, wholesalers, and recruiters are great examples of practitioners that may serve my market but don't provide the same services. Where do they hang out? Where they go, I go. You can take the same approach. If you're an architect, it makes good sense to hang out at organizations that attract construction companies and contractors. If you're a title closer, you may want to know where real estate attorneys go. Chiropractors and massage therapists may also have a common interest. And so on and so forth.

Personal Gifts

The more personal you can make a gift, the more powerful it will be. For example, I have a client who is a bulldog breeder, so I sent him a bulldog coffee-table book and a statue of a bulldog as a thank-you gift. He keeps both in his office.

Another creative idea is to make something yourself. I know someone who makes wine. They distill and bottle the wine and put personalized labels on the bottles. Their way of saying thank you is to give someone a bottle of wine with a personalized label and a quote or something about them. Naturally, tickets for a client's favorite baseball team, golf balls with the insignia of their model car and donations to their favorite charities are also nice touches.

I frequently send books or videos (usually a classic movie about sales reps like Glengarry Glen Ross or The Boiler Room), or something having to do with someone's favorite activity — yoga, horseback riding, sporting events, to people who I know would appreciate them. It's a quick and fun way to send a personal gift that people will appreciate and remind them of you.

Send Thoughtful Gifts for No Reason

Whenever I'm in a conversation with somebody I like and something comes up that is interesting (like a movie we both liked), there's a good chance that I'll send a gift (or at least a note) relevant to that discussion. If it's a gift, it's not usually something pricey, but it's something that's thoughtful, something I won't send to everybody.

As I am speaking to them at a networking event, I may jot a note down on their business card: "Send book." This serves as my friendly reminder.

Have a High Sense of Ethics

This seems like common sense, but I do need to mention it. Have a high standard for right and wrong and for what you will and won't do. I know of sales reps that are very product-driven. They want to sell a certain product, a certain type of policy, rather than looking to solve the problem for their client. Some of them will try to get things through compliance that shouldn't fly, or to stretch the truth to get more business. How many referrals do you think they get?

If people believe that you are ethical in your standards and that you're looking to do the right thing by them, they're going to refer you.

Give Awesome Referrals without Expecting Anything in Return

It's always important to think in terms of giving rather than getting. Typically, I give referrals to "great" people without expecting anything in return. But over time, if I'm generating a lot of business for somebody and they are in a position to refer me business — and they don't, I might start looking to them to refer business to me as well. And this is just a conversation away. If they are truly "great" people this should almost never be an issue. If it is, they'll tell you and you can work on resolving the issue. Giving is one thing but a relationship should never be one sided — that's not a relationship. At least not a good relationship.

Stay in Touch with Those Who Refer You Often

This gets back to OOSIOOM — Out of Sight is Out of Mind. Keep your referral sources close (your enemies closer). You should absolutely schedule meetings (phone or face to face) with those that refer you business often. Make it a regular thing — monthly, quarterly, whatever. Get it on your calendar now. Schedule it out for the whole year or you won't do it.

It's important to have a system in place to keep in touch with people — especially with those whom you have a vibrant referral relationship. It has to be scheduled, planned and deliberate.

Volunteer Your Time to Worthy Organizations

Serve on a board, head up a committee or get involved in a charity or community-service organization. Or do something with your child's PTA, school or sports team. You just never know who you will meet at an event.

I volunteer my time to job-search organizations, including the U.S. Department of Labor. I believe in donating my time to worthy causes. It's one of my favorite talks, and often a couple hundred people will be at the presentation, so I think I'm helping a lot of people. They seem to appreciate it, and it has actually turned into business for me, even though that is not why I do it.

Showcase some of the things that you do well, do it in the spirit of giving and you will create marketing gravity. If you're a financial advisor, you can speak to groups of job searchers about rolling over 401(k) accounts and 529 plans or investment strategies. People will want to hire you, work with you and refer you.

Collaborate with Your "A" Team on a Regular Basis

Your "A" team is composed of your clients, your referral sources and your true prospects (people who know you or know of you, have an interest in your product or service and are open to making a purchase today or in the future).

If you need advice about anything, why not bounce it off members of your "A" team? You get great value, you build the relationship further, they get a better understanding of the things you're working on and you create gravity. It will also keep you in touch with them.

Also, offer to give advice to your "A" team. Whatever your expertise is, offer it informally for nothing. If a client (or prospect) is not looking to hire me right now, I'm not looking to pitch them and say, "Is this the time?" I'm looking to stay in touch with them because they are in the know in the industry. They are good at what they do and are knowledgeable (presumably), and I'm looking to bounce ideas off of them. I might say, "You know that I help advisors and agencies build their practices through networking and referrals. I know that you're not in a place right now to bring me in, but feel free to call on me as a resource, even informally, if there's something that I can help you with or if you want to bounce anything off of me. I do this full-time. I am happy to help." So I'm always looking to offer that, and people are very appreciative.

The buzz I'm looking to create, other than building the relationship the right way, is "Man, this guy has really helped me with a lot of different things. If I'm not paying him, imagine how much he would help me if I did."

Keep your "A" team close to you to build those relationships.

Play Wii

There are all kinds of books out there and experts that help sales reps at generating more referrals. Yes, generating referrals is one of the biggest challenges sales professionals (in all industries) face. The fact is we make generating referrals a lot more difficult than it really needs to be.

You know the show *Are You Smarter than a Fifth Grader?* Let me take it one step further — are you smarter than a seven year old? My daughter Jessica is a fanatic about the Wii game, especially Wii Bowling, and she beats me. Badly. These days she's very caught up in Wii — and rightfully so. Jessica gets the Wii concept. Sales reps generally don't.

Sales reps tend to miss the Wii concept altogether. Wii spelled "we" that is. See where I'm going? Sales reps are so conditioned to thinking of generating referrals as a "me" thing (as in you) rather than a "we" thing (as in you and your client, prospect, referral source). Are you with me?

So instead of speaking with a client or referral source about, "How can you refer *me* more business?" turn it into, "How can *we* refer one another more business?" Now there's no reason to be afraid to ask for a referral. Fear be gone! Making your request a "we" thing removes all of the obstacles. Doesn't it? The reason *we* don't ask for referrals is because it seems self-centered. Remember, nobody cares about your business as much as you do. And others care about their own business. But if you can make it collaborative and play Wii, or we referrals, it makes it easier for everyone, profitable and more fun. Just ask my seven year old!

I was at a National Speakers Association conference with a big-time keynote speaker. I am friendly with him because we serve a lot of the same markets. He got his start at Second City in Chicago and has done stand-up comedy. He is absolutely brilliant. At this conference, I serve on a board and played bartender at an event. Talk about a networking opportunity! I was speaking with him while pouring drinks. I was telling him that a lot of my own speaking and consulting is in financial services (like his). "We should talk," I told him. "I've seen you speak in different places, and I've been at speaking engagements with you."

He replied, "That's a great idea. You could refer me business."

I don't know if he was being tongue-in-cheek with me or if that's really the way he looked at it. He had a great opportunity for me to refer him business. But he missed it. Sure, I can refer him business—no question. But he can refer me business, too. He didn't see that. I just kind of laughed, poured him his vodka and orange juice, and that was it. How many referral opportunities have you lost? Are you smarter than a seven year old?

Make Sure It Goes Both Ways—If Not, Handle It

I touched on this before but will mention it again because I run into this all the time. A sales rep will say, "You know, I've been referring a lot of business to this CPA. But he never refers me back. So I'm going to stop referring him business." Or "I'm referring a lot of business to this estate-planning attorney. He never reciprocates. You know what? I'm not referring him anymore."

I just had this conversation with a financial advisor recently. I asked, "Do you know why he doesn't refer you business?" He said no. I said, "That's your issue. You have to find out what's going on. Don't just cut him off. There may be something you don't know or may not see. Maybe he just doesn't realize it. Or maybe he doesn't know how to refer you. Or he doesn't like you or trust that you're good at what you do (tough to hear). Or he may feel that you're not experienced enough to work with his clients. Maybe there's some other problem or issue. He may have a friend or family member who does exactly what you do, and he's referring that person. You have to get to the bottom of this. You are not communicating with him."

That's when you say to the person, "Do you want to grab a drink? I'd like to speak with you and talk shop." Once you get that meeting, whether it's over coffee, dinner or a beer, say, "I want to have a conversation with you in terms of how we might refer each other more business. I know I have referred you business, and there might be an opportunity for you to refer me business, and I want to be able to discuss that and see if we can do more business together." Right there, you will discover the essence of the issue. Often, they just don't realize it. Now you're solving the problem instead of running away from it.

Make sure it goes both ways. But you don't need to keep score, as in "I referred you two. So you owe me two." It should be, in general, give and take both ways.

If it continues to be one-sided, you have to make a decision and realize that maybe the person wasn't up-front with you about something. Or if they are up-front with you and say, "Look, I do appreciate you giving me business. But my brother is also a financial advisor, and I have to give him the business," then you can respond with, "I wish you had told me that. No harm, no foul. I get it. Maybe our business practices are in a different place right now. I see your situation, and I would probably do the same thing. I'll go fish in a different pond, and we'll agree to part friends."

Then your assignment becomes finding a new CPA or estate-planning attorney with whom you can have a more collaborative relationship.

You can ask about potential opportunities moving forward—"Is there an opportunity for us to split the business or figure something else out?"

Referrals mean everything, yet so many sales producers struggle with this. Practice some of these sure-fire approaches, and you'll be more referable in no time!

Takeaways

- A referral is simply someone who is expecting your call or email with the prospect of speaking about business. As it relates to job search, it is someone who is expecting your call or email with the prospect of speaking about a career opportunity.

- One of the main reasons people don't ask for referrals is that they're afraid they will come across as a nuisance. But you will not be a nuisance if you ask for referrals as a follow-up mechanism and if you make it about reciprocal referrals, not just referrals for yourself.

- To get the right type of referral business, be specific about what you want, and tell the right people.

- It is inappropriate to ask for a referral as soon as you've made the sale. That should be your new client's moment to feel good about their investment and about the value that they will hopefully get from the product, service or concept that they've just invested in. The mechanism for asking for referrals should be in your follow-up.

- If you give referrals, you'll get referrals.

- Never try to sell to your referral sources!

- Continue networking; that can lead to referrals.

- Pay it forward—be a resource to others.

- Be referable by being likable, good at what you do and compatible to the type of business that you're looking for. Add extra value.

- Practice your PEEC Statement™ with your friends and family, clients, prospects and centers of influence.

- Follow up on all referrals immediately.

- As different situations are percolating, circle back from time to time with the person who has referred you, to let them know where things are, to take another opportunity to thank them and to ask how you can help them.

- Find out about the hangouts of the people who are in the best position to refer you, and go there.

- Send thoughtful gifts to say "thank you" for a referral or for no reason at all.

- Have a high sense of ethics. If people believe that you are ethical in your standards and that you're looking to do the right thing, they're going to refer you.

- Have a mechanism in place to keep in touch with people. It has to be scheduled, planned and deliberate.

- Serve on a board, head up a committee or get involved in a charity or community-service organization. Showcase some of the things that you do well, do it in the spirit of giving, and you will create marketing gravity.

- Your "A" team is composed of your clients, referral sources and true prospects (people who know you or know of you, have an interest in your product or service and are open to making a purchase today or in the future). If you need advice about anything, bounce it off members of your "A" team. And let them know they can do the same with you.

- Turn the referral issue into a "Wii," or "we" business instead of a "me" business. Instead of asking someone to refer business to you, ask them how you can refer business to one another. That removes the fear and obstacles.

- Give awesome referrals without expecting anything in return. But if, over time, you find that you are referring business to someone who is not reciprocating, talk to them and find out why. Handling the issue is much more effective than running from it.

Your Turn

People leave potential business on the table every day because they either do things that destroy their ability to be referable, or they fail to do things that are sure-fire ways to generate more referrals. Examine your own business to find out what you can do—and stop doing—so that you can generate more referrals. The checklist on the next two pages will help you get started.

YOUR "CALL TO ACTION" PLAN

Sure-Fire Ways to Generate More Referrals

1. Do you have a mechanism for requesting referrals?

   _____

   Do you ask for a referral as soon as you've made a sale?

   _____

   If so, will you consider asking for referrals as part of your
   follow-up procedure instead of asking for them right after
   a sale? _____

   _____

2. If you are receiving fewer referrals than you'd like, what
   do you think are the reasons? Check all that apply.

   ❑ You're afraid to ask.

   ❑ You don't know or communicate who your best
      prospects are.

   ❑ You don't have a mechanism in place to ask for
      referrals.

   ❑ You don't give enough referrals yourself.

   ❑ You're selling your referral sources rather than
      networking with them.

   ❑ You don't network enough.

   ❑ You don't spend enough time planning for your
      business meetings.

   ❑ You don't take the time to thank your referral
      sources properly—or at all.

❑ You don't pay it forward (serve as a resource to other people).

3. Which of the following strategies can you work on to generate more referrals?

❑ Try to become more referable by being more compatible to the type of business that you're seeking.

❑ Use your PEEC Statement™ more often.

❑ Follow up on all referrals immediately.

❑ Do a better job of keeping your referral sources in the loop.

❑ Spend more time in all the right places/fishing in the right ponds.

❑ Say thank you in personal, thoughtful ways.

❑ Send thoughtful gifts for no reason.

❑ Have a high sense of ethics.

❑ Give awesome referrals without expecting anything in return.

❑ Stay in touch with those who refer you often.

❑ Volunteer your time to worthy organizations.

❑ Collaborate with your "A" team on a regular basis.

❑ Play Wii—when asking for referrals, ask how you and your referral source can help one another instead of asking how they can refer more business to you.

❑ Make sure it goes both ways—if you're referring business to someone who isn't reciprocating, find out why.

4. Of the above action items that you checked, which are your biggest priorities, and what specific actions will you take to try to generate more referrals? _____

CHAPTER 12:
Networking and Job Search

"The hardest work in the world is being out of work."
—Whitney Young, Jr., Civil Rights Leader

I added this section to the book for a number of reasons. First and foremost, I have a soft spot for job searchers. I volunteer my time to countless organizations and deliver seminars on writing a resume, interviewing, and career search strategy which of course includes networking.

Hey, one day you might find yourself out of a job (I hope not) and you can refer to this section and apply your networking skills to your job search campaign.

No doubt, you have a colleague, relative, friend, enemy, someone, who has been down-sized, up-sized, right-sized, left-sized, super-sized, or whose job has simply been elimi-nated. Tell them to buy this book (or loan it to them) so they can learn how to network and apply all of the strategies we've been discussing.

I was in job search myself many years ago, although not for very long. Thankfully, I didn't have a mortgage or family at the time. I was young and renting an apartment and it was absolutely daunting. I can't even imagine what it must be like to be a job searcher right now in an economy that has helped create an unemployment rate under 10 percent. Imagine having no idea how you're going to pay the mortgage and bills, how you're going to look at yourself in the mirror.

One of the things that we pride ourselves on and what drives our ego is what we do for a living and how we go about doing our work—that's a big part of our identity. I can't even fathom what it must be like to lose that or to have that taken from you, having to face friends and family while feeling, in many ways, like you're a failure, or that you did something wrong, or that the world is against you. And you wonder how you will climb out of this hole.

This is especially hard for people who have been out of work for a year or 18 months. I know people that have been out of work for over two years. Job searchers that have been in transition for an extended period of time lose their sense of purpose and their dignity. I have conversations with some of these people, and it is absolutely heartbreaking.

One of the reasons I volunteer my time is because there is not enough of an emphasis on helping job searchers network. There may be government employees that are paid low wages to teach skills like resume writing, interviewing, and networking but there's not enough good expertise and talent to go around.

There are no high energy sales meetings organized to help job searchers strategize and celebrate. (If there are, there certainly aren't enough and not enough people that know about them.) No awards for top producer. No all expenses paid trips to the Caribbean to celebrate success.

Networking may not land a job seeker a job tomorrow — but it could! Heck, networking could be how a job seeker discovers what they want to do for work next. "Aha! I now know what I want to be when I grow up!" It's pretty exhilarating when you discover which career path to take. Then it gets back to the basic formula of where to go, what to say, and with whom?

Not enough job searchers know what networking is or know how to go about doing it. No one has taught them. Many job seekers have never had to develop these skills before because they were in jobs where networking and sales skills weren't needed much or at all. All of a sudden a computer programmer may find himself in a place he doesn't want to be, against his will — by the way. What is he supposed to do next?

He may take a lot of the traditional approaches like hitting the newspapers, contacting recruiters, monster.com, career-builder.com—all the usual stuff. But the usual stuff doesn't work as well as it once did. Even back in the day, it didn't work as well as it could have. It's so important for job searchers to know where to go, what to say and to whom.

I see the reactions of job searchers in these very large groups that I speak to. They know nothing about the information I'm sharing. There's a lot of opportunity to help those in job search and career transition to identify target markets and target companies, form a communication strategy that speaks to their target market, and go to the right places to network with an aggressive strategy in mind.

The fact remains that 76 percent of those who are landing positions are doing so through networking, according to Lee Hecht Harrison, an international outplacement firm.

Imagine what that number might be if more people knew how to network and build relationships the right way, especially since the ads in newspapers and on job-search sites account for only 13 percent of the jobs that are available. (That's right!) That means that the general public does not know about 87 percent of the jobs that may be available—you can learn about them only by knowing someone, by networking. Yes, knowing how to network will increase your odds of being able to tap into that 87 percent of all available jobs.

Here are some approaches to networking as it relates to job search.

Know What You Want

It's vital for job searchers to know what they want. Some of them have no idea what they want specifically—they just want a job. I can understand that from an emotional standpoint. But from a pragmatic standpoint, I don't get it because you can't help somebody who doesn't know what they want.

Are you focused on working in the same industry that you were in before? Or is it a career change? If so, what is that industry, and why are you looking to transition to it? Are you looking to start a business or buy a franchise? Are you looking to become a consultant in your area of expertise? Do you want to become a teacher or a writer?

I try to brainstorm with people about the possibilities. You can always change your mind—it's not like getting a tattoo on your arm. You can change your focus, that's much better than not having a focus at all.

Tell Your Friends and Family about Your Status

Most people won't share their job search with friends and family because they're ashamed. They look at it as though they've done something wrong. Or they feel that their self-worth is compromised. "If I'm not working, I must be a failure."

It's important to share your situation with people. But don't share it from a place of complaint and venting, or being a victim. Share it as "Here's where I am. This is what I'm looking for. Can you offer me some advice, insight or recommendations?" (This gets back to AIR Time™.) Your friends and family are your first line of defense. They should be there to help you.

Take Advantage of Career-Related Programs

There are tons of them out there. Some are better than others, but most of them are underutilized. I know this because I speak at engagements that are related to them, yet many people don't even know these programs are in place and don't realize the benefits that are being offered. They're just a Google search and a networking connection away.

It's important to take advantage of these programs for a number of reasons. They are typically free, they get you out of the house, they put you back into the mindset of going to work (or going someplace)—your full-time job has now become looking for a full-time job—and they get you busy with networking, interviewing, revising your résumé and being around others who can relate to you. Many of the programs that are offered focus on financial services, like what you need to do with that 401(k) and how to be careful financially. Others focus on how to write a good résumé, how to network, how to interview, how to negotiate and how to use LinkedIn.

Talk to Vendors, Prospects, Clients and Former Co-Workers

These are people that you may have a good relationship with — now it's simply a different relationship. Don't lose touch! Talk to these connections because they're in touch with people and resources within your former job. A lot of people cut those ties. But if you have a great relationship with them, call on them for networking and maybe even for social reasons.

This is a great time to catch up with these people and get reconnected. It's also a great time to reach out to your former company's competition—companies that you might want to research and network your way into.

Have a Great Résumé

Yes, I know this is obvious. As obvious as this might be, most people have resumes that are outdated and don't meet the protocol of today. Having a great résumé prepares you for the questions that come up at a networking meeting: "What is it that you do well? What are you looking to do? What are your skills?" It's fresh in your mind. Then someone may say, "You know what, I just spoke with someone who is looking for someone who does what you do. Do you have a résumé that you can forward to me?" If you have one that's already prepared, you don't lose any time.

I used to assume that people that have been through outplacement services or programs offered by the Department of Labor have a good resume. Guess what? Not the case!

Résumés today look a lot different than they did just three or four years ago.

Here are some quick highlights.

A résumé should have an objective at the top. About 90 percent of all résumés do not have a stated objective. If you know exactly what you want to do, you should state an objective on your résumé. If you're not sure or if you're open to doing different things, those are good arguments for not having one. As I mentioned earlier, it's always best to "know what you want." Therefore, if you know what you want, you should definitely have an objective on your resume. If you change your mind, you can change your objective. However, you should not have multiple résumés with multiple objectives because you'll have multiple ways of becoming confused. I'd rather see you have a résumé with no objective than to see you have four different résumés with four different objectives. You'll get confused and it's very difficult to manage.

Also, your résumé should have a summary statement in the form of a brief paragraph at the very top that talks about your profession, expertise, environments, strengths and skills. (Yes, the summary statement is actually a PEES Statement, very similar to the PEEC Statement™ from earlier.)

Generally, if you have been established in the work place for at least three years, you should probably have a two-page résumé. If you're entry-level, a new grad or new in an industry, it will more likely be a one-page résumé.

(If you have questions about how to write a powerful résumé, visit www.BuildingBlocksConsulting.com for more information and to learn about my earlier work *"You're Hired! The Building Blocks to Career Search.*)

Use an Exit Statement

An exit statement is a prepared answer that you have to the question, "So what happened to you? Why are you in job search?" Then you can say, "Funny you ask" and make your exit statement.

Your exit statement should not be used to vent or tell negative stories. It should be a networking statement. It may sound something like, "You know how Verizon has been going through a transition and downsizing? Well, they eliminated a lot of positions, and mine was one of them. But right now, I am focused on a new role, geared more toward project management, but still in telecommunications. I'm looking to learn about opportunities and companies like (and then list them). And I would appreciate any advice, insight and recommendations you could give me."

The exit statement is great to use in an interview, too, because it keeps you from going down a negative path where you start venting. You can focus on a positive, "This is where I want to go" statement. This is important because a lot of job searchers don't know how to answer that question.

You should never share any negative statements about your former company, boss or employees, for two reasons. First, misery loves company, and I don't think you want to be around others who are wallowing in their misery. And second, it's a small, small, small, small world. The negative things I hear in job-search venues make me think, "No wonder you're not working."

Create a Target List of At Least 20 Companies

The list should include companies you would like to work for—your bucket list. Write the list on an index card, or put it in Word, and that becomes your hit list. Hang it above your computer or mirror. You should have a number of criteria for how you have decided on those particular companies. Consider organizations that reflect:

- Your desired industry
- The size of organization you want to work for—a small, family-owned business or a large corporation
- Your desired location—Are they local? Are you willing to commute into the city or relocate?
- The kind of culture do you want to be a part of

When you're in job search for a long time, you may feel like you don't care about some of these things. But the more focused you are, the better able you will be to tell people what you are looking for. This becomes part of what you will research and talk about at networking events. Maybe you will research five companies a week—look for press releases, look on LinkedIn, etc. And now you have a focus. Those companies now become your call to action. Now you can say, "I am looking to meet or be introduced to a manager who is connected with the project-management department within Verizon." Maybe you have learned the name of a contact from someone else or from LinkedIn.

Now you have the name of a person you would like to connect with. It's no accident that people land in companies that they're targeting. If you're not targeting a company, what are your chances? Be proactive rather than reactive. Have a target to shoot for.

Read Newspapers and Trade Publications in Your Chosen Field

Look at the help wanted ads and know what's out there, but also be very well-read in the profession that you come from or are gravitating toward. You don't want to fall out of the loop. Be on top of your game in terms of trends, mergers and things that are going on so that you have that much more insight into what's happening.

Post Your Résumé on Job-Search Sites

Naturally, keep your resume posted on all the necessary job search sites. I'm all about the networking, but this puts another line in the water. Whatever you do, don't look at this as being the only way to search for a job, though; it's yet another approach. I know people who update their résumé every week on monster.com, and they've been doing so for months. Have people landed jobs on monster.com, careerbuilder.com, and other job search sites? No doubt. But most jobs aren't landed through websites.

Reach Out to Recruiters in Your Industry or Profession

There are a number of important questions that you should ask when you connect with recruiters:

- **Are they in your industry or profession?** This is not a generalist strategy; it's a specialist strategy. You want a recruiter who has contacts and connections in that industry, someone who is well-connected. You don't want someone to just see you as a number and a job title. Industries have recruiting specialists—pharmaceuticals, retail, telecommunications, etc. They often have expertise and their own target list of companies that they work with and for, and they have connections.

- **Are they retained or contingency-based?** Retained means the recruiting firm receives a retainer, a fee to keep the recruiter focused on finding the best candidate for the job. Contingency-based means the recruiter gets paid when they find the right candidate. See the difference? This is important because as a job searcher, your preference is to work with a retained firm rather than a contingency-based firm. You want them to be focused on finding the best person for the job. You don't want them to throw jobs at you that aren't a fit just so that they can get paid. Recruiters focused on high level positions tend to be retained, as are recruiting firms that are much more established. This is not a show-stopper, but it is something you should know. And if they won't tell you, hang up the phone and call another recruiter. There are plenty of recruiters out there and they are suffering in this economy, too.

- **Do they have a good track record with placing those who do what you do?** Say, "These are my skills, this is the type of job I'm looking for. How many people like me have you placed, and what is the time frame?"

- **Are they reliable?** Do they do what they say they will do? Do they return your calls? Do they respect your decisions? Do they value what you have to say?

- **Will they ever cost you money?** I don't think you should ever have to pay a recruiter. There are too many of them out there, and the companies that retain them should foot the bill. What some recruiters do, because it's all about supply and demand, and they know that people are desperate—is say, "Pay me this fee, and I guarantee that you will get the job that you're looking for at the income level you're looking for." But there are no guarantees.

I know somebody who was in a recruiter's office. As she was looking over the application and all the paperwork, she was about to sign her name, and then she saw in fine print that the transaction was going to cost her $15,000 up-front. She left the office crying.

Conduct Yourself as a Business Person, Not as a Job Searcher

Maintain your dignity. You were a business person or other professional before, and you will be again. Be positive and excited to be exploring new opportunities. Fake it if you have to. Remember, the first person you ever sell is you.

Practice The Pool Rules of Networking™

Have your tools of the trade with you (but no résumés!). No selling. Have an array of questions to ask. Have a goal and a plan. It is never about you. (It's important to help others, especially other job searchers).

Create and use your elevator pitch, plan to take the initiative to follow up and have fun (no, really!).

Be Active in Job-Search Networking Groups

Also explore professional associations in your chosen field, Chambers of Commerce and your college alumni organization. The key phrase is "be active." Don't just show up. See if you can have a role in the meetings. See how you can help people. Volunteer your time. Spend as much time as you can there.

Volunteer to Do Talks at Industry Meetings

If you have expertise or skills that are of value in your industry, you can talk to the board members of associations, and they will book you to speak. In some cases, they may pay you. But that's not why you're there—you're there to showcase how good and smart you are and to network your way in. Not too many ways are better than that. Job searchers look at themselves as job searchers only and do not realize the value they can add. Always look for opportunities to promote your expertise. No one can take that from you!

Don't Get Stuck on LinkedIn or Other Business/Social Media

Remember the guy I mentioned who was proud of his "networking" skills because he was on LinkedIn for 11 hours? OK, he gets an "A" for effort, but that's time he will never get back. These online communities have a place, so spend your hour a day to update, post, connect and come up with names—and then log off.

Be Ruthless About Staying Positive

If you can, let someone else handle your finances. That way, you are disconnected from it. If your spouse or someone else can insulate you from having to focus on that directly, then make those arrangements if it doesn't compromise you in any way.

Hang Out with Positive People

Positive people do positive things and tend to hang out with other positive people. That goes for family, friends and new contacts. You don't need people discouraging your every move. There are enough people out there touting that there are no jobs and that the economy is bad. Stay clear of all the Negative Nellies that get in the way of productivity. Who needs them? People are being offered jobs every day. Stay positive and focused and spend time with others that make you feel good and can be of help. (I'm positive of that!)

Stay in Touch with Those in Your Network

Especially the centers of influence in your chosen industry, profession, and target companies. Send articles, give referrals, make an occasional call, offer to help them in any way you can. "But I can't help anybody because I'm in job search." Really?

Don't Stay Home

If you do, you'll get caught up in the drama of Oprah and Dr. Phil, and it will take you away from where you need to be. You can log on to the Internet and your email at *Panera Bread* for free. Go to a library or a Department of Labor office. Go to somebody else's office if you can. Create an environment that makes you feel like you're productive, like you're a business person. If you feel productive, you have a better chance of being productive. If you stay home all day, it doesn't do a lot of good for your psyche. As a business owner, I have an office at home, but often I don't work here, for the same reason. Getting out helps me keep focused and stay busy.

Get Involved with Outside Activities

Do what you can to keep busy. It will put you in contact with more people and help you maintain a positive outlook and a balanced life. Take a class, join a gym, teach a class (if you can!), find a hobby, get involved in a book club. You might discover a new career while not losing your sanity. If you can, use your outside activities as a reward for being productive in your career search.

Keep Doing the Things You Love

That is, if it makes sense. If you like fitness, playing golf or whatever, do it, as long as it's not putting too much of a pinch on the budget. I'm not saying you should renew that country-club membership, but do what makes sense to keep your life in balance.

Actions speak louder than words. When job search is your full-time job, it's important to keep busy, keep learning, keep helping people and keep positive.

Continue to Use and Develop Your Networking Skills to Meet New People, Learn and Advance Your Career—Forever

Networking does not end when you land the job. A lot of people think, "OK, cool. I don't have to network anymore." It's important to keep in touch and continue to grow your network because also there is networking that happens internally, within an organization. Now that you've learned how to do this effectively enough to land a job, stay in touch with the people who got you there, in part for social reasons, but also, you never know—who's to say that company won't go belly-up in two months or that your new job is short-lived, or maybe you won't like it? That network should be there as your security blanket.

I'm doing a networking talk soon to a pharmaceutical firm about internal networking to help the employees work more effectively in project teams and to build their careers. As a new person in a company, you want to showcase your networking skills so that you can learn more about what you need to do and network with people you'll be working with on cross-functional teams. They probably won't do a good job of reaching out to you. So reach out to them. Find out what you need to say and to whom, what you need to learn, what you can do to help. It's the same networking model, but it's executed under one roof.

Also, people often get promoted not because of what they do but because they're very well-networked with decision makers and people know who they are.

In a country with just under a 10 percent employment rate, job seekers may need to consider reinventing themselves. I think the new term for this is "re-careering". Job seekers and career changers should think about the new skills they need to develop in their chosen profession or industry. Maybe they need to focus on a new profession or industry, in which case they'll need additional skills and expertise.

People need to reinvent and rebrand themselves, tell people what they're thinking, have a different focus than they may have had in the past, be more creative and open-minded, and more open to change.

Change after all is a good thing.

Takeaways

- Networking speaks to one of the biggest problems in the country today—a 10 percent unemployment rate.

- About 76 percent of those who are landing positions are doing so through networking, according to Lee Hecht Harrison, an international outplacement firm.

- Ads in newspapers and on job-search sites account for only 13 percent of the jobs that are available. That means that the general public does not know about 87 percent of the jobs—you can unearth them only by networking.

- It will be easier for other people to help you in your job search if you can articulate what type of job you want.

- Your friends and family are your first line of defense. Make sure they know what type of job you are seeking.

- Get involved with career-related programs because they are typically free, they get you out of the house, they put you back into a place of going to work—your full-time job has now become looking for a full-time job—and they get you busy with networking, interviewing, revising your résumé and being around others who can relate to you.

- Seek the help of vendors, clients, prospects and former co-workers in your job search.

- Look for job opportunities in the companies that are competitors of your former employer.

- Make sure your résumé contains an objective and a summary statement that showcases what sets you apart from your peers.

- Prepare and practice your exit statement, which is the answer that you will give to the question, "So what happened to you? Why are you in job search?" It will help keep you focused on what you're looking for and will keep you from venting about your former employer.

- Keep a target list of at least 20 companies updated and with you at all times. It's no accident that people land in companies that they're targeting.

- Read newspapers and trade publications in your chosen field to keep up-to-date.

- Post your résumé on job sites, but realize that doing so is just one small part of your overall job-search campaign.

- Reach out to reliable recruiters in your industry or profession who have a good track record, who are paid on a contingency, not retained, basis and who do not charge job searchers a fee for their services.

- Conduct yourself as a business person, not as a job searcher.

- Practice The Pool Rules of Networking™.

- Be active in job-search networking groups.

- Volunteer to do talks at industry meetings.

- Spend no more than one hour a day on social media.

- Be ruthless about staying positive, and hang out with positive people.

- Stay in touch with those in your network, especially with your centers of influence, and help other job searchers.

- Get out of the house, and get involved with outside activities.

- Keep doing the things you love, if the cost is not prohibitive.

- Continue to use and develop your networking skills to meet new people, learn and advance your career—forever.

Your Turn

Being in job search can drain you of your dignity and sense of purpose if you let it. Enlist the help of those around you to embark on a positive journey toward finding your next job or career.

YOUR "CALL TO ACTION" PLAN

Networking and Job Search

1. When people ask, "So, what kind of job are you looking for?" What will your answer be? _____

   _____

   _____

2. When someone asks you, "So what happened to you? Why are you in job search?" What will your answer (exit statement) be? _____

   _____

3. List some career-related programs in your area in which you can get involved. _____

   _____

4. List newspapers and trade publications in your chosen profession or field that you will begin reading.

   _____

   _____

5. List at least 20 companies that you would like to work for.

   _____

   _____

   _____

   _____

CHAPTER 13:

Business Practices You Should Practice

*"Practice does not make perfect.
Only perfect practice makes perfect."*
—Vince Lombardi

The essence of networking is being able to relate to other people, empathize with them and have a giving nature. If you don't realize that by now, go back to Chapter 1. (Do not pass go. Do not collect $200.)

If you can make other people feel good about what you do and say, that plays into every networking approach that I can think of.

This chapter takes the approaches discussed throughout this book and applies those approaches to day-to-day practices that you can...well, practice.

These practices may seem like small potatoes—but they are important ingredients in creating and maintaining a networking attitude and ultimately a networking brand. I promise that if you put these approaches in motion, people will notice and think highly of you. That's a good thing.

Update Your Voice-Mail Greeting Daily

Clients and other associates that call you regularly will absolutely notice that you change your voicemail daily and update your whereabouts. They will compliment you and feel that you care about the impression that you leave every day. (Kind of like "tweeting" on your voicemail greeting.)

Let people know if you'll be out of the office and when you will return. It leaves an impression with people that every day, you have a fresh perspective, and you're giving them up-to-date information. It shows that their call *really* is important to you. I know people who add quotes and anecdotes. I just keep mine short and sweet — but current.

Just leave a quick voice-mail greeting to let people know that you'll be in the office in the afternoon but that you will be traveling on business after that. Ask them to leave a message, and say that you'll return their call as quickly as possible. Then do it!

Often enough, when I call someone and listen to their voice-mail greeting, it says, "…please leave a message and I'll call you at my earliest convenience."

That doesn't leave me with the best impression. It implies that my call isn't all that important at all and you'll return my call when you get around to it. Is that really good enough?

Return All Messages within 24 Hours or the Next Business Day

Try to return phone calls or emails within 24 hours. Or, if the message was left on a Friday or the day before a holiday, then return the message the next business day. And I mean all phone calls—even those from people you don't know or people who are soliciting business. You like *your* calls to be returned. I pride myself on returning everybody's call within 24 hours. I even mention that on my voice-mail greeting: "Please feel free to leave a message. You can rely on me to return your call within 24 hours or the next business day." Then I do so, and people realize that I'm true to my word.

When you are leaving your phone number as part of a voice mail message, mention it twice. That way, the recipient of your message doesn't have to play the message back to capture your phone number. They might be driving, or they might be reaching for a pen or you might speak quickly and they didn't get your number down. I know I speak quickly. So I will mention my number at the beginning of the message, and then I'll say, "I'll leave you my number at the end of this message again."

I also believe all emails should be returned within 24 hours unless you're traveling internationally (or happen to be in a submarine) and don't have access. You may not be able to solve a problem or follow through on something within 24 hours, but at least return their email and let them know that you got their message, that you're working on it and that you will be back in touch in the next couple of days.

Send Handwritten Notes on a Regular Basis

In an earlier chapter, I mentioned that I send out five handwritten postcards or regular cards out every day. That's 25 a week, 100 a month. Yes, I actually lick a stamp and fill out an address on an envelope and stick it in a mailbox. (If you're a Gen Y'er or Gen Z'er you probably have no idea what I'm talking about. If you're a Gen X'er or a Boomer, I'm sure you realized that we don't actually "lick" stamps anymore.)

I get a lot of feedback about the cards. I often receive handwritten notes back or at least emails and people think that it's really thoughtful that I take the time to add a personal touch. Many times, my notes and postcards will get posted on the wall (an actual wall, not a fan page or homepage), whereas emails get deleted. With the volume of emails that are received daily, handwritten notes are remembered forever. When was the last time you received a handwritten note?

Statistics show that business owners will make better connections and land more business just by taking a few minutes out of the day to put pen to paper. It's a little old-fashioned, and when I mention this to the students in the class I teach at Rutgers University, they think I'm insane. It seems most students don't even know the price of a U.S. Postage stamp!

Send someone a handwritten card to say thank you if they've done something to help you, or as a follow-up. Do it right now and see what happens!

Call or Email to Confirm All Scheduled Meetings a Day in Advance

The few times that I didn't do so, I either got stood up or otherwise discovered that there had been a miscommunication. This is especially important if you're traveling—just call or email to confirm the meeting because it makes both parties feel good. If the location or time needs to be changed, you can make the adjustment right then, and there's no harm, foul or wasted trip.

Be 15 Minutes Early to All Meetings

People have a different perception of you if you're always early to a meeting. It means that the meeting was so important to you that you made sure you were there in plenty of time. Also, it will give you a buffer if there's construction, heavy traffic, an accident, if you get lost or if life gets in the way. Too many people fail to allow for these things. Of course, it you *are* running late let the person you are meeting know as soon as possible.

When I leave myself plenty of time to get to where I'm going, I feel less stressed and concerned about getting there. When I arrive early, I can relax, collect my thoughts and grab that cup of coffee. More importantly, I feel calm, collected, and prepared for my meeting.

Do Your Homework

Google the person you will be meeting with. People are flattered when you know a little bit about them and have taken the time to research their background.

Before I meet with somebody, I'll Google them, then print their Web site and any profiles about them that I find. I joke with my Rutgers students, "I'll bet you didn't know that you can print Web pages." So I print them and paper-clip the pages together. As I'm reviewing them, I write on them with a red pen and highlighter. I write questions down that I may have about the material and highlight sections that I want to bring up in the meeting.

When I get to the meeting, I remove the paper clip and spread the pages out across the table to let the other person know that I've done my homework and that I'm really interested in some of the things that they are doing. Then I bounce some questions off of them. They are flattered that I went to such trouble to do that. Talk about an impression!

I tell job searchers to do this, too, in preparation for job interviews. It will help you ask questions as a *result* of your research, not as a result of *not doing* any research. It will allow you to ask better questions and feel more confident about your level of preparation. You will always have a better meeting because of it.

Be Humble and Self-Deprecating

I worked with a firm recently, and spoke to a group of brand-new financial advisors. I mentioned that I teach at Rutgers, and that resonated with them because Rutgers is just over the bridge from where this group is. One guy in the back of the room, a very nice and inquisitive guy, asked me why I don't mention my college degrees in my materials.

He almost called me out on it. I told him that I appreciated his asking, but, I said, "There's no reason for me to mention it. It's not relevant. I don't think it gets me any business, per se, and it just sounds very self-promoting when people talk about their degrees—unless there's a reason for it. It almost compromises the message." (Often enough, people brag about their college education and degrees if they don't have much of a message to brag about.)

I told the group a story about how, at a networking meeting, I met a social worker, and his introduction to me was, "I have a master's degree in social work." I wasn't disrespectful to him, but I was thinking, "Big deal. So what?"

Not to downplay education, but that shouldn't be your lead. If that's your lead, what else do you have to talk about? When people meet you, they want to like you. They want to feel good about what you're saying. They want you to come across as being competent but also compatible in helping them solve a problem. Your college degrees and other credentials won't get you liked, make you compatible, or get you hired. This also goes for licenses, designations, and the type of car you drive.

Just be humble and self-deprecating about your accomplishments. If somebody compliments you, just thank them for their kind words. If you can crack on yourself from time to time and get a laugh out of it, I think that's a good thing. The more humble and soft-spoken you are about your accomplishments and success, the more marketing gravity you will create. Also, you will make people feel good about you — and about themselves.

Don't Dominate a Conversation

Let other people talk. Conversations should be two-sided. I know too many people who make it all about them. Nobody wants to be around someone who does nothing but talk about their job, their activities, their kids, and their life without any interest in yours. Follow The Pool Rules™ and make it a tennis (or swimming) match back and forth. Be interested in others and you will become interesting to others.

Maintain Your Integrity and Honesty

Be up-front and true to yourself and others. Most people will appreciate it, even if it's not what they want to hear. If you can do the job or solve the problem, great. If you can't, be honest about it: "That's not my forte, but I can connect you with somebody who would do a really good job with that." Or you might need to tell someone, "I botched this. I didn't do a great job with it, and next time I will be better." Then tell them how and why. It's a small, small world and the last thing you need as a business owner, sales rep, or job searcher is a bad reputation.

Remember People's Names and Details about Their Lives

Bill Clinton was famous for doing this. He used to carry index cards and notes that would refresh his memory about people he was about to meet. He could then follow up on details about their lives. You can't possibly remember everybody's name and details about all of their lives. But if you can be pre-pared and do a little homework to refresh your memory—bring the details from the back of your mind to the front of your mind—that's always a powerful thing.

I love it when people come out of the woodwork and remember something that I might have said way back when, or they remember to ask me about something I shared with them. "How did the research on that recruiting article go?" It's always flattering when people remember something about you or are at least interested enough to refresh their memory and ask the right questions.

Focus Less on "Me" Language and More on "We" Language

When there are great accomplishments, it's important to use "we" language, especially if the accomplishments were made as a team. Say, "Yes, I think we did a great job with that." Even if you were the heavy, give everyone else credit. But if something didn't work out well, and you are making a critique, make it a "me" thing: "Yeah, that whole fiasco was on me. I dropped the ball with that. I could have done a better job. That was my fault."

To that end, I find it really annoying when people say things like "my secretary," "my assistant," "my office," or "my department." It comes across as being egotistical. It's not right or wrong—it's all about how it makes people feel. So instead of saying "my administrative assistant," say, "the admin in the department did a great job."

Or even better, use the person's name. "I'll ask Bill to handle that for you." When people use "me/my," it makes it all about them and may come across as pretentious. They may not mean it to sound that way (they probably do), but it could. That's the power of language!

Follow Through on All Promises Promptly

It's best to establish a time frame and stick to it. Don't just say, "I'll get to that." Say, "You can rely on me to get to this by tomorrow before noon." If you want something done, give it to a busy person. Busy people tend to get things done pretty quickly, that is, if they're busy for the right reasons.

Be a Mentor to Others

Give back. Think about the people you connect with who are where you might have been not all that long ago. Is there advice that you can give them respectfully, without coming across as a speak-easy or know-it-all? You can say something like, "Would you be open to hearing some lessons learned and some mistakes that I made along the way?" People will appreciate it.

For example, I am mentoring three up-and-coming speakers right now as part of a program through the National Speakers Association. They are nice, and I think they have a lot of skill and talent and a lot to offer. They can't under-stand how I can take the time to help them — work I normally charge for. But I don't even think twice about it because people helped me along the way, too.

On the other hand, don't let others take advantage of you — or they will. This is not a mentor/mentee relationship. There will always be people looking to shoplift your time. If people appreciate your help and the time spent, great. Just don't waste your time on people that don't appreciate it or won't make a difference because of it.

Also, don't get in the habit of offering unsolicited advice — especially to people you don't know or don't know well. Nobody likes to be given advice unless they ask for it or if it's evident that it's coming from a credible source.

Hey, that's my unsolicited advice.

Never Speak Negatively About Anyone

I mentioned earlier that negative people attract negative people and not to be a Negative Nellie. There is one exception to this rule. If you are about to do business with someone, and I know firsthand that this person is not ethical, not good at what they do or has a bad reputation, I need to tell you that before you invest time and money in them. If I don't tell you, and you find out later that I knew about this the entire time it will reflect badly on me and on our relationship. It's best to just be honest and give accurate feedback when your intentions are good and you are looking to help. It may be awkward but it's the right thing to do.

Make Sure that Referrals You Offer and Introductions You Make Are Worthy of Your Endorsement

I don't think it's a coincidence that great people seem to be connected with other great people. One of the best compliments you can receive—"You always put me in touch with such great people." I also find the opposite to be true—slugs tend to hang out with other slugs. It's guilt by association. Yes, I have stories.

Be Creative about Saying Thank You

We don't say "thank you" enough. If somebody does something really significant to help you, such as referring you business, I think a creative thank you is in order. What ends up happening is that it might quietly incentivize somebody to help you even more. Plus it shows how much you appreciate the help because you've taken the time to be creative in expressing your gratitude.

If someone is a Kansas City Royals fan, send them something Royals-related. If they have a certain hobby, send them something related to that. Find out a little about people, and make it personal.

Be Persistent—Never, Never, Never, Never, Never Give Up

Remember Lorenzo, from earlier? He was a referral who was supposed to call me but didn't. So I called him every Tuesday for seven months, and he finally called me back. Don't give up on prospects or others you might be pursuing for one reason or another. Some people just play hard to get. Others are busy, preoccupied or not prepared to speak with you. Often enough, they just don't know how to respond to you. Sometimes they're just plain rude. As long as you were connected to them through an introduction or referral, be tastefully persistent.

Also, if there is a goal or a dream you have (to start your own business, to pursue a certain career, to write a book, to get that designation, to earn that degree), use your network to help you. Be clear on what you want, make a SMART Goal out of it and have someone you trust hold you accountable to achieving that goal. Don't ever give up. Most people do.

There's a line in one of my favorite movies, Up in the Air, where George Clooney (a hired gun who terminates company employees) says to a guy he's firing, "How much did they pay you to give up on your dreams?" Go out and get back to the dream job you gave up to take this job nineteen years ago. This is your wake up call.

Most people get sold a bill of goods to give up on their dreams. If you're looking to build that business, where do you need to go, what do you need to say, and who do you need to meet to make that happen?

The same thing goes for your career aspirations and whatever else.

Be Genuinely Interested in Other People

I find that the greatest people I know tend to be more interested in what others are doing than what they are doing. They keep up with other people, and they truly care. Again, the more interested you are the more interesting you become, the more gravity you create and the more people will become interested in you, too.

Be a Connector

Always look to connect people who you meet with other people they need to meet. Now, I'm not suggesting that if you meet someone for the first time, you put him or her in touch with your best clients. You don't know them well enough yet, unless you have a really good vibe. But by being a connector, you are in the habit of looking at the value of other people and seeing how they might help one another. Heck, that's a great way to be!

Be in the habit of connecting other people. And don't just connect people just for the sake of doing it; there has to be a good reason for it. It has to add value to people's objectives whether it's landing that job, getting that business, learning that topic, solving that problem, or meeting the love of their life.

Maintain a Positive Attitude, No Matter What

I have always believed that, through your words and/or actions, you make people feel one of two ways: OK or not OK. Rarely is there an in-between. Some of your words or actions are unavoidable. But most of the time, we have complete control over how we make people feel, and it's all about your attitude toward other people and toward yourself.

Way back in the day, I was operating a very busy restaurant in New York City and late on a Sunday night, was held up at gunpoint. Three guys ate their meal, paid their bill, tipped their waitress, and stuck a 9 mm 14 clip weapon in my face. Well, only one of the men did that, the other assaulted an armed security guard (working security in the restaurant) while the third went outside to start the car.

Without getting into the details, nobody was shot and thankfully everyone lived to fight another day. I was viewed as a hero for keeping my cool and for not panicking. (It's not how it looks on TV.) I gave a very detailed report to the police who eventually caught the three gunmen in a car chase in Florida. This was after the gunmen shot and killed a kid in a McDonald's days after I had the pleasure of meeting them. I must admit that the seriousness of the situation hit me when I learned about this.

This experience changed my life and my perspective about everything. I realize that every day that has followed has been a gift — a second chance in many ways.

One of the things that helped me cope with the situation was a one-page story that was left anonymously in my mailbox by somebody who worked in the restaurant. I researched the story and learned that it was published in the *Reader's Digest*. Here's the story but the author and date are unknown.

Jerry was in the restaurant business. He was the kind of guy you love to hate. He was always in a good mood and had something positive to say. When someone would ask him how he was doing, he would reply, "If I were any better,

I'd be twins." He was a unique manager because he had several waiters who had followed him around from restaurant to restaurant. The reason the waiters followed Jerry was because of his attitude. He was a natural motivator. If an employee was having a bad day, Jerry was there telling the employee how to look on the positive side of the situation.

Seeing this style made me curious, so one day I went up to Jerry and asked him, "I don't get it. You can't be a positive person all the time. How do you do it?"

Jerry replied, "Each morning, I wake up and say to myself, 'Jerry, you have two choices today. You can choose to be in a good mood, or you can choose to be in a bad mood.' I choose to be in a good mood. Each time something bad happens, I can choose to be a victim, or I can choose to learn from it. I choose to learn from it. Every time someone comes to me complaining, I can choose to accept their complaining, or I can point out the positive side of life. I choose the positive side of life."

"Yeah, right. It's not that easy," I protested.

"Yes, it is," Jerry said. "Life is about choices. When you cut away all the junk, every situation is a choice. You choose how you react to situations. You choose how people will affect your mood. You choose to be in a good mood or a bad mood. The bottom line is that it's your choice how you live your life."

I reflected on what Jerry said. Soon thereafter, I left the restaurant industry to start my own business. We lost touch, but I often thought about him when I made a choice about life instead of reacting to it. Several years later, I heard that Jerry did something you are never supposed to do in the restaurant business. He left the back door unlocked one morning and was held up at gunpoint by three armed robbers. While trying to open the safe, his hand, shaking from nervousness, slipped off the combination. The robbers panicked and shot him. Luckily, Jerry was found relatively quickly and was rushed to the local hospital. After 18 hours of surgery and weeks of intensive care, Jerry was released from the hospital with fragments of bullets still in his body.

I saw Jerry about six months after the accident. When I asked him how he was, he replied, "If I were any better, I'd be twins. Do you want to see my scars?"

I declined to see his wounds but did ask what went through his mind during the robbery.

"The first thing that went through my mind was that I should have locked the back door. Then as I lay on the floor, I remembered that I had two choices. I could choose to live, or I could choose to die. I chose to live."

"Weren't you scared? Did you lose consciousness?" I asked.

Jerry continued, "The paramedics were great. They kept telling me I was going to be fine. But when they wheeled me into the emergency room and I saw the expressions on the faces of the doctors and nurses, I got really scared. In their eyes, I read, 'He's a dead man.' I knew I needed to take action."

"What did you do?" I asked.

"Well, there was a big burly nurse shouting questions at me," said Jerry. "She asked if I was allergic to anything. 'Yes,' I replied. The doctors and nurses stopped working as they waited for my reply. I took a deep breath and yelled,

'Bullets!' Over their laughter, I told them, 'I am choosing to live. Operate on me as if I am alive, not dead.'"

Jerry lived, thanks to the skill of his doctors, but also because of his amazing attitude. I learned from him that every day, we have the choice to live fully. Attitude, after all, is everything.

Keep your attitude in check. If you have a positive attitude, you will attract others who have a positive outlook. If you don't, you will tend to attract those who do not.

Incorporate these other best practices into your daily life so that you can make people feel good about themselves and great about you.

> *"A positive attitude may not solve all your problems, but it will annoy enough people to make it worth the effort."*
>
> —Herm Albright

Takeaways

- The essence of networking is being able to relate to other people, empathize with them and have a giving nature. If you can make other people feel good by what you do and say, that feeds into every networking approach that I can think of.

- Update your voice-mail greeting daily. Let people know if you'll be out of the office and when you will return. It leaves an impression with people that every day, you have a fresh perspective, and you're giving them up-to-date information.

- Return all calls within 24 hours or, if your initial contact was on a Friday or a holiday, by the next business day.

- Send handwritten notes on a regular basis to say thank you or to follow up after an initial contact.

- Call or email to confirm all scheduled meetings a day in advance. It may save you a wasted trip.

- Be 15 minutes early to all meetings. It shows that the meeting is important to you. It will also buffer you against construction and other delays.

- Do your homework. Prepare for meetings by printing out the Web site of the person you're going to meet with, and write comments and questions on the pages.

- Be humble and self-deprecating.

- Don't dominate a conversation.

- Maintain your integrity and honesty.

- Remember people's names and details about their lives. Use index cards or notes to help you remember those details.

- Focus less on "me" language and more on "we" language.

- Follow through on all promises promptly.

- Don't get in the habit of offering unsolicited advice.

- Be a mentor to others. Share lessons learned and mistakes you've made along the way with those who want to hear them.

- Never speak negatively about anyone. The one exception is an instance in which you need to warn somebody about doing business with an unethical person or saving them from a negative experience.

- Insure referrals your offer and introductions you make are worthy of your endorsement.

- Be creative about saying thank you.

- Be persistent—never, never, never, never, never give up.

- Be genuinely interested in other people.

- Be a connector—always look to connect people whom you meet with other people whom you know or have met.

- Maintain a positive attitude, no matter what—even in the midst of life-threatening or life-altering events.

CHAPTER 14:
Your Networking Action Plan

"If you don't paddle your own canoe, you don't move."
—Katherine Hepburn

A networking plan is a lot like a business plan. It gets and keeps you focused on the basic components of your business.

When you're starting a business, one of the first things a business coach or consultant might tell you is that you need a business plan. If you go to www.bplan.com, you can see a lot of sample business plans, and you will see that they all follow a similar model.

What's nice about having a business plan is that you can refer to different parts of it, and because it follows a model, it forces you to think about the things you haven't thought about. For example, it will force you to think about how to build a new component of your business—what will it look like? What is your vision? Who are your prospects? What will your marketing look like? What will your budget be? How will you generate that budget—is it an investment that the owner will fund fully, will it be funded through venture capital or will you get a bank loan? Is it a partnership, a proprietorship or a corporation? It makes you ask questions of yourself and then get help from people in getting those questions answered. It also forces you to see your vision.

What is your business going to look like moving forward? Where will you be in three or five years?

Another reason to formulate a business plan is so that you can make a case to get funding. It shows that you've thought about it, and you can ask someone if they think the business could succeed.

And a business plan will help keep you on track. When I revisit my business plan each year on my birthday in November, what's really fun for me is to see what I've already accomplished because the plan is there. I can say, "I did that," or "I fell short here," or "I really blew this away." I can see if it went the way it should have gone or if something didn't play out the way I thought it would.

It is just as important to have a Networking Action Plan (NAP). It helps you plan out your networking approaches. How will your marketing and business development approach look in the context of networking and establishing important relationships? Think about what you want your practice to look like and how a networking strategy is going to fit within that plan.

Let's look at the various components of your Networking Action Plan.

Your Networking Goals

The first thing you need to think about is your goals. Are they SMART—Specific, Measurable, Actionable, Reasonable and Time-driven?

Your goals should be far-reaching. They shouldn't be unrealistic, but they should be somewhat of a stretch. A goal is not a task—a task is to make 10 phone calls today, whereas a goal might be to implement a seminar aspect to your business, become a board member of a group, create a niche with physicians or transition your business to become 40 percent referral-based. It's the activity that drives the result, not the result itself. A goal has to prompt activity.

When I say this to advisors, they will say that their goal is to make Leader's Conference or earn a certain amount of commission. That can be valid, but to me that is the result of doing other things well. Maybe that's your vision, where you want to go. But the goal is what you will do to get there. Wanting to make Leader's Conference next year is great, but how do you know if you're on track? Your NAP (hopefully you're not taking one) helps to keep you headed in the right direction through your relationships at any given time.

People and Organizations with Whom You Should Network

Your Target Market

Your target market is whom you serve best and therefore wish to serve most. Be very specific in terms of who you think your target market should be. It's always better to focus on only one or two markets. Three is too many. Remember, if you're serving everyone—corporate executives, young professionals, business owners, soon-to-be retirees and college graduates—then you don't have a target market. Have a good reason why you are focused on a particular marketplace. That will impact your Networking Action Plan in a big way because your target market drives how you spend your time—where you go; with whom you speak; and what you say, read and write.

Natural Market

This is a term that's used in the insurance industry. Your natural market is composed of your friends, relatives and neighbors—people who know you well. Don't assume that they all know exactly what you do and what your goals are. Find opportunities to share your vision with them and see how they may help you. Of course, help them right back. Who knows — family members and friends may become your clients over time.

Unnatural Market

Your unnatural market is composed of those in your network who are in the outer circle just beyond your natural market. I look at that market as being your doctor, dentist, chiropractor, therapist, CPA, property and casualty rep, banker and broker—people whom you tend to do business with, and for whom you are their client or patient.

We tend to be very shortsighted rather than thinking like a networker. You may think, "I see my doctor only when I get sick." But your doctor is a business person who knows people as well. So why not look at him or her as being a potential referral source, or someone you can bounce your PEEC Statement™ off of? You can say, "Doc, I don't know if you know this, but I'm in the credit card process business. I'm focused on helping health care professionals streamline their credit processing system while saving money. Maybe, from one business person to another, we can talk shop at some point when I'm not paying you for a visit."

Years ago, I hurt my lower back while weight lifting on a Sunday. Most doctors' offices were closed. My friends had to carry me out of the gym. Somebody mentioned a chiropractor he really liked, and they took me there. I didn't know anything about chiropractic care at the time, but the chiropractor did a great job. He put blocks under me and stretched out my back. I was intrigued at the newfangled techniques. As I was waiting in agony, lying on those blocks, I was forced to look at some charts that the chiropractor had on the wall about nerve endings, the human body, chiropractic approaches. When he came in, I asked him questions.

I found out that he had gotten into the chiropractic business because chiropractic care had helped him after he sustained injuries in a serious car accident. Then he asked me what I do for a living. I told him that I help insurance agencies generate more referrals through networking, and he started referring me people—giving me names. It certainly wasn't my purpose—I was in agony—but it turned into a reciprocal referral relationship because I began sending him business, too. I began to go to him for regular appointments, and he would bring in newspaper clippings and magazine articles that were relevant to the insurance industry. That experience showed me that there is a lot of opportunity in places where you might not expect to find them.

Religious, Alumni and Professional Organizations

Think about the people in this segment if you are active in a church or temple. Consider people from religious organizations, alumni chapters and professional associations. We take many of these people for granted. We don't want to look at them as prospects we are going to sell to—but maybe there is an opportunity to collaborate with them on business. You might say, "Hey, Bill, we always talk about religion when we get together. What type of work do you do?" They will most likely ask what type of work you do, and all of a sudden, you may have created an opportunity.

Consider your children's' sports teams as an opportunity, too. I found someone who writes and designs print ads from my daughter's sports team. She is the mother of one of my daughter's friends, and she runs a business out of her home. I never would have found out that she writes ads if we hadn't talked about it at a game. And she is right down the block. She brings prints over, and my wife walks them back with the corrections. Thankfully, she does great work.

Former Co-Workers, Suppliers and Customers

Focus on the people you worked with where you have the strongest relationships. We often don't consider these people as resources or potential referral sources. These are great candidates for your PEEC Statement™ and to elicit advice, insight, and recommendations (AIR™ again).

Community and Political Groups

Look for people you already have relationships with and can build further relationships with. You could be just a conversation or two away.

Your Spouse's or Partner's Network

A sales rep who serves the physician market was telling me recently that his wife and a friend had reconnected at an alumni event, and the friend's husband just happens to be a heavy hitter in a physician's association. The rep asked me what the right approach would be for asking his wife's friend to approach her husband about doing business. I suggested he go through his wife, have his wife approach her friend, and then he could follow up and say, "I am a sales rep, financial advisor or whatever, and my professional niche happens to be physicians. I know that your husband is a shaker and a mover, and I would love to be able to brainstorm with him to see if we could be a resource to one another."

When leveraging your relationship with your husband, wife, boyfriend, girlfriend, or some sort of significant or insignificant other, tread lightly. You have more to lose here than merely a sale.

True Prospects

Do your prospects know you? Do they know what you do? Do they know whom you serve? Do they care? If they don't, they're not prospects. Given my definition of prospects, who are the 10 whom you should be thinking about approaching from a networking standpoint? I am always working my lists. I like to focus on a list of 25 true prospects at any given time (which may be any given month). That may be too ambitious for some people, so 10 is a good number to start with.

Referral Sources (Centers of Influence)

These are your chickens, as I call them. Who comes into contact with your prospects all day, every day? With whom do you need to build better relationships?

I have a list on the white board in my office that says "key chickens." I have 12 names on that list. They are my key referral sources. Some of them I speak to monthly, at least; others I probably don't speak to enough.

Your Top Clients

Who are your top clients, and how can you help one another? How often should you stay in touch, and can you refer them business? It's really important to focus on your top clients because they're likely to refer you to people and prospects that are like themselves. You don't want to say, "I'd like to work with really affluent people"—I know reps who want to work with very successful people or thriving companies (not a bad thing), but it's difficult and somewhat pretentious to say that in a networking situation. But if you're speaking to your top clients—the ones who are the most successful and whom you like the best—chances are that without having to say that, they may refer you to quality people.

From a strategic standpoint it's smart to focus on your top clients. Why wouldn't you? You don't want to neglect other clients, but from a networking standpoint, ultimately, you want all of your clients to be your top clients (or like your top clients), and you should end up firing the people who are bad clients or those you don't like.

I'm lucky because I love all my clients at this point in time. (No really!) But a couple of years ago, I wasn't so lucky. It's a drain to work with bad clients.

What constitutes a bad client? Good question. Does your client:

Pay you on time?
Pay you enough money?
Follow through with your advice?
Return your messages promptly or at all?
Create opportunities for repeat or additional business?
Recommend and refer you to other prospects?
Help you to continue learning and growing?
Take up more of your time than they should?
Make you feel like a valued member of the team?
View you as a business partner?
Value your time?
Have accountability for the success of your work together?
Allow you to have fun?

If any of these questions prompted a NO, you might need to re-think the relationship with this client. Also, this is not the client that you wish to clone. That said, focus on cloning the clients that you like and respect the most.

Your best clients—those you want to continue building relationships with—should be part of your networking plan. Keep a list of your top 10 or so and go from there.

Which clients do you enjoy serving the most? How often should you stay in touch? Can you refer *them* business?

Which clients deem you referable? How often should you stay in touch? Can you refer *them* business?

Whom would you clone—your absolute favorites? How often should you stay in touch? Can you refer them business?

Here, I'm making a distinction among clients whom you can help the most, the ones you enjoy serving the most and the ones who deem you referable. I have clients who refer me all the time, and others I would like to have refer me more.

It's important to think about this and make these distinctions because as you're putting pen to paper, you can make good decisions about the types of people you want to work with.

Advocates

Your advocates are those who would take a bullet for you, who understand your work and are powerful enough to help you. Again, my 90-year-old grandmother doesn't qualify here because she may not have the power to get me where I want to go professionally.

What will your strategy be to stay in touch with your advocates every 30 days? Can you refer *them*?

Networking Events You Should Attend and/or Join

What events do you need to attend (or what ponds do you need to fish in) that would allow you to meet and greet the type of people you need to know? Networking doesn't happen on its own. You have to schedule the time to actually attend group meetings. Do a search for the appropriate meetings, put the dates on your calendar and go.

Preparation for Networking Events

What are you prepared to do in all of these events moving forward as they relate to your networking and how you spend your time? What will your research look like?

And how will you know that when you get there, it's a fit? When I go to a meeting, I know whether or not it's a fit usually within seconds. I judge the experience on how I'm greeted at the door as I'm signing in. I judge it by the people I'm speaking with as I'm in line to sign in. When I tell them it's my first time to this meeting, I notice how endearing and welcoming they are to me, and are they looking to make me feel welcome and comfortable?

What tools of the trade will you need?

This gets back to name badges, your business cards, your pens, your questions and anything else you might need that will make you feel comfortable and potentially a good fit with this particular venue or group.

How will you contribute?

What can you do beyond just showing up to get involved and in touch with more people? What can you do to help the board members or coordinators of the meeting? Can you help out at the registration table? Give out paperwork to attendees? Help make connections for people? You won't know unless you ask!

What are you prepared to do as it relates to this venue?

For example, let's say that one of my clients has invited me to an art gallery because there's a showing there. I'm with other clients, and it's all about the art. I'm not there to pitch my wares. It's about the art, and the person who is sponsoring it. I would be looking to contribute, to see if there's some way I can help the host of the event, to find out if I can support him or her to help sell more art, schedule more showings or create more venues. How can I help?

Is the organization relevant to your target market?

If not, why not? I think most organizations you attend should be relevant to your target market or at least a specific goal you may have. If these venues are not, that's fine, just have a compelling reason.

Conversation Starters and Opening Questions

I mentioned these in earlier chapters. But what are the opening questions and conversation starters that will work best for you? Jot them down.

What will you say after you introduce yourself? What questions will you ask to learn more and to help? They can change depending on the type of event you go to, the market you serve, your personality and communications style, etc.

Conversation Finishers and Closing Statements

This is important because a lot of people don't know how to disengage from a conversation the right way. So again, you can get a refresher in Chapters 2 and 3 about ending conversations gracefully, but what is the best approach for you?

The key to your Networking Action Plan is to come up with your own variation on all of the components. Remember, it's always best to be a first-rate version of yourself rather than a second-rate version of somebody else.

PEEC Statement™

Remember, from Chapter 5, your PEEC Statement™ incorporates your Profession, Expertise, Environments and Call to Action. Get it down to 30 seconds or less. You're going to put it into action now that you have a Networking Action Plan, so practice it.

Follow-Up Strategy

There's a whole segment on follow-up in Chapter 10. What does your step-by-step process look like? Always remember that not following up after an event, or with someone whom you've connected with at an event, is the same thing as not having gone at all.

Follow up within 24 hours, or as close to that as possible.

Maintenance Plan

What will you do all day, every day, to maintain and continue to grow your networking campaign, the connections in your database, and your prospect, client, and advocate lists?

Call to Action

What is the next step toward implementing your networking strategy? Once you have all of this information down, now what? And when will you follow through and start working your networking plan of action?

The time is now!

Takeaways

- A Networking Action Plan (NAP) is a lot like a business plan. It gets and keeps you focused on the basic components of your business, helps you make a case to get funding and forces you to think about components of your business that you might not think about otherwise.

- Your networking goals need to be SMART—specific, measurable, actionable, reasonable and time-driven.

- A goal is not a task. It's an activity that drives the result, not the result itself. A goal has to prompt activity.

- Your NAP should focus on all of the people you know whom you can network with and potentially have reciprocal referral relationships with, including your target market, natural market and unnatural market; people from religious, alumni and professional organizations; former co-workers, suppliers and customers; community and political groups; your spouse or partner's network; true prospects; referral sources (centers of influence); the people who come into daily contact with your true prospects; your top clients; and your advocates.

- Fire clients who are preventing you from doing your best work and with whom you dread doing business. Eventually, all of your clients should be your top clients.

- Joining networking groups and attending networking events will help put you in touch with more people. To prepare for these meetings and events, research them in advance, know how to introduce yourself, decide how you will start and end conversations, know what questions to ask, be able to deliver your PEEC Statement™ in 30 seconds or less and offer to take on a leadership role.

- You must have a follow-up strategy, maintenance plan and plan of action before you can reap the rewards of your Networking Action Plan™.

Your Turn

Your Networking Action Plan (NAP)™ pulls together everything we've discussed in the previous chapters. The checklist on the next page will help you build your NAP™ so that you can have your entire networking strategy in one document. Remember, the time is now!

YOUR "CALL TO ACTION" PLAN

Your Networking Action Plan™

1. **Goals**—What are your networking goals? They need to be SMART—specific, measurable, actionable, reasonable and timed. And remember, a goal is not a task; it's a major activity that drives a result. _____

2. **Target Market**—Whom do you serve best and therefore wish to serve most? _____

3. List names in the following categories to build your list of prospects.

   Natural market (friends, relatives, neighbors)

   Unnatural market (banker, broker, CPA, lawyer, doctor, dentist)

   Religious, alumni and professional organizations

   Former co-workers, suppliers and customers

   Community and political groups

   Spouse/partner's network

True prospects (people who know you or know of you, have an interest in your product or service and are open to making a purchase today or in the future)

Referral sources (centers of influence)

People who come in contact with your prospects—all day, every day

---

Top clients—Which clients do you enjoy serving most? How often should you stay in touch? Can you refer *them* business? Keep your standards high; list at least 10.

Which clients deem you referable? How often should you stay in touch? Can you refer *them* business?

Whom would you clone? How often should you stay in touch? Can you refer *them* business?

Advocates (those who love you enough to "take a bullet" for you, who understand your work and whom you help, and are powerful enough to get you where you need to go) What will your strategy be to stay in touch every 30 days? Can you refer *them*?

---

4. **Networking Events**—What are some networking events you will attend and/or join? (Consider chambers, networking groups, professional associations and community groups.)

Preparation for these events—What will you do to research these venues?

How will you know if they're a good fit for you?

What "tools of the trade" will you need?

How will you contribute?

Are the organizations relevant to your target market? If not, why are you including them?

Conversation starters and opening questions—How will you introduce yourself?

What will you say after you introduce yourself?

What questions will you ask to learn more and to offer to be of help?

Conversation finishers and closing statements—How will you finish conversations? What will you closing statements be?

5. **PEEC statement**—What is your PEEC statement—
profession, expertise, environments and call to action?
(Refer to the worksheet in Chapter 5 if necessary.)

_____

_____

_____

6. **Follow-Up Strategy**—What does your step-by-step
follow-up process look like?

_____

_____

_____

7. **Maintenance Plan**—What will you do all day, every
day, to maintain and continue to grow your networking
campaign?

_____

_____

_____

8. **Call to Action**—What is the next step toward implementing your networking strategy? And when will you do it?

_____

_____

_____

CHAPTER 15:

What Now? Set a Goal and Put Your Networking into Action!

"Everyone has a plan until they get punched in the mouth."

—Mike Tyson

It's not every day that you see Katherine Hepburn and Mike Tyson quoted in the same book. Well, you've seen it here folks. Both have it right.

This chapter is less about content and information and more about focus, goal setting, and implementation. Having a business plan or a Networking Action Plan (NAP) is great but how do you put your plan into place?

I will let you in on a little secret; *most people* don't put a plan into action after reading a business book (like this one). They look at the last chapter as being the ending point rather than the starting point.

If you don't apply any of the principles in this book (assuming the information is helpful and applies to your work as a sales professional, business owner, or job searcher), than really, what's the point?

Hey, you may have the best intentions in the world after reading this book. You may commit to joining every networking group under the sun. You might completely embrace networking as your modus operandi for promoting and marketing your business. You might etch out the perfect target market. You may develop the best PEEC Statement™ this side of the Mississippi. And the referral strategy you implement may generate more business than you know what to do with. Yes, the best intentions in the world.

What's going to prevent you from accomplishing any and all of this?

Funny you ask!

- You'll decide that you're completely overwhelmed by all of the great information, anecdotes, approaches, examples, philosophies, techniques, and principles highlighted in this book. Naturally, you'll need time to process everything before deciding how you're going to put everything into action.

- You'll make the conscious decision that networking is simply not for you. You're more of a "behind the scenes" kind of person. Besides, it takes a lot of work to educate and establish better relationships with your clients, prospects, and referral sources. What you've been doing all along in your marketing and business development is probably working just fine.

- You just don't have the time to network. You're very busy in the day to day activities of your business, going to networking meetings, having conversations with clients, and contributing to the success of others just doesn't fit into your schedule right now.

- Networking is not only an investment of time; it's an investment of money. You just don't have the extra cash available to join a group because you're just starting out in your business. When things pick up and money starts rolling in, then you'll re-read this book, refresh your memory and infuse networking and referral marketing into your business.

- It's a bit intimidating going to a networking meeting where you don't know anyone. Besides, the approaches in this book look good on paper, but actually going to an event and having a conversation with someone about your business is completely daunting. There are much easier ways to drum up some business.

- You're as successful as you want to be and simply don't want any more business. Besides, all of these strategies and techniques seem like a lot of work.

- You will get to it tomorrow.

- You've already forgotten what you've read and you're excited about the next business book you're going to download on your Kindle.

I'm sure you can think of some other excuses but the point is that you will get bogged down and in the way of *your own* success. Despite having all the information about networking you need in this book, in essence, you will punch *yourself* in the mouth better than even Mike Tyson ever could.

Without a set of goals in place and someone holding you true to them, you won't make it out of the first round. (I see this every day in my work with sales reps, financial advisors, sales managers, business owners, and job searchers. What's the outcome? They fail.)

Don't get me wrong. Some of you might very well be driven, focused, and self motivated. No doubt about it! You may already have your *Networking Action Plan (NAP)* filled out and you're ready to go. Locked and loaded, baby!

Of course, some of you, many of you, most of you, well, are not. If this is you, don't feel bad. You're in the majority. Most sales people need to have their feet held to the fire. No worries. That's what this chapter is all about.

Where do you go from here?

At this point, it's important to set goals (the right goals) and stay focused on them. Without specific goals, I wouldn't get anything done. Most sales people are the same way.

What activities are you involved in that are important enough for you to set goals in the first place? Think of all of those New Year's resolutions and broken promises.

Putting that fitness program in place, losing that weight, spending more time with friends and relatives, improving that golf swing, making those investments, saving that money, cleaning that shed, growing that garden, learning that dance step, reading that book, overcoming that fear, making that apology, asking that cute brunette out on a date.

As you can see, you can set goals in many different areas of your life, not just business. There are 8 areas of life that I like to talk about with audiences— Career, Financial, Health, Family, Self Improvement, Spiritual, Adventure, and Business.

Since the purpose here is to apply goal setting to your networking activities, I will assume that this will fall into the Career or Business areas of your life. Of course, if you're focused on that cute brunette, we might be moving into Adventure or Self Improvement. I'm just saying.

Anyway, the 8 areas of life are pretty self explanatory but let me offer a few thoughts and you can apply goal setting to them as you see fit.

Career

Is your career going in the right direction? Are you happy with what you're doing and where you're doing it? Is your salary and/or commission structure fair? What would you change about your career if you could if you had absolutely nothing to lose? What would your career plans be if you lost your job today?

Financial

Are you making as much money as you would like? Are you being paid as you should given your industry, profession, education, years of experience, and accomplishments? Are you planning and investing wisely for retirement, children's college, vacation, that 1951 Studebaker, a rainy day? Are you where you want to be financially? What debts are excessive and need to be paid off? Is there a financial plan in place? Do you have a financial planner?

Health

Do you feel good everyday or at least most days? When you look in the mirror do you like what you see? Do you exercise? Do you watch what you eat? Have you had a physical in the last year? How is your cholesterol level? When was your last visit to the dentist? Are you at your desired weight?

Family

Do you spend enough time with your immediate family? Should you have a better relationship with certain members of your family? Are you as involved as you would like to be in your children's school activities? Are you making the same mistakes with your kids that your parents made with you (if any)? What mistakes are you making with your family relationships and what can you change today?

Self Improvement

What have you always wanted to accomplish but never had the chance to do? Is there a skill you always wanted to learn? What language would you learn if you could? If you could hire a coach to help you master any activity, what would it be?

Spiritual

The term *spiritual* may mean different things to different people. It could relate to religion or your beliefs and values in a more holistic sense. Being spiritual could also mean how you can be at peace with yourself. Whatever it means to you, do you see an area in your life that you want to improve that fits into this category?

Adventure

Have you always wanted to climb Mount Kilimanjaro? Jump out of an airplane (with a parachute)? Become a white water rafting instructor? Compete in an ironman competition? Learn a martial art?

Business

Have you ever wanted to start your own business? How could you double your commission next year? How could delivering educational seminars grow your business? How could you become a better networker? How could you become legendary in a specific marketplace? What would you need to do to improve your business model?

You may have noticed some natural overlap from one area of life to another. Career can easily overlap with Financial, Health with Adventure, and so on.

Bottom line, are there areas of your life outside the realm of Business and Career that you should be paying attention to? Consider what they might be and feel free to apply the approaches discussed in this chapter to them. This might be an excellent time to focus on other important areas of your life and take them "along for the ride".

Goals

What is a goal anyway? I don't want to get into a battle of semantics. You hear about goals all the time. Often, people use terms like task, objective, mission, vision, wish, and even value proposition in place of the term *goal*. (Of course, if we're talking about scoring a goal — as in soccer, this will prompt a completely different discussion.)

A goal for our purposes here is simply a statement that commits to a specific outcome (or set of outcomes) in a predetermined timeframe. Easy enough?

There are 7 MUSTS to be considered to correctly set goals or to at least get the most out of your goals.

1. Goals MUST have Passion

If there is no passion behind your goal, again, what's the point? It's easy to lose momentum and focus if you weren't that passionate about it in the first place. How do you know if you are passionate about your goal? Well, you must consider the specific activity. Let's use my passion for boxing as an example.

Do you love it so much; you will move time when no time appears to exist?

No matter how busy I am, how much business travel I have, or what appears on my calendar, I will schedule time in my week to hit the heavy bag or speed bag, jump rope, run (or do road work as we say in the trade), shadow box, or go a few rounds in the ring with a willing sparring partner.

Do you (or would you) invest your time, energy, and money in the pursuit of excellence?

It pains me to say this (pun intended), but I actually pay a guy to hit me. In the ring that is. Yes, he teaches me how to stand, the proper footwork, how to throw a punch, take a punch, and how to push myself to the level of conditioning needed to survive in the ring. But at the end of the day, I pay a guy to hit me. And he's worth every penny.

Do you feel a sense of loss when you can't be the best you can be at it?

One of my greatest thrills was attending the finals for the Golden Gloves competition in Ohio. One of my clients took me and we were seated ringside. In order to qualify for the Golden Gloves, other than being a good fighter, you have to be between the ages of 16-36. Most of the fighters were on the lower range of the scale. As excited as I was to watch the fights, I couldn't help thinking how much better I would be in the ring if I had started at the age that most of these kids had started. I'm trying to make up for lost time now but at my age, you can only do so much.

Do you have a tough time hiding your excitement when you talk about it?

I use boxing examples all the time when I'm speaking from the stage or delivering a seminar. Anyone that knows me sees how excited I get when I'm asked about my escapades in the ring or about any of the classic fighters of old — Jack Dempsey, Gene Tunney, Stanley Ketchel, Joe Louis, Harry Greb, and Sugar Ray Robinson. Go ahead, just ask me about them!

A lot of sales people feel this way about golf. (I'm not really sure why.) They move heaven and earth just to get 9 holes in, pay for lessons, go to the driving range.

If you can get this excited about a goal you are working on that relates to your Career or Business, imagine how successful you will be.

2. Goals MUST be SMART

Of course, the goal should be *smart* in every sense of the word. I'll just have to trust you on this one. What I mean here is that SMART goals are Specific, Measurable, Actionable, Realistic, and Time driven. (Yes, another acronym!) Your goal must be specific enough to be focused; measurable enough to know when you've hit your mark, actionable enough to determine what needs to be done, realistic enough to be possible, and timely enough to create urgency.

3. Goals MUST be a bit Lofty

This may be where a goal differs from a task. A goal must be far reaching and lofty enough where it can't be crossed off of your checklist moments after writing it down. For example, *joining a networking group* should not be a goal. After researching the group online, attending a couple of meetings, and paying your membership fee, you're pretty much done. So what's a loftier purpose? How about *being elected president of my Rotary group and creating an improved membership process by December? Creating at least 10 important referral based relationships within the Rotary club in 3 months?* Your goals should be a bit of a stretch so make them count.

4. Goals MUST be about Process

Your goal should be about putting a process or system in place, not hitting a specific result. Of course, the result is important. But the premise here is if you focus on the process, the result will be there. Sales people are notorious for setting a commission amount (the result) as their goal.

I will earn $120,000 in commission by the end of the fiscal year.

That's all well and good but so what? What will you do to earn this commission?

I will deliver 4 educational seminars a month to my target market insuring at least 16 additional sales appointments and $10,000 in monthly income.

Here we focused on the process with a "dash of result" thrown in for good measure. See the difference?

5. Goals MUST be Accountable

Some people can hold themselves accountable to their goals. Most can't. What can you do to insure that you will stay focused on your goals? Maybe for every week that you don't move forward on a goal, you have to contribute a specified sum of money to your rival college. Or make 20 cold calls. Or sing karaoke with your friends. Or whatever. The point is there has to be a negative consequence. (Negative consequences are much impactful than positive ones.)

Hiring a business coach is another way to establish goals while staying focused on them. Part of the value that a business coach offers is holding you accountable to and for your actions (or lack thereof).

One of the best things you could do is choose an accountability partner. It could be a fellow sales rep or business owner. You could hold each other accountable to goals and compare notes during weekly or monthly meetings.

What gets measured gets done. And peer pressure is an excellent way to be held true to your school and get the things you need to get done, done.

6. Goals MUST be Written

A Harvard Business School study found:

> 83% of the population does not have any clearly defined goals
>
> 14% have goals but not written down
>
> 3% of the population has goals that are written down

The study concluded that the 3 percent that did have written goals were earning an astounding 10 times more income than that of the 83 percent group. In addition, similar studies have shown that individuals with written goals also tend to have better health and happier marriages than those without goals. You must sign your soul to the devil.

The power of written goals is indisputable. Writing your goals down is the first step to any action. And write them the old fashioned way — with pen and paper, not typed in a computer. Why is writing your goals so important? It creates a commitment in your mind that gives you the momentum to achieve your immediate goals. Writing them is even more crucial for your long term goals.

7. Goals MUST be Visible

Put your goals in a place where you can see them every day. If they're in a Word file somewhere, you'll never look at them. Again, write them out long hand and keep them on a clipboard at your desk. Hang them on your bathroom mirror, attach them to the remote control for your TV, post them on the fridge, keep them in your wallet, or tape them to the GPS. Or all of the above. I keep mine written on white boards in my office. Get creative and try to have fun with it.

Cindy, a colleague of mine, works for a college in a job she hates. The only thing Cindy hates more than her job is her boss. She jokes that when her boss has temper tantrums (I did say temper tantrums) it reminds her of the cartoon character Yosemite Sam. Cindy dreams of quitting her job and starting her own business as a career coach. I helped her establish some goals to expedite the process. Cindy posted the goals on her bathroom mirror next to a newspaper clipping of Yosemite Sam. Every morning she laughs at the picture that serves as a friendly reminder to pay attention to her goals.

Objectives

I mentioned objectives earlier. Objectives are the smaller tasks you may need to tackle to accomplish the goal. Objectives are the rungs to the ladder that must be climbed to reach your goal.

I'm trying to help Andrew lose 40 pounds by his wedding day. Just in case you're wondering, Andrew approached me at a business meeting and asked for my help. (I'm not sure if there's more pressure on me or him.)

Here's his goal.

Become physically fit and gain self confidence by implementing a daily fitness regimen, healthy diet, and active lifestyle (to lose 40lbs) by March 2011.

Here are his objectives.

- *Eliminate all white bread, rolls, dessert, and reduce alcohol consumption by 50% by August 1.*
- *Make doctor's appointment to get physical by August 17.*
- *Move treadmill from parent's house to basement by September 1.*
- *Join gym by September 1.*
- *Read <u>Body for Life</u> by Bill Phillips by September 7.*
- *Mail diet/daily workout routine to Michael Goldberg by September 8.*
- *Schedule weekly calls with Michael Goldberg every Friday to report changes in weight and other progress.*

You get the point. Andrew has lost 15 pounds at the time of this writing and is doing a great job. He's not as focused on these objectives as I'd like him to be but he's a lot further along than he might have been without goals and objectives.

When Andrew accomplishes all of his objectives, it may be time to establish more detailed objectives that have more meaningful milestones — bench pressing a certain weight, running a certain distance, or consuming a certain number of grams of protein.

Objectives tend to be living, breathing targets designed to grow as you grow. Or shrink as is the case for Andrew.

Examples

Here are some examples of business or career goals to get you thinking about your own goals moving forward.

Overcome fear of public speaking by January 1, 2011.

Deliver 3 educational seminars a month to target market by February 1, 2011.

Create referral process insuring at least 5 additional clients per month by March 1, 2011.

Establish 10 scheduled sales appointments with physician marketplace by April 1, 2011.

Land 2 job interviews with hiring managers with target companies starting May 1, 2011.

Develop PEEC Statement™ from Goldberg's book and practice it with 5 clients a week for their feedback by June 1, 2011.

Can these goals be better? Loftier? More specific? Sure. But this ain't a bad place to start!

Your Turn!

Run, don't walk! Write your goals down now! Once you have them written, quickly review the 7 MUSTS from earlier to see if you can make improvements.

Then make them.

I'll get you started! Take out a legal pad and start writing.

Craft 3-5 goals from Goldberg's book to insure focused networking strategy TODAY. (As in right now.)

Networking is absolutely the best way to grow a business, land a job, learn something, solve a problem, and meet the love of your life. Really, what can be more important? And if you don't help your own cause, who will?

My shop teacher in the eighth grade, Mr. Azarelli, used to point to a ten word sentence that was painted on the wall, above the blackboard, in the front of the room. "Az" would remind us that these ten words strung together formed the most important sentence in the English language and was ultimately the meaning of life. He would make us recite these ten little two letter words before each class. They read:

If it is to be it is up to me.

Now, it's up to you.

ABOUT THE AUTHOR

 Michael Goldberg is a networking expert and the founder of Building Blocks Consulting, LLC. The programs he has developed are responsible for hundreds of thousands of dollars of increased revenues, retention, and employment opportunities.

Michael speaks at conferences and associations, runs sales meetings, and delivers "results driven" programs on networking, referral marketing, sales presentations, leadership, communication, service, and career search.

For most of his career, Michael has worked in the service industry in regional positions with a focus on training and development. He has also worked in academia teaching a variety of business and communication courses in Boston, New York, and New Jersey. Michael is among the 7 percent of speakers worldwide who have earned the Certified Speaking Professional (CSP) designation from the National Speakers Association and the International Federation for Professional Speakers.

Today he spends his time helping firms in financial services increase their level of production and ability to recruit top flight talent through networking and referrals. Clients include MetLife, New England Financial, Amalgamated Life, NY Life, Mass Mutual, Securian Financial, Genworth,

Principal Financial, Northwestern Mutual, Prudential, Aflac, and Chubb & Son.

Michael has been quoted in the *Harvard Business Review* and the *Wall Street Journal,* and has regular columns in *Agent's Sales Journal, Producer's Web,* and *Producer's E-Source.* He has spoken at numerous conferences in the financial services industry including LAMP, NAIFA, NAHU, and Sales Mastery Forum.

Michael is currently an award winning adjunct faculty member at Rutgers University and frequently volunteers as a speaker for the Department of Labor and organizations focused on career search.

A graduate of Lesley University, Michael has lived in New York, Los Angeles, Boston, and New Jersey.

Check out his blog at **www.BuildingBlocksConsulting.com** or follow him on Twitter @MEGoldberg.

INDEX